D0031414

Contemporary Women's Writing in German

CONTEMPORARY WOMEN'S WRITING IN GERMAN

Changing the Subject

Brigid Haines and **Margaret Littler**

OXFORD
UNIVERSITY PRESS

OXFORD
UNIVERSITY PRESS

Great Clarendon Street, Oxford OX2 6DP

Oxford University Press is a department of the University of Oxford.
It furthers the University's objective of excellence in research, scholarship,
and education by publishing worldwide in

Oxford New York

Auckland Bangkok Buenos Aires Cape Town Chennai
Dar es Salaam Delhi Hong Kong Istanbul Karachi Kolkata
Kuala Lumpur Madrid Melbourne Mexico City Mumbai Nairobi
São Paulo Shanghai Taipei Tokyo Toronto

Oxford is a registered trade mark of Oxford University Press
in the UK and in certain other countries

Published in the United States
by Oxford University Press Inc., New York

First published 2004

British Library Cataloguing in Publication Data
Data available

Library of Congress Cataloging in Publication Data
Data available
ISBN 0-19-815967-6

1 3 5 7 9 10 8 6 4 2

Typeset by Graphicraft Limited, Hong Kong
Printed in Great Britain
on acid-free paper by
Biddles Ltd.
King's Lynn, Norfolk

For Davey and Nick

Acknowledgements

Chapter 2 is a revised and extended version of Brigid Haines, 'Beyond Patriarchy: Marxism, Feminism, and Elfriede Jelinek's *Die Liebhaberinnen*', *Modern Language Review*, 92/3 (1997), 643–55. Chapter 5 is a reworking of Margaret Littler, 'Beyond Alienation: The City in the Novels of Herta Müller and Libuše Moníková', in Brigid Haines (ed.), *Herta Müller* (Cardiff: Cardiff University Press, 1998), 36–56, and Brigid Haines, ' "The Unforgettable Forgotten": The Traces of Trauma in Herta Müller's *Reisende auf einem Bein*', *German Life and Letters*, 55 (2002), 266–81.

All English translations of German quotations are our own and thus responsibility for any errors they may contain is ours. Where published English translations are known to exist they are listed in the Select Bibliography.

For their help in reading and commenting on sections of the book we should like to thank Adrian Armstrong, Çiğdem Balım, Stephanie Bird, Elizabeth Boa, Alexandra Clarke, Allyson Fiddler, Katharina Hall, Helen Hills, Beth Linklater, Lorraine Markotic, Lyn Marven, Hilary Owen, and John J. White. In addition Brigid Haines would like to acknowledge the support of the Arts and Humanities Research Board, whose award of a period of leave under the Research Leave Scheme greatly facilitated completion of the volume. Both authors are also grateful to the British Academy for funding the appointment of Sabine Rolle as Research Assistant, and to Sabine herself for her work on the bibliographical apparatus of the book.

BH
ML

Contents

Abbreviations

The following abbreviations are used throughout for primary texts:

K Kassandra
L Die Liebhaberinnen
M Mutterzunge
R Reisende auf einem Bein
S Simultan
Ü Übergang

References are given in the form: (*S* 40).

Full details of the editions used can be found in the Select Bibliography.

Introduction

Changing the subject

The six literary works that are the focus of this study attempt nothing less than to change the subject of German literature. 'Changing the subject' is deliberately ambiguous. On the one hand it indicates the differing themes and concerns of works authored recently by women in a literary tradition where most established writers have been men. But also, and more importantly, it denotes the challenge contained in these works and others to the universalist notions of the subject on which that literature has traditionally been based, which, crudely expressed, assumed a subject that was unified, stable, and normatively male. 'Subject' and 'subjectivity', terms deriving from psychoanalysis, philosophy, and critical theory, and explained in more detail below (as well as briefly in the Glossary), are thus central to this study, which of necessity takes an explicitly, though we hope not heavy-handedly, theoretical approach to the analysis of literary texts. For the study of literature is in fact always in some measure theoretical: even naive readers of texts start with certain assumptions about what literature is, who writes it, and how it achieves its effects, though they may not question them. Critical theory helps make these assumptions visible, gives us a common terminology, and facilitates complex readings of texts which see their narrative strategies not as separate from but as a response to other contemporary discourses.

This study offers detailed, theoretically informed readings of six significant prose texts by women writers from the German-speaking world. In each chapter we respond to the specificity of the particular text, and provide a new reading which goes beyond its critical reception to date and in which the consequences of different theoretical approaches are rendered explicit. The chapters are presented in chronological order of the texts' publication but are intended also to stand alone. They can thus be read in any order, although a chronological reading will highlight certain progressions in both the development of women's writing in the post-war period—in particular from modernist towards postmodern conceptions of subjectivity—and in recent moves in feminist critical theory, beyond 'images of women', psychoanalytic, and Marxist feminisms towards theories of performativity, embodiment, and new materialism. The book will also repay a second reading or at least a certain amount of cross-checking, for recurring concerns in the writing, for example trauma and the legacy of Germany's fascist past, will emerge, as will interesting parallels between the texts, such as the multilingualism of several of the female protagonists. We also hope that the indispensability of critical terminology will become increasingly apparent. What follows in this introduction both anticipates complex arguments spelled out in the chapters and draws out some of their implications; the introduction concludes with summaries of the individual chapters which list the main arguments and highlight the ways in which theory has been deployed. It too will therefore yield more if reread by way of a conclusion.

Six texts

As our title indicates, the six prose texts examined in detail in this book have at least three fundamental things in common: they were all written in German, by women, in the recent past (they were published between 1972 and 1990); they also have in common that they have met with critical acclaim. From the many texts of which these things could be said (for women's writing in German is an extensive, significant, and growing field) we have chosen these six because, in our view, they are aesthetically challenging—each author achieving a distinctive voice—and raise pertinent questions for feminism in their representation of women's experience.[1] In particular they show that 'identity', with its connotations of stability and control, is a less adequate term for describing how a modern person sees him- or herself than the term now current in various strands of critical theory, 'subjectivity', with its dual meanings of 'a subject which acts' who is also 'subject to' the forces which define it. In different ways the texts all reflect the rise of a feminist consciousness in Europe since the start of the second women's movement in 1968. They also reflect, in common with much literature in German from this period, the tumultuous events of twentieth-century history in and beyond Germany and Austria—in particular the Holocaust—and

[1] For a survey of the field of recent German women's writing see Chris Weedon (ed.), *Post-War Women's Writing in German: Feminist Critical Approaches* (Oxford: Berghahn, 1997). We regret that two significant categories could not be represented in the current volume; namely, texts by Jewish and Swiss writers.

explore the resulting interrogation or renegotiation of Austrian and, in particular, German identities. Beyond these shared characteristics, however, it is difficult to generalize because the texts are so diverse in terms of the experience represented and the aesthetic strategies employed.

Thus although the first two texts are conceptually and formally very different, they share a distinctly Austrian flavour, by virtue both of their settings (Vienna and Carinthia for Ingeborg Bachmann's story cycle *Simultan* and the Austrian countryside for Elfriede Jelinek's novel *Die Liebhaberinnen*) and of their common intellectual heritage (for example, the influence of Wittgenstein's philosophy of language). Bachmann's stories, ostensibly thematizing mundane and everyday aspects of five women's lives, also engage with the limitations of language in a post-Holocaust world and convey a powerful sense of historical catastrophe and suffering, while Jelinek's novel mounts a scathing Marxist-feminist critique of capitalism and patriarchy through its satirical portrayal of two women's attempts to obtain husbands on the marriage market. Bachmann's subtle narrative voice conveys, through its closeness to her characters, their subjection to the dominant discourses of the day, while also revealing their compliance with the social roles held out for them. This contrasts with Jelinek's obtrusive and dominating narrator, whose presence structures the narrative of *Die Liebhaberinnen* tightly in order to enlighten the reader about oppressive power structures, while simultaneously revealing through mimicry the inevitably ideological nature of language itself.

The next two texts represent aspects of post-war German experience, but again in markedly different ways. 'Übergang', the title story of Anne Duden's story cycle of that name, is set in the late 1970s in West Berlin, a city the author left in 1978 for London, having moved to the Federal Republic from the German Democratic Republic with her family as a teenager. Through its account of a traumatic attack on its female protagonist and its exploration of violence in Germany's past, it examines the legacy of the Holocaust through a narrative of physical and subjective disintegration, with the erasure of traces of damage amounting to a further act of violence. Christa Wolf, who, like Bachmann, was born before the Second World War, lived through both the Weimar Republic and the Third Reich, and was, when she published the novel *Kassandra* in 1983, living through her third of four incarnations of a German state, namely the GDR; uniquely among our six authors she chose a mythological setting as a way of commenting indirectly on the cold war which was then threatening to wreak nuclear catastrophe on German soil. Duden's text represents a kind of *écriture féminine*: its slippage between first- and third-person narrative, its rhythmic patterns, and its play with ambiguity point beyond the symbolic dimension of language to a repressed feminine space, while its foregrounding of the materiality of the body suggests a critique of the mind/body dualism of western culture. Wolf's novel is feminist in a quite different sense: presented in the form of Kassandra's monologue looking back over her life as she is about to die, it articulates directly women's experience of marginalization by allowing a female figure who has traditionally been silenced to be heard. *Kassandra* is much more conventional in its structure than 'Übergang', although the 'closure' of the narrative is countered by the openness of form of the lectures on poetics which accompany and comment on the text. And like Duden's text Wolf's lectures also mount a critique of western thinking, this time of the instrumental reason which leads to war, and attempt to envision alternatives by looking for the point where western culture took a wrong turn.

The final two texts suggest other, more hybrid and mobile, German identities; they mount a challenge to hegemonic notions of 'Germanness', and indeed to totalizing discourses of all kinds, including feminism. Irene, the protagonist of Herta Müller's novel *Reisende auf einem Bein,* is, like the author, a German, but from outside Germany: she is an ethnic German who arrives in West Berlin towards the end of the 1980s from a repressive East European country (a thinly disguised Romania). The narrative records her gradual and only partially successful acclimatization in the first few weeks and months after her arrival, and reveals that her present alienation is caused at least in part by the trauma she has suffered in the past. The unnamed protagonist of 'Mutter Zunge' and 'Großvater Zunge', two stories in Emine Sevgi Özdamar's story cycle *Mutterzunge,* is, like the author, a Turkish woman living in Berlin who decides to learn Arabic as a way of filling in some of the gaps in her identity. The love affair with her teacher which ensues cannot be sustained, but it enables her to encounter the various historical layers present in contemporary Turkish culture and to explore the complex and ambivalent heritage of Islam. The aesthetic of both works supports their preoccupation with decentred forms of subjectivity: the gaps and silences in *Reisende auf einem Bein* are symptomatic of the gaps in Irene's psyche, while the poetic style employed by Özdamar, which draws on imagery from Turkish, forces the German reader to share the sense of linguistic estrangement experienced by the protagonist.

The ethnic and political diversity of the contemporary German-speaking world and the profound impact of twentieth-century historical events on it are therefore represented here, as is a wide range of innovative aesthetic strategies. The experience of dictatorship, for example, resonates throughout Wolf's and Müller's texts, while those by Bachmann and Jelinek critique repressive power structures left over from a previous era within the particular western capitalist democracy that is Austria. The central significance of the Holocaust, as perhaps the defining moment of twentieth-century European history, haunts Bachmann's, Wolf's, and Duden's texts. From the vantage point of the early twenty-first century, the texts collectively remind the reader that the cold war division of Europe into East and West, which seemed so permanent at the time, was always already a temporary affair, and that the German-speaking lands have always been a place of border traffic.[2] The evocation of Vienna in *Simultan* and that of Berlin in 'Übergang', *Reisende auf einem Bein*, and 'Mutter Zunge'/'Großvater Zunge' illustrate this well: Bachmann's Vienna is founded, at least for its men, on a nostalgia for the lost territories of the Austro-Hungarian empire, while Duden's West Berlin reflects both the controlling role of the United States of America (in the presence of GIs in the city) and a certain limited degree of ethnic diversity (in the presence of a black doctor). Müller's and Özdamar's later texts, published shortly before and just after the fall of the Berlin Wall respectively, depict Berlin as a multicultural city.

The focus on women's experience in the chosen texts raises the question of autobiographical influence, which in several of them is quite strong. Müller is the most explicit about this, happily employing the term 'autofiction' to describe her literary output. We hope to show that the close link between lived experience and literary expression does not in any way involve a narrowing of focus, because of the diversity of that experience and the subtleties of its expression. In particular these texts all interrogate the role of language in the acquisition of subjectivity, through the media (in Jelinek), through propaganda (in Wolf), through the discourse of denazification (in Duden), and, indeed, even when the emphasis is on the protagonists' refusal to respond positively to the ways in which they are positioned by language, as in Bachmann's Nadja and the polyglot protagonists of Müller and Özdamar. This makes for protagonists who are somewhat unstable and who exist in an often complicitous relationship with the discourses which constitute them. They do not unambiguously seek victim status as women, as some of the protagonists of early second-wave feminist texts such as Verena Stefan's *Häutungen* (1975) and Brigitte Schwaiger's *Wie kommt das Salz ins Meer* (1977) did, though Wolf's *Kassandra* reminds us of the recurring pattern whereby women become objectified in time of war. The texts also raise both lighthearted and deeply serious questions about women's relationship with their bodies, from Bachmann's Beatrix's use of make-up, to the

[2] See Elizabeth Boa, 'Writing About Women Writing in German: Postscript and Perspectives', in Jo Catling (ed.), *A History of Women's Writing in Germany, Austria and Switzerland* (Cambridge: Cambridge University Press, 2000), 254–64 (260).

preoccupation with the materiality of the body in Duden, the breaking down of boundaries between the protagonist's self and her surroundings in Müller, and the concern with eroticism in Özdamar.

The focus on women's experience and subjectivity is not necessarily typical of these authors, each of whom has produced a large body of work, some in a variety of genres other than prose fiction: Bachmann is to this day known as much as a modernist poet as for her later prose texts; Jelinek is a prominent playwright; Duden's later works are mostly poetry; Wolf is usually discussed in the context of GDR literature, and is even sometimes read as *the* representative GDR author; Müller places her own work within twentieth-century literature of trauma rather than within women's writing; and Özdamar's novels are frequently viewed as the outstanding example of Turkish-German writing. Indeed, despite their common concern with articulating women's experience, these six texts too could and should be read in many contexts other than that of women's writing. But the risk of ghettoization which inevitably accompanies a project such as ours is, in our view, worth taking, because collectively the texts raise important questions of concern to women readers about the construction of female identity, the possibilities for agency, and women's complex, often complicitous relationship to hegemonic power structures.

Aesthetic form is a crucial element in the literary exploration of subjectivity and power, and the texts operate with a variety of means, from the modernism of Bachmann to the postmodern language play of Özdamar. The authors' aesthetic choices often reveal the desire to break with existing conventions: both Wolf and Müller explicitly write to counter the stifling norms of socialist realism, the prescriptive aesthetic rules of eastern-bloc states, while Jelinek satirizes the cosy genre of romantic fiction and seeks to shock with her abandonment of the traditional rules of capitalization in the German language. Duden perhaps goes furthest in terms of formal experimentation, attempting something paradoxical; namely, the expression of embodied subjectivity through language. But the majority of the texts at the same time adopt some conventionally masculine discourses and narratives unproblematically, or rework them to give them a new slant: Jelinek presents Marxist arguments without irony, Özdamar engages without prejudice with Islam, Wolf perceives many truths in traditional myths, while also reinterpreting them, and Bachmann, like Virginia Woolf before her, attempts with her text to insert a distinctly female voice into the male narratives of modernism. It is, significantly, only Duden and Müller, those writers whose texts are most strongly marked by trauma, who regard all hitherto dominant frames of reference with scepticism.

Theoretical approaches

These writers' appreciation that subject-formation is a complex process, their diverse aesthetic strategies, and their differing placement of themselves in relation to the political, historical, philosophical, and literary discourses of their times suggest that any naive or single-aspect reading of their works will fail to do justice to them. We therefore present readings which adopt a range of different approaches, readings which we hope are authoritative but which do not attempt to have the last word. Our approach could be termed heuristic, in that we prioritize the texts themselves, using theory as a way into them and to show how they relate to contemporary debates about issues such as gender, subjectivity, and representation. As *Germanistinnen* we are concerned to locate our interpretations in specific cultural and historical contexts, being committed to grounded, historical readings as well as to theoretical pluralism. The theories used to approach the texts are not all feminist, although we endeavour to highlight the gendered implications of theory, and to indicate incompatibilities and parallels between different conceptual frameworks. We aim to encourage a scholarly yet pragmatic approach to the use of theory, which should be an empowering interpretative tool, not a daunting or exclusionary practice.

While we did not set out with a theoretical template to guide our readings, certain emphases have emerged which reflect both recurrent themes in the literature (such as language and trauma in a post-Holocaust world) and current philosophical concerns (such as the mind/body dichotomy in western thought). An important theoretical context for at least four of our authors (Bachmann, Jelinek, Duden, and Wolf) is Frankfurt School *Kulturkritik* (critiques of culture), as is well-documented in existing (especially German) criticism of their work. Our own theoretical approach is a self-critical post-structuralist feminist one. Post-structuralism offers a theory of subject-formation indebted to twentieth-century Marxism, psychoanalysis, deconstruction, and Foucauldian discourse theory. In place of the Hegelian self-conscious subject in pursuit of absolute knowledge, it sees the subject as an effect of culture, being psychologically, socially, and discursively constructed, and called to occupy subject positions not of its own making. Post-structuralism's usefulness for feminism lies in its analysis of the competing and contradictory subject positions held out to women, and in the insights it affords into the psychologically compelling nature of these positions. We adopt this theoretical stance self-critically, recognizing critiques of post-structuralism: that it posits only one theory of subject-formation in a world where multiple possibilities coexist; that it foregrounds subjectification at the expense of agency; that it shares the limitations of its 'source' narratives, and thereby reinforces the absolute distinction between representation and the material world which some contemporary feminist philosophy is now challenging. Three specific impulses in contemporary feminist theory permeate our textual analysis: psychoanalysis, performativity theory, and what we have called 'new materialism'. However, cutting across these are Marxist, post-colonial, and trauma theories, which provide different perspectives on subjectivity, attending to categories such as class, race, and ethnicity, as well as gender. In contemporary usage it is most common to encounter these theoretical impulses in their intersections with each other: for example, Marxism with feminism; performativity with Althusserian Marxism; psychoanalysis with post-colonial theory and trauma theory. Not all of these avenues can be pursued in any detail here, but the paragraphs below outline in brief a particular trajectory within feminist theory which has informed the readings which follow.

Only Bachmann's *Simultan* (the oldest text) is considered in terms of 'images of women' criticism, and this is only to demonstrate the limitations of this approach; the implication that literature represents femininity in a 'distorted' way implies a 'true' alternative which is itself problematic as soon as attempts are made to define it. As the discussion of Bachmann's stories seeks to demonstrate, only a complex analysis of psychic and discursive female-identity acquisition does justice to the subtleties of her cultural critique. Psychoanalysis, whilst initially critiqued by feminism as a discourse which has itself contributed to women's oppression, is important for the significance it accords to the unconscious, and for the instability it acknowledges in subject-formation. Indeed, psychoanalytical understanding of gendered identity acquisition was crucial in identifying the limitations of feminist consciousness-raising, with its naive and optimistic assumption that insight into the causes of oppression would lead directly to women's emancipation. In taking seriously the impact of the unconscious on human life, psychoanalytic theory offers explanations for contradictory and complicitous behaviours. In positing subjectivity as gradually and laboriously achieved, it opens up the possibility that it can be constructed differently.

Thus even the patriarchal view of the symbolic posited by Jacques Lacan need not be construed as inevitable, because of the priority accorded to culture in his theory. By virtue of the human infant's premature birth, it is uniquely dependent on the care and example of others; the trajectory from need to demand and ultimately desire demonstrates how completely language and culture take the place of instinct, so often invoked to legitimize male aggression and female passivity.[3] As revealed in the discussions of Bachmann and Duden in this volume, Lacan's notion of the symbolic order has been important for an understanding of the marginal position of the feminine in mainstream culture, as also for the difficulties encountered by women authors in writing from a specifically female subject position. Necessarily speculative and open to rival interpretations, psychoanalysis has produced persuasive models for analysing certain forms of aesthetic modernism, as well as for understanding phenomena such as post-traumatic stress. Both rely on Lacan's notion of the real, as that which cannot be known, symbolized, or mediated, the constitutive 'outside' of the symbolic. It exists before entry into the symbolic (for example, it is manifest in the infant's body before any training), and is residually present in the symbolic in material effects such as rhythm, or in logical impossibilities in the signifying chain. In trauma, unprocessed experience causes a fixation or blockage in the patient's psyche, and the role of psychoanalysis is to encourage him or her to symbolize that element of the real which is causing distress. This is relevant to the discussions of Duden and Müller, both of whom depict the psychic consequences of specific historical instances of trauma.[4]

The limitations of psychoanalytic theory are also discussed in the chapters which follow; it can be gender-blind (as in some readings of Duden as a modernist writer), universalizing, and ahistorical, suggesting that subject-formation has always and in all places occurred in an identical way. Thus whenever 'woman' is invoked in psychoanalytic theory the term inevitably reduces the diversity of female experience to a single, implicitly normative account. Psychoanalysis, with its debt to Freud and Lacan in particular, is also fundamentally Eurocentric (hence the doubts expressed regarding its relevance to Özdamar's text). For the new-materialist theorists such as Christine Battersby and the Australian School it is the radical split between body and psyche, real and symbolic in Lacan's thinking which limits his usefulness for rethinking an embodied female subjectivity. This dualism is indebted to Kant's noumenal/phenomenal divide, which posits an inaccessible 'being' of things beyond the world constructed by our senses, imagination, and understanding. Similarly, Lacan's view of the necessity for a

[3] See Dylan Evans, *An Introductory Dictionary of Lacanian Psychoanalysis* (London: Routledge, 1997), 37.

[4] For further explanation of the real see Bruce Fink, *The Lacanian Subject: Between Language and Jouissance* (Princeton, NJ: Princeton, University Press, 1995).

cut from the Other in subject-formation is indebted to Kant's view of self-knowledge as possible only in opposition to the phenomenal world which is other than the self.[5] From this perspective Lacanian theory offers too little potential for thinking subjectivity differently, except perhaps via Luce Irigaray's concept of mimicry: the subversive appropriation of culturally feminine modes of discourse to expose the operations of power from within.

The concept of mimicry—recently reclaimed for feminist and post-colonial theory and liberated from its historically negative connotations—has opened up new ways of conceptualizing agency for marginalized subjects.[6] The proximity of mimicry which emulates and mimicry which parodies the dominant culture is the source of its destabilizing power. It is related to the notion of performativity, as formulated by Judith Butler, which envisages resistance to social conditioning without positing a subject with free will who resists. Whereas a performance is carried out by a subject who precedes the performance, Butler's notion of performativity (used in the sense of performative speech acts) contests the very notion of a continuing self. As in post-structuralist theory, Butler sees the subject as the product of social power structures, not a free agent, but she accentuates the temporal and iterative process by which subjectivity is formed. Different aspects of subjectivity (such as gender) are acts which produce the very thing they name. This does not occur once and for all, but in a sequence of repeated gestures which give rise to the impression of something stable and authentic. While this does not imply that different genders can be performed at will, it does contain the potential for agency and change. That this is available only within existing constraints, and may not occur at all, is perhaps most cruelly evident in the lives of Jelinek's protagonists. In *Bodies that Matter* (1993) Butler discusses performativity in terms of 'citationality', referring to Derrida's claim that the possibility of failure is intrinsic to any performative utterance. Thus the perfect iterative performance is precarious and can always fail or be subverted, as suggested in the Butlerian reading of Bachmann's story 'Ihr glücklichen Augen'. Nonetheless one could argue that there is an uneasy marriage of Freudian psychoanalysis (with its focus on the subject) and deconstructive linguistic theory (which dethrones the subject) in Butler's work, a tension identified in our analysis of Bachmann's story.

[5] See Christine Battersby, *The Phenomenal Woman: Feminist Metaphysics and the Patterns of Identity* (New York: Routledge, 1998), 62, 86–9.

[6] When opposed to mimesis, the Aristotelian term for the ennobling and self-conscious imitation constitutive of art, mimicry was traditionally the form of adaptation of which animals were capable, devoid of humanizing power.

Butler collapses the distinction between sex and gender which underpinned the challenge to essentialism in the 1970s from those who saw identity as constructed rather than given. Butler insists instead that there is only gender, even sex being discursively constructed. This Foucauldian move is dependent on a view of discourse as simultaneously prescriptive and productive, both presupposing the subject positions it is possible to occupy at a given historical moment and producing their illegitimate alternatives. Hence, while there is no stepping outside discourse to some realm of 'freedom', there is the potential for the proliferation and subversion of discursive formations from within. Butler's thinking is also profoundly Hegelian, in assuming that the being of a thing is identical with the mode in which it is thought; hence, because the body is *thought* by means of discourse, it is an *effect* of discourse.[7] Discourse posits its outside (matter) and thereby constitutes it. This gives rise to one of the major criticisms of Butler's work in recent debates on feminist ontology. Christine Battersby for one, while sympathetic to Butler's political agenda to challenge the heterosexist bias in contemporary culture, criticizes her view of all matter as discursively produced. For Battersby, Butler shares the epistemological bias of much post-structuralist theory, focusing on representation at the expense of theorizing subjective agency, or of redefining substance in a way which would validate women's bodies.[8]

The branch of feminist philosophy which we have dubbed 'new materialism' loosely incorporates figures such as Adriana Cavarero, Rosi Braidotti, Battersby, and the 'Australian School' including Elizabeth Grosz, Moira Gatens, and Genevieve Lloyd. They are all interested in theorizing embodied subjectivity and in challenging the body/mind, matter/representation divide which even Butler's work upholds (despite her apparent concern with 'matter'). Drawing more on Spinoza than on the Kantian tradition informing much post-structuralist thought, and more influenced by Deleuze than by Lacan, these theorists challenge the absolute boundary between representation and the real, and posit meaning as emerging at the level of the body, not just retrospectively through discourse. This is a challenge to Butler's *ex post facto* logic, and an assertion that what is only known after symbolization is nevertheless there before it. For Spinoza there is no radical mind/body divide; being

[7] See Claire Colebrook, 'From Radical Representations to Corporeal Becomings: The Feminist Philosophy of Lloyd, Grosz, and Gatens', *Hypatia*, 15/2 (2000), 76–93, for a critical discussion of Butler's Hegelian legacy.

[8] See also Seyla Benhabib's suspicion that Butler's radical anti-foundationalism is a threat to women's hard-won subjective status (Benhabib, 'Feminism and Postmodernism: An Uneasy Alliance', in Seyla Benhabib, Judith Butler, Drucilla Cornell, and Nancy Fraser, *Feminist Contentions: A Philosophical Exchange* (London and New York: Routledge, 1995), 17–34 (22)).

is synonymous with becoming, and meaning begins at the level of the corporeal. His 'philosophy of immanence' is fundamental to Deleuze's view of human sociability as a dynamic substance in a state of constant molecular mobility.[9] This dynamic view of intersubjective movement informs the positive reading of bodily fragmentation in Duden's text.

Battersby's attempt to think subjectivity on the basis of a body which can give birth is not a retrogressive step, imprisoning women once more in their reproductive destiny, but goes hand in hand with a reconceptualization of matter as capable of radical novelty.[10] She is also concerned to reinstate metaphysics as potentially useful for feminism, but basing her ontology on a view of substance which is dynamic and can change.[11] This critique of a particularly western philosophical tradition is echoed in the erotic imagery of Özdamar's poetic prose, which is rooted in the Islamic tradition of Ottoman romance. A related concern with relocating the political from lofty abstractions to the level of relations between unique individuals in Cavarero's work finds resonances in Wolf's novel, and a transnational dimension is opened up in Braidotti's cartographic metaphor for self, the nomadic subject. This figure of mobile, polyglot subjectivity is relevant to our discussions of both Müller's and Özdamar's texts, where fractured and fragmented identity is a painful but ultimately life-affirming condition.

This brief outline only touches on some of the ideas we have found useful, and none is entirely displaced by the others. Nor do they exist in isolation, and we attempt to indicate their intersections (or incompatibilities) with other frameworks where relevant. So, for example, in Wolf's *Kassandra* the Enlightenment project is modified, but not abandoned, by means of a new understanding of the subject and of politics. In fact, Wolf's reclaiming of Enlightenment values is paralleled in Cavarero's and Battersby's mining of western culture for other, more productive models than those commonly used and abused by dominant philosophical traditions. In Duden's text a tension is identified between

[9] For a discussion of the synergy between feminism, Spinoza, and Deleuze see Moira Gatens, 'Feminism as "Password": Rethinking the "Possible" with Spinoza and Deleuze', *Hypatia*, 15/2 (2000), 59–75.

[10] A parallel may be drawn with Adriana Cavarero's reinterpretation of the figure of Demeter, who embodies the power, though not the obligation, to reproduce life: 'to generate is an exclusively female experience, but it is not an automatic and obligatory process where women are mere vehicles' (Cavarero, *In Spite of Plato: A Feminist Rewriting of Ancient Philosophy* (Cambridge: Polity, 1995), 64).

[11] For Battersby essentialism is only problematic if an Aristotelian view of essence as unchanging, inert substance is adopted. Instead she looks to thinkers such as Henri Bergson for a view of essence as a 'snapshot', or temporary stability in an underlying fluid matter (Battersby, *The Phenomenal Woman*, 34).

the priority accorded to matter in 'Übergang' and the fascination with the unapproachable real; between the celebration of 'intensities' and the psychoanalytical notion of *jouissance* (which is both traumatic and pleasurable). In Özdamar's text unexpected parallels emerge between a pre-modern and a postmodern critique of the mind/body distinction. Most notable in Jelinek's novel is the tension between a Marxist-feminist agenda and a post-structuralist scepticism about representation, which poses still urgent questions about women's material being and the viability of Enlightenment narratives of emancipation. These and similar tensions in the texts and the critical approaches used raise a fundamental issue of balancing the affirmative force of postmodernism with the critical purchase needed to bring about social change.

Chapter summaries

Ingeborg Bachmann, Simultan

The focus of *Simultan* is intimate but the implications wide-ranging: each of the five stories in the volume outlines a personal crisis in the life of a different woman, but, as the title, with its reference to simultaneous translation, implies, the overarching concern is with the limitations of language in a post-Holocaust world. The five damaged protagonists inhabit a world in which the evil that spawned National Socialism lives on in the everyday inhumanity of post-war Austrian society. 'Images of women' approaches are shown to be of limited value: they merely distinguish between the two frame stories, in which the protagonists, the interpreter Nadja and the photojournalist Elisabeth, are successful career women, and the middle three stories, in which the myopic Miranda, the narcissistic Beatrix, and the neglected old Frau Jordan are defined primarily by the men in their lives. Chapter 1 reads the stories using insights from psychoanalysis, the performativity theory of Judith Butler, and the dialogism of Mikhail Bakhtin, but always with an eye to the locatedness of the women's experience in the real space/time of post-war Austria.

The influence of Wittgenstein's theory of language games can be detected in the title story; this reading is contrasted with a gendered psychoanalytic one which proposes that Nadja's crisis occurs as a result of her having successfully taken up a position in the symbolic. The protagonists of 'Ihr glücklichen Augen' and 'Probleme Probleme' are read as ambiguous characters: Miranda's selective vision is both symptom and creative impulse, while Beatrix is an unconsciously ironic commentator on the social roles imposed on women, simultaneously demonstrating her complete complicity with them. Beth Linklater's performativity reading of 'Probleme Probleme', which questions whether there is any psychic reality underneath the masquerade of femininity, is shown to be fruitful but also critiqued for the fact that it cannot account for the hints of unconscious resistance in Beatrix, and indeed the other protagonists. 'Das Gebell', the story most explicitly linked to Austria's fascist past through the figure of the successful psychoanalyst Leo Jordan, is read using Bakhtin's theory of hybrid constructions in language: the young and the old Frau Jordan are constrained in their interaction by the power of the absent son. While many of the stories could be said to operate with a polarized view of gender, the last and longest story, 'Drei Wege zum See', unsettles gender identity in its exploration of destructive modernity and historical loss.

Elfriede Jelinek, Die Liebhaberinnen

Die Liebhaberinnen is an anti-romance, an ironic take on the familiar tale of a woman's search for a husband. Chapter 2 explores the apparent contradiction between the novel's engagement with overtly feminist subject matter (women and work, domestic violence, marriage, and motherhood) and the narrator's lack of empathy with the characters and pessimism regarding the possibility of change. Beginning with an examination of the high degree of intertextuality of the novel, it then unravels the complex interplay of Marxist, feminist, and post-structuralist ideas in the text to explore the tension between the novel's debt to Enlightenment ideology and the complicity of its discourse in the power structures it seeks to expose.

The female protagonists' complicity in their own oppression by patriarchal capitalist power structures is explained in terms of Althusser's notion of interpellation, taken up also by Judith Butler: although responding in different ways to the ideological discourses of romance, marriage, and motherhood, Paula, Brigitte, and Susi all actively desire the conditions of their own exploitation and fail to resist the relations of power which construct them. That they also derive their identity from their role as objects of exchange in a social and symbolic order which cements the relations between men (Luce Irigaray) shows that Jelinek locates the source of their oppression in their internalization of exploitative economies which pre-date and exceed capitalism.

The enlightening message and didactic frame are undermined by the aesthetics of mimicry practised by the narrator, who repeatedly draws attention to the unreliability of language, casting doubt on the possibility of enlightenment's leading to social change. The sustained attack on language shows that a critique of capitalism itself is not enough, and exposes the implication of language itself in the power relations which feminism seeks to challenge.

Anne Duden, 'Übergang'

'Übergang' recounts the autobiographically inspired story of a sudden, unprovoked, violent attack on an unnamed female protagonist in a West Berlin nightclub, and of the apparent dissolution of her identity as a result. The story can partly be read as a trauma narrative, as the protagonist attempts to embed the horrific attack in the story of her life, in which the unspoken trauma of the Holocaust dominates; this attempt, however, only partially succeeds.

The text is approached in Chapter 3 from two distinct psychoanalytic viewpoints before being examined using postmodern theories of difference and embodied subjectivity. First a Lacanian reading, such as that of Sigrid Weigel, proposes that the attack dislodges the protagonist's anchoring in the symbolic, enabling a partly welcome release of all that was repressed in her unconscious during the process of subject-formation. The text thus celebrates feminine excess in a patriarchal symbolic order. But its foregrounding of the body, of damaged flesh, and intense physical sensation begs a more negative interpretation in the light of Julia Kristeva's theory of the abject; that is, the challenge mounted by such things as body fluids, excreta, and dead bodies to subjective boundaries. The wiring of the protagonist's jaw as part of her medical treatment, experienced as a second violation, subjects her to the humiliation of abjection, and the end of the text is suggestive of her despair and paranoia. This raises the problem of reader identification, for Stephanie Bird has highlighted the fascination in Duden's protagonists with the role of violence in the assertion of identity. As a member of the nation responsible for the Holocaust and also of the self-destructive human race, the protagonist is thus not just a victim but also complicit in destructive power structures.

Leslie Adelson's postmodern awareness of multiple differences is used to show up the limitations of the Lacanian argument—a too universalizing view of 'woman' and a too willing acceptance of her exclusion from the symbolic—and to re-embed the text in its place and time; Adelson also raises the question of whether the text's depiction of the black GIs who perpetrate the attack is racist. The unusual priority given to matter by the text is revisited with reference to the work of feminist philosopher Christine Battersby, who challenges the Kantian system inherited by Lacan and thus by many feminists. While theories of identity derived from Kant rest on a firm inside/outside distinction and see the passive body as essentially a container of the active and superior mind, Battersby breaks down these distinctions; thus the abject in Duden's text is not simply a signifier of the feminine but shows how libidinally invested the body is. Music also functions to dislodge fixity, allowing the protagonist to be porous in a more utopian sense than in her experience of abjection, a sense which does not necessitate the collapse of her subjectivity. The chapter asserts the legitimacy of a pluralistic approach to Duden's work, for the crisis experienced by the subject in the text remains open to contrasting interpretations, consonant with Duden's positioning between modernism and postmodernism. Indeed, to privilege one approach over the other would be to impose a unity on female experience which is unsupported by Duden's text.

Christa Wolf, Kassandra

The novel *Kassandra* is a contemporary retelling of the story of the Trojan prophetess who spoke the truth but was not believed. Chapter 4 explores the novel's feminist message by reading it in the contexts of GDR literature, the tradition of German *Kulturkritik* (critiques of culture), and the cold war, and in relation to recent theories of myth and the feminist philosophy of Adriana Cavarero. It attempts to address two problems highlighted by critics: first, the—for feminism—uncomfortable 'strength' of the central figure, Kassandra, and her self-sacrificial status within a closed narrative; secondly, the tension between the novel's powerful critique of instrumental reason and the 'weakness' of the political solutions envisaged.

The potentially retrogressive aesthetic trajectory in Wolf's work from discursively constructed subjectivity to autonomous selfhood is explained as a response to cultural policy in the GDR. The coexistence of the novel and the accounts of its genesis in the poetics lectures militates against the narrative closure of Kassandra's story, constituting a narrative fabric in which different meanings are held open. Vattimo's typology of contemporary approaches to myth is used to explain the tension between

Wolf's critique of the classical tradition and her debt to it in the novel. If seen as both mythography and mythopoeia, her use of myth can be understood not as postmodern cultural relativism but as a pragmatic form of limited rationality with some leanings towards archaism. She does not abandon Enlightenment ideals entirely, but opposes to them a flexible form of thought based on the formal structure of myth itself.

Kassandra's self-knowledge, proclaimed by her with such confidence, is shown to be partial, narrative in nature, and a function of her desire for unity (Cavarero). Her critique of patriarchal power structures has not prevented her from internalizing them, but while she herself valorizes the mind over the body, the text calls this hierarchy into question and demonstrates the importance for her continuing identity-formation of unconscious processes, her body, and her interaction with others. And whereas the Scamander community is a fragile utopia, it is not an abstract political symbolic order that dictates roles, but a community of unique, embodied subjects for whom subjectivity is founded on an altruistic relation to a necessary other (Cavarero). Wolf's attempt to redefine politics in ways which allow the individual to flourish still owes a debt to the Enlightenment project, while proposing alternatives to its conventional understanding of subjectivity and sociability.

Herta Müller, Reisende auf einem Bein

Reisende auf einem Bein, which depicts the arrival in West Berlin of an ethnic German immigrant from Eastern Europe in the late 1980s, is unusual in Müller's œuvre in that it is not set in her native Romania. However, traces of trauma, the central concern in Müller's autofictional œuvre, and a reflection of her experience of dictatorship, are present throughout. Chapter 5 uses trauma theory and Rosi Braidotti's theory of nomadism to explore the gaps in and fluidity of the protagonist's subjectivity, and to read the work, with its fragmentary aesthetic, both as literature of trauma and as a postmodern city novel.

Irene's estranging view of West Berlin, which ignores its recent history yet gives an intimate picture and contextualizes it in unexpected ways, does not constitute a sustained critique of capitalism; rather it results from her trauma and is characteristic of the anti-systematic aesthetic which is Müller's response to the experience of totalizing systems. Irene's compulsive behaviour, automatic responses to triggering situations, and attraction to sites of violence in Germany's past are read as symptomatic of her trauma.

However, her positioning with regard to the city is also read as that of a postmodern female embodied subject: her gaze does not seek to dominate what she sees; she is, as a woman, always aware of the threat of violence; and her identity is fluid, as demonstrated in her liking for collage. Like Braidotti's nomadic subject, Irene is sustained by desire and enjoys inhabiting the multilingual space of the polyglot, though she does not seek connections with other women. While the appreciation of urban anonymity is unquestionably rooted in a very specific historical experience of totalitarian rule, the novel's exploration of open form and fluid subjectivity demonstrates the conceptual links between trauma theory and the postmodern condition.

Emine Sevgi Özdamar, 'Mutter Zunge' and 'Großvater Zunge'

The female protagonist of 'Mutter Zunge' and 'Großvater Zunge' attempts to reconnect with her Turkish heritage by learning Arabic, which might seem a retrogressive step, as the abolition of the Arabic script by Atatürk in the 1920s heralded a widespread westernization of Turkey that contributed to the emancipation of women. Chapter 6 probes the protagonist's apparently perverse desire by exploring her situatedness as a young, left-wing Turk living in Berlin. It employs psychoanalytical, post-colonial, and new-materialist thinking to illuminate the texts, though always in the awareness that the different parameters of Islamic culture mount a challenge to these western discourses.

The protagonist's initial sense that she has been cut off from her mother tongue is related to a widespread critique in 1980s Turkey of the legacy of Kemal Atatürk's brand of modernization. The Koranic texts by means of which she learns Arabic are strict in their injunctions but poetic in their effects and thus challenge the western mind/body dualism. The love affair which develops between the protagonist and her teacher, in which she temporarily succumbs to the attraction of the roles held out for women in Islam, involves a similar move, showing the assertion of a sexually embodied desire which is outside the Kantian model of a self based on opposition to brute matter. Though the lessons give them an opportunity to perform a common oriental identity, the relationship founders on their different conceptions of corporeality. While the protagonist has by the end undoubtedly acquired a sense of cultural continuity, her identity is not restored to a sense of wholeness, for the Turkish culture to which she gains enriched access is revealed to be itself hybridized.

1 Ingeborg Bachmann, *Simultan* (1972)

Introduction

The title of Ingeborg Bachmann's second volume of short stories points at once to one of her most enduring concerns, that of the limitations of language in a post-Holocaust world. Simultaneous interpreting implies a faith in the transparency of language and the transmissibility of meaning, a faith called into question by the unspeakable horrors perpetrated by National Socialism. At the same time the female narrative voice and the focus on the everyday details of women's lives ground her perspective on recent Austrian history in a gendered subjective experience which is of particular interest to feminism.[1] Ingeborg Bachmann was born in 1926 in Klagenfurt in the Austrian province of Carinthia, in the so-called 'Dreiländereck' ('three-countries corner') bordering on Yugoslavia (now Slovenia) and Italy. The significance of this region, with its history of borderland cosmopolitanism on the one hand and its provincial enthusiasm for National Socialist ideology on the other, resonates throughout her work.[2] She was twelve years old at the time of the *Anschluß*, and is often quoted as saying that the entry of Hitler's troops into Klagenfurt was the traumatic event which inaugurated her memory.[3] She finished school in 1944, and after the war studied philosophy, German literature, psychology, and psychotherapy in Vienna. She was awarded her doctorate for her work on the critical reception of Martin Heidegger's existentialist philosophy in 1950, in the course of which she distanced herself from the neopositivist tradition in which she had been trained, and became increasingly fascinated by the language philosophy of Ludwig Wittgenstein.[4] It was for her poetry that Bachmann first became famous,

[1] In Bachmann's first collection of stories, *Das dreißigste Jahr* (1961), the narrative perspective is predominantly male.

[2] Hans Höller points out that Bachmann's father was among those teachers in Carinthia to join the NSDAP in the early 1930s (Höller, *Ingeborg Bachmann* (Reinbek: Rowohlt, 1999), 25–6).

[3]. Höller notes that Bachmann was not actually in Klagenfurt on this day, 12 March 1938, but that this does nothing to invalidate the symbolism of the *Anschluß* as the violent experience which marked the end of childhood (Höller, *Ingeborg Bachmann*, 18).

[4] Neopositivism is an empirical approach to philosophy which regards observable evidence as the only basis of human knowledge and precise thought. It does not pose questions the answers to which cannot be publicly verified. Wittgenstein was probing the boundaries set to philosophy by neopositivism, and was thus challenging the dominant orthodoxy at the University of Vienna in the first half of the twentieth century.

when she read from her first collection of verse *Die gestundete Zeit* (1953) at the Niendorf meeting of *Gruppe 47* in 1952 alongside Paul Celan and Ilse Aichinger, winning the *Gruppe 47* prize in 1953. Having made her name as a poet in West Germany and caused a media sensation, she went to Italy, where she lived for prolonged periods over the next twenty years.[5] A further volume of poetry followed, *Anrufung des Großen Bären* (1956), then two volumes of short stories, *Das dreißigste Jahr* (1961) and *Simultan* (1972), as well as radio plays, essays, and libretti. The second volume of stories is very different from the first, both in terms of narrative perspective and in its links to the trilogy of novels on which she was working at that time, the 'Todesarten-Projekt' ('Ways of Death Project'), of which only one, *Malina*, was completed; it was published in 1971.[6] The project was to remain unfinished because of Bachmann's untimely death from injuries sustained in a fire in her Rome apartment in 1973.

Although *Malina* was a popular success, both the novel and *Simultan* were rejected by the critics who had seen Bachmann as a great modernist poet and did not welcome what was perceived as a shift of focus to the daily concerns of women's lives. She was dubbed a 'gefallene Lyrikerin' ('a fallen poetess') by the influential critic Marcel Reich-Ranicki, who saw in *Simultan* nothing more than a cynical departure into 'Trivialliteratur'.[7] The stories were indeed concerned with the private sphere at a time when overtly political literature was in vogue, and they did not offer the role models of successful emancipation current in the discourse of second-wave feminism. It was not until the 1980s that feminist criticism began to see in Bachmann's late prose a radical critique of the structures of patriarchal language and society, and she was heralded posthumously

[5] For Bachmann Italy was not an exotic or a romantic location but a country to which she had always felt very close because of its proximity to her childhood home (Bachmann, *Wir müssen wahre sätze Finden: Gespräche und Interviews* (Munich: Piper 1991; 1st pub. 1983), 130).

[6] The other novels, *Das Buch Franza* and *Requiem für Fanny Goldmann,* exist in fragments only. The four-volume critical edition *'Todesarten-Projekt',* edited by Monika Albrecht and Dirk Göttsche, under the direction of Robert Pichl (Munich: Piper, 1995), uses the title *Das Buch Franza*, which was Bachmann's final choice. Its more familiar title is *Der Fall Franza.* The interconnections are seen most clearly in the names which recur in the novels and stories: Elisabeth Mihailovics is the disconcertingly successful cousin of Beatrix in 'Probleme, Probleme', but also an acquaintance of Elisabeth Matrei in 'Drei Wege zum See'; indeed, her unexplained murder is reported in this story. In 'Drei Wege' there is mention of Fanny Goldmann, the eponymous heroine of one of the novel-fragments, and the Franziska of 'Das Gebell' is the female protagonist of *Das Buch Franza.* Many of the names (such as Altenwyl and Trotta) are drawn from the works of Hugo von Hofmannsthal and Joseph Roth, and together they construct the fictional Viennese world of the novels and the stories alike.

[7] Höller quotes Reich-Ranicki's review in the *Berliner Allgemeine Zeitung* of 16 March 1973, in which he describes the stories as 'Lesestoff für jene Damen, die beim Frisör oder im Wartezimmer des Zahnarztes in Illustrierten blättern' ('reading material for those ladies who browse at the hairdresser's or in the dentist's waiting room') (Höller, *Ingeborg Bachmann*, 159).

as a feminist *avant la lettre*.[8] The focus on the 'ways of death' rather than on the lives of women in the texts began to be seen as a devastating attack on the destructiveness of male-dominated culture. Since the 1990s many critics have called for a more historically grounded reading of Bachmann's prose, warning against the temptation to tailor the author to fit the latest feminist, post-structuralist, or other theory.[9] Indeed, her preoccupation with fascism is crucial, in particular her critique of the Austrians' self-image as the 'victims' of National Socialism rather than its willing perpetrators.[10] However, as Elizabeth Boa has pointed out, the fact '[t]hat Bachmann's work continues to resonate through the shifting phases of feminist debates is a measure of its dense complexity'.[11] This chapter will argue that the insights of recent feminist theory can legitimately supplement our knowledge of Bachmann's own historical and intellectual contexts, in order to demonstrate the continuing relevance of her work to women readers today. In the discussion of the stories that follows the intention is to show how feminist psychoanalytical, Bakhtinian, and performativity theories can offer new perspectives on Bachmann's stories, without invalidating what we know about her specific coordinates; as an intellectual conscious of writing after Auschwitz, and as a trained philosopher exploring the limits of philosophy and the possibilities of going beyond it in art.

'Wienerinnen': centre versus periphery[12]

The Austrian capital, the Italian landscapes of 'Simultan', and the Carinthia of 'Drei Wege zum See' ('Three Paths to the Lake') have personal and historical resonances for Bachmann, as places she knew as

[8] For a good summary of the feminist reception of Bachmann in the 1980s see Sara Lennox, 'The Feminist Reception of Ingeborg Bachmann', *Women in German Yearbook*, 8 (1992), 73–111.

[9] Sara Lennox, 'Constructing Femininity after 1945: Ingeborg Bachmann and Her Readers', in Robert Weninger and Brigitte Rossbacher (eds.), *Wendezeiten, Zeitenwenden: Positionsbestimmungen zur deutschsprachigen Literatur 1945–1995* (Tübingen: Stauffenberg, 1997), 173–92; Sigrid Weigel, *Ingeborg Bachmann: Hinterlassenschaften unter Wahrung des Briefgeheimnisses* (Vienna: Zsolnay, 1999).

[10] In 'Drei Wege zum See', for example, Trotta comments on the paradox of Austrian 'victimhood', stating that the German fascist bureaucrats were by no means as evil as the Austrian Nazis (S 396–7).

[11] Boa, 'Reading Ingeborg Bachmann', in Chris Weedon (ed.), *Post-War Women's Writing in German: Feminist Critical Approaches* (Oxford: Berghahn, 1997), 269–89 (286).

[12] 'Wienerinnen' (Viennese Women) was Bachmann's working title for *Simultan*. See Robert Pichl, 'Das Wien Ingeborg Bachmanns: Gedanken zur späten Prosa', *Modern Austrian Literature*, 18/3, 4 (1985), 183–93 for the significance of Vienna in Bachmann's late prose.

'home', and as locations with a legacy of fascism. Any feminist reading of the stories must take account of their highly specific settings, and of the historical continuum in which these are embedded.[13] It is well documented, for example, that 'Drei Wege zum See' draws on characters from Joseph Roth's novels about the demise of the Austro-Hungarian empire *Radetzkymarsch* (1932) and *Die Kapuzinergruft* (1938).[14] This accounts for the sense of anachronism in the narrative, which combines nostalgia for the cosmopolitanism of the old empire with a critique of its authoritarianism and warmongering. The region of Carinthia is as much a metaphorical border area as a geographical location, in contrast to the stagnation, decadence, and repression of the past often associated with Vienna, the setting of the three middle stories. Only the simultaneous interpreter Nadja in 'Simultan' and the photojournalist Elisabeth in 'Drei Wege' have escaped from the suffocating provincialism of the capital; both travelling the world in their successful careers. Yet in their own ways Beatrix and Miranda also cross borders, resorting to extreme strategies which point to their dissatisfaction with the social order they inhabit. The two longer and more complex stories frame the three, shorter cameos of female existence. 'Simultan' is the story of Nadja's brief affair with Ludwig Frankel, a fellow Austrian (with a wife at home in Vienna) whom she meets when she is interpreting at a UN conference in Italy. Despite their common language, they communicate in a mixture of Italian, French, and English, and the story raises questions not only about problems of translation but also about the limits of what can be expressed linguistically at all. 'Drei Wege zum See' concerns the fifty-year-old Elisabeth Matrei, who returns home from Paris to visit her father in Carinthia after attending her brother's wedding in London. While rediscovering the walks of her childhood, she reflects on the rootlessness of her existence, the lovers she has known and lost, and

[13] See Almut Dippel, *'Österreich—das ist etwas, das immer weitergeht für mich': Zur Fortschreibung der 'Trotta'-Romane Joseph Roths in Ingeborg Bachmanns 'Simultan'* (St Ingbert: Röhrig, 1995). Dippel dates each of the stories specifically between 1955 and 1970. Siobhan S. Craig explores the historical resonances of the Italian setting of 'Simultan' in 'The Collapse of Language and the Trace of History in Ingeborg Bachmann's "Simultan"', *Women in German Yearbook*, 16 (2000), 39–60.

[14] For the references to Joseph Roth in Bachmann's work see Irena Omelaniuk, 'Ingeborg Bachmanns "Drei Wege zum See"', *Seminar*, 19/4 (1983), 246–64; Leo A. Lensing, 'Joseph Roth and the Voices of Bachmann's Trottas: Topography, Autobiography, and Literary History in "Drei Wege zum See"', *Modern Austrian Literature*, 18/3, 4 (1985), 53–76; Peter West Nutting, '"Ein Stück wenig realisiertes Österreich": The Narrative Topography of Ingeborg Bachmann's "Drei Wege zum See"', *Modern Austrian Literature*, 18/3, 4 (1985), 77–90; David Dollenmeyer, 'Ingeborg Bachmann Rewrites Joseph Roth', *Modern Austrian Literature*, 26/1 (1993), 59–74; Dippel, *'Österreich'*.

the entwinement of her own identity with the fate of Austria in the twentieth century.

'Probleme Probleme' is the story of the twenty-year-old Beatrix, whose addiction to sleep and obsession with the artificial, perfumed world of the beauty parlour are symptomatic of her contradictory attitudes to femininity. While she refuses to engage with social reality by taking on any form of employment, she appears to conform to the images projected on to her by her married lover Erich, and reinforced at the hairdressing salon. 'Ihr glücklichen Augen' depicts the short-sighted Miranda, who refuses to wear glasses (in a comparable gesture to Beatrix's sleeping) to avoid facing up to the ugliness and cruelty of the world. She constructs a world for herself which is both self-deceptive and a survival mechanism, to the extent that when Josef, her great love, leaves her for another woman she fabricates an affair of her own to conceal from herself and others her pain. 'Das Gebell' gives insight into the relationship between Franziska Jordan, third wife of the successful psychiatrist Leo Jordan, and her mother-in-law Frau Jordan. The old woman's conversations inadvertently reveal years of neglect and cruelty by her son, a story which forms the background to the nightmare vision in *Das Buch Franza* of the triumph of western political and cultural imperialism, embodied in Leo Jordan.

Two contrasting feminist readings of the stories illustrate a shift in feminist reception of Bachmann in the course of the 1980s particularly clearly. Gudrun Mauch saw the figures of Nadja and Elisabeth as models of emancipated, independent women, while the myopic Miranda, the narcissistic Beatrix, and the neglected old Frau Jordan were defined primarily by their relationships to the men in their lives.[15] Twelve years later Friederike Eigler detected a more unsettling subversion of gender norms in the three shorter stories than in the supposed liberation of Nadja and Elisabeth.[16] Indeed, when challenged on her sometimes very conventional depiction of women, Bachmann distanced herself from contemporary feminist notions of emancipation:

> **Für mich stellt sich nicht die Frage nach der Rolle der Frau, sondern nach dem Phänomen der Liebe—wie geliebt wird. Diese Frau [the 'ich' in *Malina*] liebt so außerordentlich, daß dem auf der anderen Seite nichts entsprechen kann. Für ihn [Ivan] ist sie eine Episode in seinem Leben, für sie ist er der Transformator, der die Welt verändert, die Welt schön macht. Vielleicht ist**

[15] Gudrun Mauch, 'Ingeborg Bachmanns Erzählband *Simultan*', *Modern Austrian Literature*, 12/3, 4 (1979), 273–304.

[16] Friederike Eigler, 'Bachmann und Bachtin: Zur dialogischen Erzählstruktur von *Simultan*', *Modern Austrian Literature*, 24/3, 4 (1991), 1–16.

> **das sehr merkwürdig für Sie, wenn ausgerechnet eine Frau, die immer ihr Geld verdient hat, sich ihr Studium verdient hat, immer gearbeitet hat, immer allein gelebt hat, wenn sie sagt, daß sie von der ganzen Emanzipation nichts hält. Die pseudo-moderne Frau mit ihrer quälenden Tüchtigkeit und Energie ist für mich immer höchst seltsam und unverständlich gewesen.**[17]

This quotation shows both an ambivalence towards contemporary feminist discourses (also explicit in the words of Beatrix in 'Probleme Probleme') and the suggestion of a fundamental incompatibility in the relations between the sexes, one which concerns their capacity to love, from which one might extrapolate the incompatible structures of their desire. It is this dimension of Bachmann's writing which has given rise to reconsiderations of the relative status of the 'emancipated' and 'oppressed' protagonists in *Simultan*, and to readings which focus not just on 'images of women' but on psychoanalytical dimensions of the texts and in particular on the relationship between language and desire.

Psychoanalytical readings

Many critics have identified the significance of Ludwig Wittgenstein's philosophy of language for the story 'Simultan', based on the essays and broadcasts Bachmann devoted to his work.[18] There is certainly more than a suggestion that Nadja's crisis derives from a questioning of her own professional use of language, which presupposes the presence of extralinguistic meaning and the possibility of its perfect transmission from one language to another. Wittgenstein's *Tractatus Logico-Philosophicus* (1921) had been important for Bachmann's Ph.D. thesis, as it proposed that there are aspects of our emotive, aesthetic, ethical, and spiritual

[17] 'For me it is not a question of the role of women, but of the phenomenon of love—how people love. This woman [the I in *Malina*] loves in such an extraordinary way that nothing can reciprocate it. For him [Ivan] she is an episode in his life, for her he is the transformer who changes the world, makes the world beautiful. Perhaps it is very strange for you to hear a woman who has always earned her living, paid for her studies, always worked, always lived alone, for her of all people to say that she doesn't believe in the concept of emancipation. The pseudo-modern woman with her agonizing efficiency and energy has always been very strange and incomprehensible for me' (Bachmann, *Wir müssen wahre Sätze finden*, 109).

[18] See in particular Sara Lennox, 'Bachmann and Wittgenstein', *Modern Austrian Literature*, 18/3, 4 (1985), 239–59. It is possibly no coincidence that Nadja's lover is called 'Ludwig', although she avoids using his first name. Siobhan Craig has pointed out that Frank(e)l is a Jewish name, and could be a specific reference to the Austrian-Jewish writer Ludwig August Frankl von Hochwart (1810–94) (see n. 13). It is perhaps also worth noting that Bachmann studied psychotherapy under Viktor Frankl in Vienna, pointing to a link between her philosophical and psychoanalytical concerns in the story.

experience which exceed the boundaries of language and of philosophy. The Ph.D. thesis cast doubt on the truth claims of Heidegger's metaphysical existentialism, concluding that the questions he was posing belonged to the domain of art, not philosophy.[19] In Wittgenstein's later, posthumously published *Philosophische Untersuchungen* (1953) he abandoned the notion of a monolithic, abstract language, denoting a 'real' world for all people in a similar way, in favour of the coexistence of different language games, representing the partial understanding of the world of different groups of speakers. In place of language as a universal system he posited a multiplicity of languages in use, corresponding to the needs and experiences of its speakers. There are echoes of these ideas in 'Simultan', where Frankel repeatedly poses the question to Nadja of whether there will one day be a universal language. She either ignores him or laughs off the idea as 'romantic', while actually recognizing that his vision would mean the end of her professional existence ('Für mich wäre es eine große Erleichterung, wenn die Sprachen verschwänden, sagte sie, nur würde ich dann zu nichts mehr taugen').[20] More fundamentally, however, his vision represents the monolithic view of language which Wittgenstein rejected, and which Nadja also instinctively resists. Instead she struggles to articulate her own ideal, driven by the desire for a language which would correspond precisely to her experience: 'sie kämpfte erbittert und wild für ihre Erfindung und sprachlos der einzigen Sprache entgegen, auf diese eine zu, die ausdrücklich und genau war'.[21]

Plausible though this reading is, it leaves out of account the gendered nature of the female protagonists' relationship to and positioning in language. Although both Nadja and Elisabeth are multilingual, independent, and successful in a man's world, they are both still marginalized in the powerful discourses of their society. The interpreter mediates only other people's ideas, existing only in the language of others, and the journalist records world events, but in a discourse which cannot

[19] There is a debate, which lies beyond the scope of this study, about the relative importance for Bachmann's work of Heidegger's philosophy and of Frankfurt School theory. Gudrun Kohn-Waechter argues for the influence of Heidegger in 'Das "Problem der Post" in *Malina* von Ingeborg Bachmann und Martin Heideggers "Der Satz vom Grund"', in Anita Runge and Lieselotte Steinbrügge (eds.), *Die Frau im Dialog: Studien zu Theorie und Geschichte des Briefes* (Stuttgart: Metzler, 1991), 225–42. Sigrid Weigel maintains in *Ingeborg Bachmann* that she was opposed to what she saw as the irrationalist impulse in Heidegger's work, aligning her with the thinking of the Frankfurt School.

[20] 'It would be a great relief for me if languages were to disappear, she said, only then I wouldn't be good for anything any more' (*S* 127).

[21] 'she fought bitterly and wildly for her discovery, and struggled mutely towards the one language, the only language that was explicit and precise' (*S* 125).

represent her own, specifically female, concerns. A report which Elisabeth researches on the topic of abortion merely highlights the gulf between language, knowledge, and experience, as the male gynaecologist's 'expert' knowledge prevails over, and silences, the experience of the women concerned.[22] In 'Simultan' the elaborate sign system developed by Nadja and Frankel when swimming off the treacherous rocky coast illustrates metaphorically both their language game as lovers and her subordination to his signifying power; she has to respond 'blindly' to his instructions in order to negotiate the hazards in safety. The enormous statue of Christ above the village of Maratea evokes not only the 'monolithic' view of language (from its vantage point the whole bay is visible) but the unequivocally phallic power of the signifier, rendering Nadja speechless. She is horrified when Frankel insists on the vertiginous ascent to the top of the cliffs where the Christ figure stands, prostrating herself on the ground in abject fear. In contrast, when on their last day together she swims alone she gains a partial and no longer threatening view of the coastline, seeing the statue now as a great bird preparing for flight.

This view of language as medium of patriarchal power corresponds with Ingeborg Dusar's (1990) psychoanalytical reading of 'Simultan', which sees Nadja's crisis as a result of her having successfully taken up a position in the symbolic; the immediacy of pre-Oedipal experience is forgone once the individual is mediated by language. The image of the simultaneous interpreter's mind as a kind of mixing desk for the language of others conveys the subject's alienation in language to great effect. Both Nadja and Frankel search in their common origins and Viennese dialect for the truth of their own identity, but cannot find it in language. The characters' nervous disturbances and their failed communication point to the existence of an 'other scene' of action, and to the realization that the ego is a mere rhetorical figure. Hence Nadja struggles to bring herself into the 'here' and 'now' with Frankel, drifting off instead into thoughts of a previous painful relationship which this liaison seems doomed to mirror. At the same time Frankel is thinking of fishing, and of how he had wanted to shoot the cernia fish in the neck, when Nadja feels a sudden pain in her neck, indicating that the real drama is being played out somewhere else, displaced in the unconscious (*S* 140). The relief experienced by Nadja at the end of the story when she fails to translate a line from the Bible in her hotel room can be explained as the recognition that language is not transparent, it has a material opacity which

[22] *S* 420–1. Elisabeth's report on abortion could be a topical reference to the campaign led by Alice Schwarzer in 1971, in which three hundred prominent West German women declared in an article in *Stern* that they had had illegal abortions.

resists functionalization and translation. This reading sees language not just as an oppressive straitjacket but also as the repository of a residue of *jouissance*, the pleasure in the text which cannot be reduced to its signifying function.

Dusar sees the central concern of the whole volume as being 'die radikale Darstellung einer verletzten weiblichen Innenwelt',[23] and the stories 'Probleme Probleme' and 'Ihr glücklichen Augen' as Bachmann's most eloquent elaborations of this theme. She is among those critics to have interpreted 'Ihr glücklichen Augen' with reference to the dedication of the story to Georg Groddeck (1866–1934), who was known for his psychoanalytical approach to psychosomatic medicine.[24] Groddeck's view of illness was as a 'production' akin to a work of art, which required interpretation rather than cure. It was the non-verbal expression of the id, which he saw as governing both physical and psychic reality. Thus visual disorders such as myopia were a result of the individual's repressed complexes, both an expression of and a defence against forbidden wishes. Unlike the destructive rationality of psychoanalysis as embodied in Leo Jordan (in *Das Buch Franza* and 'Das Gebell'), Groddeck represents a holistic understanding of mind and body, and a view of organic disorders as creative states. Also significant for the story is Groddeck's distinction between the physical, passive sense of sight and a more creative envisioning which is an act of projection of something 'internal' outside ourselves, from which latter phenomenon visual disorders derive.[25] Thus the story begins with a clinical diagnosis of Miranda's short-sightedness and her astigmatism, but the reader is

[23] 'the radical representation of a damaged female psyche' (Dusar, *Choreographien der Differenz: Ingeborg Bachmanns Prosaband 'Simultan'* (Cologne/Vienna: Böhlau, 1994), 255). As will become clear, this emphasis on surface versus depth, inner versus outer reality, is not compatible with the performative reading of the texts.

[24] Groddeck's work on vision was published posthumously in the 1960s, when Bachmann was working on these stories. Linda C. Hsu psychoanalyses the protagonist Miranda for the psychosomatic causes of her myopia in 'A Favourite Selection at the Beauty Parlour? Rereading Ingeborg Bachmann's "Oh Happy Eyes"', in Gudrun Brokoph-Mauch (ed.), *Thunder Rumbling at my Heels: Tracing Ingeborg Bachmann* (Riverside, Calif.: Ariadne Press, 1998), 76–91. Robert Pichl links the story's dedication to the title quotation, from the 'Türmerlied' of Lynkeus in *Faust II*, treating references to vision as a theme which determines the text's immanent structure, in 'Ingeborg Bachmanns "Ihr glücklichen Augen": Eine Apologie der Strukturanalyse', in Irene Heidelberger-Leonard (ed.), *Text Tollhaus für Bachmann-Süchtige? Lesarten zur Kritischen Ausgabe von Ingeborg Bachmanns Todesarten-Projekt* (Opladen/Wiesbaden: Westdeutscher Verlag, 1998), 118–29. Only Ingeborg Dusar in *Choreographien der Differenz* (p. 91) moves beyond the thematic treatment of short sight, pointing to the multiple levels of intertextuality which call for a more complex and allegorical interpretation.

[25] This is suggested also by the title's intertextual reference to Goethe's 'Türmerlied' ('watchman's song'), which evokes the distinction between mechanical sight (*sehen*) and poetic vision (*schauen*).

increasingly plunged into her own perspective, from which her blurred vision is a 'blessing' and a productive state of uncertainty. According to Groddeck's theory her myopia is the expression of a conflict between social and individual morals, and of a desire to be blind to aspects of society she finds intolerable. Indeed, it does relieve her of the necessity to confront suffering and ugliness, allowing her to construct a reality which protects her from cruelty, even that of betrayal by her beloved Joseph. However, with its multiple intertextual references, the story invites us to go beyond clinical diagnosis of the protagonist and to read it as a reflection on unconditional love and an allegory of literary production. Dusar has noted that the continuous present tense and the scenic, rather than sequential, nature of the narrative point to the reproduction of the absolute present of the lover's discourse, dominated by a drive to eliminate separation which is doomed to failure.[26] At the same time the very name 'Miranda', etymologically being both 'astonished' and 'worthy of admiration', suggests an ambivalence in the narrative attitude towards her as both subject and object of the narrative. Her creative myopia is a form of affective, aesthetic filtering of reality, yet she also affords the reader an insight into the 'secret suffering' which Bachmann considered it was the role of literature to disclose. In keeping with Groddeck's challenge to the scientific claims of psychoanalysis, Miranda's selective vision points to a knowledge which only a synthesis of aesthetic, philosophical, and psychoanalytical perspectives can achieve.[27]

In 'Probleme Probleme' Beatrix is a similarly ambiguous character, simultaneously conforming to social roles (such as the beautiful younger woman with whom Erich has an affair—albeit platonic) and resisting social expectations (to train, earn money, or marry). For all her escapism (in sleep, at the hairdresser's) there are moments when her behaviour does appear as a more or less conscious self-defence mechanism in a hostile world. She allows Erich to pour out his troubles to her, and to feel responsible for her welfare, projecting on to her the image of immature, unthreatening sexuality, calling her a 'demi-vierge' ('semi-virgin') and 'Mädchenfrau' ('girlwoman'). She even reinforces this by insisting that her birthday (29 February) permits her to claim eternal youth. She shows no trace of female solidarity with Erich's suicidal wife, but as she ponders her own role as sympathetic ear for his 'problems' a moment of resistance emerges in the transition from free indirect speech to inner monologue: 'Demi-vierge war ganz schön, aber immer konnte sie

[26] See Dusar, *Choreographien der Differenz*, 73.

[27] Dusar, *Choreographien der Differenz*, 89–91.

ihm dieses Vergnügen nicht machen, sie so problemlos zu sehen. Ich bin eine Frau—das mußte ein Problem werden für ihn.'[28]

Beatrix's double life, in which she both plays the game and illuminates its rules, makes her an unconsciously ironic commentator on her situation. Yet the scenes at the hairdresser's throw her complicity into sharp relief. When surrounded by mirrors she finds in them her real 'Zuhause' ('home'), indicating the extent to which she has internalized social constructions of femininity. Sigrid Schmid-Bortenschlager has read this story in terms of Lacan's 'mirror stage', suggesting that Beatrix is a case of arrested development, narcissistically entranced by her own imaginary ideal I.[29] The references to her immaturity indicate a pre-oedipal psychic state, a rejection of mature female sexuality on the terms available in the symbolic (hence her refusal of sex with Erich). The moment of crisis in the story, when an inexperienced beautician disturbs the illusion of perfection, could be seen as a moment of insight into the constructedness of the image. Nonetheless Schmid-Bortenschlager contends that Bachmann stops short of challenging the symbolic construction of femininity on the level of the narrative itself. This view will be revisited in the light of the Bakhtinian reading of Bachmann's narrative technique which follows.

From psychoanalysis to performativity

Ingeborg Dusar interprets the mirror scenes in 'Probleme Probleme' as the site of positive psychic rebellion. Beatrix's excessive sleeping is a fetishistic return-to-the-womb fantasy, and her waking behaviour a parodic playing out of hysterical femininity. Hysteria, usually taken to be the result of a sexual disturbance, was seen by Freud as an indicator of the inadequacy of gender identity to support the differences between the sexes. For Lacan it was the hysteric who had insight into the fundamental lack in desire and knowledge, revealing the incapacity of any human subject to satisfy the ideals of symbolic identifications. Thus Beatrix's knowing use of her 'favourite' words, such as 'grauenvoll' ('horrific'), 'Gewissen' ('conscience'), 'Schuld' ('guilt'), and 'Verantwortung' ('responsibility'), points to an awareness of the inability

[28] 'Semi-virgin was all very well, but she couldn't always give him the pleasure of letting him see her as so unproblematic. I am a woman—this had to become a problem for him' (S 196).

[29] See Sigrid Schmid-Bortenschlager, 'Spiegelszenen bei Bachmann: Ansätze einer psychoanalytischen Interpretation', *Modern Austrian Literature*, 18/3, 4 (1985), 39–52.

of words to deliver meaning, while her vanity is a form of subversive mimicry of psychoanalytical myths of femininity.[30] This is understood in terms of Irigaray's notion of mimicry, a masquerade of patriarchally defined femininity in order to reveal the mechanisms of its construction. However, Dusar detects a pleasurable intensity in Beatrix's narcissism at the beauty parlour; when she dismisses the clumsy young apprentice and is transfixed by her own reflection, doll-like and expressionless, it is narrated as a quasi-mystical moment. She sees herself as 'ein einsames unverstandenes Kunstwerk . . . unerreichbar und zum Glück unverstanden'.[31] This remains an intriguingly ambiguous moment in the text, evoking simultaneously the cliché of a 'feminine mystique', and the suggestion of an ecstatic moment of what Dusar terms '*jouissance* jenseits des Phallus'.[32]

In contrast to this reading, which posits an internal psychic reality underlying the text's emphasis on surface appearances, Beth Linklater proposes a performative reading of 'Probleme Probleme', based on the work of Judith Butler. For Linklater, Beatrix is 'performed as a woman through repeated citation of feminine gender norms', and the challenge to the stability of those norms comes when that repetition momentarily fails.[33] Instead of detecting in the superficiality of the text intimations of inner pain or moments of ecstatic *jouissance*, this reading questions whether anything *does* lie beneath the masquerade of femininity created at the beauty parlour. While the role of mirrors in the story may suggest the narcissism of imaginary identity, the proliferation of reflections can also be seen as undermining the notion of any 'original' being reflected in the glass. As Beatrix is prepared for the hairdryer we read that 'Sie versank förmlich in dem Spiegel', becoming no more than her mirror image.[34] Clothes and make-up are also significant in Beatrix's performance of femininity, but, rather than being a victim of the 'beauty myth', her adornments are arguably the most substantial thing about her. As

[30] Dusar, *Choreographien der Differenz*, 288.

[31] 'a lonely work of art which is not understood . . . inaccessible and fortunately not understood' (*S* 202).

[32] Dusar, *Choreographien der Differenz*, 293. '*Jouissance* beyond the phallus' is what Lacan posits as the 'Other', ineffable feminine desire which is possible because women are not as wholly subject to the symbolic order as men. As Bruce Fink puts it, 'Feminine structure proves that the phallic function has its limits and that the signifier isn't everything' (in *The Lacanian Subject: Between Language and Jouissance* (Princeton, NJ: Princeton University Press, 1995), 107).

[33] Beth Linklater, '"Ein einsames unverstandenes Kunstwerk": Performing Gender Through Make-up in Ingeborg Bachmann's "Probleme Probleme" and Cindy Sherman's *Untitled Film Stills*', in Carolin Duttlinger, Lucia Ruprecht, and Andrew Webber (eds.), *Performance and Performativity in German Cultural Studies* (Oxford: Lang, 2003), 201–20.

[34] 'She positively sank in the mirror' (*S* 185).

she stands in front of the mirror trying to decide what to wear, she is described as 'fast durchsichtig' ('almost transparent') and 'wächsern im Gesicht' ('with a wax-like complexion'), and this prompts her to put on make-up and assert a presence in the world (*S* 163). The climax of the text comes when she is made up at the beauty salon, at first 'as normal' by Frau Hilde, but then by a new member of staff who brings about the catastrophic collapse of the image, by failing to sustain the repetition on which the consolidation of subjectivity depends. It could be understood in terms of the 'potentially productive crisis' which can disrupt every process of repetition, undoing the effects by which 'sex' is stabilized.[35] The scene which Dusar interprets as a moment of *jouissance* can be seen instead as the performance of yet another artificial image of femininity, 'märchenhaft' and 'geheimnisvoll' ('fairy-tale-like', 'mysterious'). The self-love experienced in this moment when Beatrix gazes at her doll-like face and the ringlets in her hair is described explicitly as a romantic *coup de foudre*, 'wie in den Filmen, so romanhaft' ('like in the films, or in a novel', *S* 201). Even her distress at the end of the story, when her make-up is finally removed by the rain and her tears, reproduces in Linklater's view 'another stock personality', that of the deserted lover in a 'private moment of despair'.[36]

Suggestive and radical though this reading is, because it casts doubt on a psychic reality underlying surface appearances, it cannot account for the hints of unconscious resistance in Beatrix. There is the suggestion of an inner opposition to the performance of *any* social identity, as she repeatedly falls back into sleep: 'sie war noch gar nicht bei sich, wo tief inwendig etwas lautlos zu einem Rückzug rief, immer zu einem Widerruf'.[37] Similarly, while she uses the 'empty' word 'grauenvoll' to describe her reluctance to keep her appointment with Erich, we also read: 'Sie empfand dumpf etwas als unerträglich.'[38] While there can be no doubt that Bachmann was concerned with social constructions of femininity, and even with the possibility of their conscious appropriation, there are limits to the ways in which the texts support such radically anti-foundationalist readings, denying any essence of subjectivity. In 'Simultan' Nadja is a consummate performer of the sophisticated woman of the world (*S* 131–2), and in 'Drei Wege zum See' Elisabeth is

[35] See Judith Butler, *Bodies that Matter: On the Discursive Limits of 'Sex'* (New York/London: Routledge, 1993), 10.

[36] This is the lavatory attendant's interpretation of Beatrix's appearance, prompting her sympathetic comment: 'Ja, die Männer' ('Oh, *men!*') (*S* 207).

[37] 'She wasn't yet fully with it when deep inside something called silently for a retreat, repeatedly for a withdrawal' (*S* 162).

[38] 'She had the vague feeling that something was unbearable' (*S* 161).

aware of having been transformed from a plain Viennese woman into an elegant beauty in Paris (*S* 381–2), but the texts resist a reading which would collapse the distinction between inner and surface reality. Miranda's focus on surface appearances in 'Ihr glücklichen Augen' is unequivocally a form of escapism, however legitimate, rather than a questioning of the existence of 'depth'. Nevertheless it is indubitable that Bachmann's conformist protagonists often articulate unintentional social critique. Beatrix's observations on female emancipation, for example, are a poignant comment on the apparent independence of Nadja and Elisabeth, and point to an underlying awareness in the stories of the material inequalities underpinning gender relations: 'Besonders grauenvoll kamen ihr alle Frauen vor, die arbeiteten, denn sicher hatten die alle einen Defekt oder litten an Einbildungen oder ließen sich ausnutzen von den Männern.'[39] Much of the central three stories' critical impact derives from their narrative ambiguity. They call for a view of textuality as a site of competing meanings, as well as an understanding of language as structuring the individual psyche or as a law governing culture.

A Bakhtinian reading

Friederike Eigler has read *Simultan* in terms of the theories of the Russian linguist and literary critic Mikhail Bakhtin, arguing that there is a productive synergy between his view of heteroglossia (the intersection of different ideolects and sociolects in language) and feminist theories concerned with agency and social change.[40] While Bachmann may not have shared Bakhtin's redemptive view of literature, his notions of hybrid construction and the fool are useful ways of understanding some of the ambiguities in her prose style.[41] Bakhtin evaluated positively the existence of multiple voices in prose, where 'voice' refers not to any metaphysical notion of 'presence', nor simply to the 'voice of a character', but to the coexistence in the text of different

[39] 'She found working women particularly frightful, because they were of course all deficient or suffered from delusions or allowed themselves to be exploited by men' (*S* 174).

[40] This discussion is indebted to Friederike Eigler, 'Bachmann und Bachtin', and 'Feminist Criticism and Bakhtin's Dialogic Principle: Making the Transition from Theory to Textual Analysis', *Women in German Yearbook*, 11 (1995), 189–203.

[41] Bakhtin saw literature as a completion of subjective reality from the perspective of otherness. In this respect parallels may be drawn between his aesthetic and Frankfurt School theory, by which Bachmann was undoubtedly influenced.

discourses shaped by concrete social, professional, or ideological factors. He resisted 'monologic' readings which would seek to harmonize these voices and produce singular meaning. Importantly, also, what Bakhtin sees as the dialogic principle operating in texts is not just the willed product of the author but is a function of the discourses which constitute the author's socio-historical context. Unlike the common use of the term 'dialogue' (indicating a willingness to cooperate in an equal exchange), the notion of dialogism may include tensions and struggle between antagonistic voices which refuse to enter into a dialogue. This is the source of its usefulness for feminist criticism, which is attentive to the disruption of dominant ideologies and interested in the possibilities of subjective agency. According to this reading the female characters in *Simultan* can be seen as part of the Austrian upper middle class, sharing its values and prejudices, yet simultaneously more or less socially marginalized. Even Nadja in 'Simultan' communicates largely in the voices of others, talking in set pieces and clichéd phrases in a variety of languages. In the figures of Miranda and Beatrix, however, both exploited by patriarchy and maintaining a certain independence from it, their critical distance brings them close to Bakhtin's notion of the fool.[42]

The coexistence of complicity and resistance is seen at the end of 'Ihr glücklichen Augen', when Joseph finally ends the relationship with Miranda, and a previously unheard tone of outraged fury interrupts both the narrator's voice and that of the naive Miranda: 'Und eine inwendige andere weniger sublime Miranda weiß sich nicht zu fassen: Mein Gott, ist dieser Mann blöde, er ist einfach zu blöde, ja merkt er denn überhaupt nichts.'[43] A more complex confusion of shame, compassion, and cowardice is going through Joseph's mind at the same time. As he attempts to extricate himself from the situation with staged nonchalance, his gaze falls compulsively on the street name outside Miranda's window, which reads 'Blutgasse' ('Blood Lane'):

> **Einen Augenblick lang nimmt er Miranda in die Arme, er berührt mit seinem Mund ihr Haar und ist unfähig, etwas anderes zu sehen und zu fühlen außer dem Wort 'Blutgasse'. Wer tut uns das alles an? Was tun wir einander an? Warum muß ich das tun? und er möchte ja Miranda küssen, aber er kann nicht, und so denkt er nur, es wird noch immer hingerichtet, es ist eine**

[42] The fool was Bakhtin's idea of a figure who could stand apart from social convention, and afford the reader a critical distance from it: 'a man who is in life, but not of it, life's perpetual spy and reflector' (Eigler, 'Bachmann und Bachtin', 6, quoting from Mikhail Bakhtin, *The Dialogic Imagination*, trans. C. Emerson and M. Holquist (Austin, Tex: University of Texas Press, 1981), 161).

[43] 'And another, inner, less sublime Miranda cannot contain herself: My God, this man is stupid, he is simply too stupid, doesn't he notice anything at all' (*S* 268).

> **Hinrichtung, weil alles, was ich tu, eine Untat ist, die Taten sind eben die Untaten.**[44]

This is one of the moments in the text when the character's insight momentarily coincides with the voice of the narrator, but is immediately repressed as Joseph takes flight from Miranda's devastating forgiveness. There is a striking parallel between Miranda's loving transfiguration of reality and Bakhtin's view of the author's production of the hero, as both aesthetic act and an act of love: 'Love is the culmination—or even the condition—of the aesthetic.'[45] This supports the reading of the story advanced above, in which Miranda's astonished gaze on the world is an allegory of aesthetic production. It also evokes her Shakespearean namesake in *The Tempest*, who exclaims: 'How beauteous mankind is! | O brave new world | That has such people in't!'[46]

In hybrid constructions, where more than one voice coincides, the force of ideological constraints operating in the text is laid bare. This is particularly striking in 'Das Gebell', in which the power of the absent son and husband determines what can and cannot be said between the old and the young Frau Jordan.[47] The narrative confronts us immediately with the incongruity of the old Frau Jordan's poverty and her son's successful career as an internationally acclaimed psychiatrist. The old woman hears imaginary dogs barking, which Franziska notices is not just a sign of senility, but is related to a history of neglect and cruelty by her son. Leo had forced her to get rid of a dog, Nuri, her only companion, because it took a violent dislike to him, and she lives in fear that he will put her in an old people's home. Franziska takes over responsibility for visiting the old woman in order to relieve her husband of a burden, but is increasingly unable to suppress the knowledge of his professional opportunism and cruelty to his mother.

[44] 'For a moment he takes Miranda in his arms, he touches her hair with his lips and is unable to see or feel anything other than the words "Blood Lane". Who does all this to us? What do we do to each other? Why do I have to do this? and he wants to kiss Miranda, but he can't, so he just thinks, the executions are still going on, it's an execution, for everything I do is a misdeed, deeds simply are misdeeds' (*S* 270–1). Several critics have noted that the name 'Blutgasse' commemorates a massacre of the Knights Templar in 1312, a factor which contributes to the subtext of violence underlying contemporary Viennese social reality (see Pichl, 'Ingeborg Bachmanns "Ihr glücklichen Augen"' and Dusar, *Choreographien der Differenz*).

[45] Anne Jefferson, 'Bodymatters: Self and Other in Bakhtin, Sartre and Barthes', in Ken Hirschkop and David Shepherd (eds.), *Bakhtin and Cultural Theory* (Manchester: Manchester University Press, 1989), 152–77 (155).

[46] *The Tempest*, Act 5, Scene 1.

[47] The very fact that they are referred to thus suggests the interchangeability and dispensability of women in marriage. It takes on sinister connotations when Leo announces to his mother that there is a new woman in his life, after the unexplained disappearance of Franziska.

The third-person extradiegetic narrative voice is focalized largely through Franziska, but also occasionally supplements her perspective, highlighting the limitations of what she is able to think. The old Frau Jordan is constrained by the discourse of maternal gratitude and pride, Franziska by admiration and love for her husband. Very early in her relationship with her mother-in-law she notices the old woman's fear of her son, although the narrative voice notes: 'sie unterdrückte ihr erstes Begreifen'.[48] When she buys things for Frau Jordan, or even pays for her medical treatment, she does so from her own money, as we learn by means of a hybrid construction that echoes Leo's words for the small amount of financial independence he grants her, but includes an ironic comment on how little it is: 'sie . . . griff ihr weniges Geld auf dem Sparbuch an, von dem abgemacht worden war, daß es ihre eiserne Reserve sein solle für irgendeinen Notfall, der hoffentlich nie eintreten würde und auch nur kleiner Notfall hätte sein dürfen'.[49] When she grasps the significance of the dogs' barking, having learned the story of Nuri from the old woman, Franziska is still unable to formulate the full implications of her knowledge: 'Franziska hörte ihr verkrampft zu, und sie sagte in sich hinein: Das also ist es, das ist es, und sie hat ihren Hund für ihn weggegeben. Was sind wir für Menschen, sagte sie sich—denn sie war unfähig zu denken, was ist mein Mann für ein Mensch.'[50] While the narrative could not be said to uncover unconscious contents by means of *écriture féminine* (see Schmidt-Bortenschlager's criticism of Bachmann's work above), it discloses unwelcome truths by juxtaposing voices revealing incompatible versions of reality.

A particularly unnerving revelation, which Franziska pieces together only gradually (and reluctantly), is the story of Leo's relationship with his distant cousin Johannes. While inwardly amused at the old woman's prudish embarrassment about Johannes' homosexuality, Franziska struggles to understand her husband's hostility to this relative. Only gradually does she understand that her husband's medical studies in the early 1930s had been paid for by Johannes, who was later interned as a homosexual in a concentration camp during the war. While Leo uses his cousin's experience in his research into the psychological

[48] 'she suppressed her first realization' (*S* 287). This implies further that Franziska, also, is afraid of Leo.

[49] 'she . . . broke into her small savings account, which they had agreed should be her iron reserve for any emergency, which would hopefully never happen and would in any case have to be a small emergency' (*S* 288).

[50] 'Franziska listened to her tensely, and said to herself: So that's it, that's it, and she gave her dog away for his sake. What kind of people are we, she said to herself—because she was incapable of thinking, what kind of a person is my husband' (*S* 303–4).

disturbances of ex-concentration-camp inmates, his antagonism towards Johannes betrays his own ingratitude and homophobia. His reticence about this part of his family's history suggests also unreconstructed prejudices among the bourgeois medical circles in which he moves. However, this all emerges only implicitly in the course of the two women's conversations. Franziska's frustration at the old woman's allusive style mirrors the reader's experience of the narrative itself, which repeatedly points beyond the characters' thoughts and exposes their self-deception:

> **Sie blieb aber etwas verstört, denn die alte Frau hatte manchmal eine so umständliche Art, Dinge zu sagen und doch nicht zu sagen, und sie fand sich dann nicht zurecht, obwohl sie auf einmal ganz von Stolz erfüllt war, daß jemand aus Leos Familie etwas so Furchtbares durchgemacht hatte, und daß Leo, in seiner taktvollen bescheidenen Weise, ihr nie etwas darüber gesagt hatte, auch nicht in welcher Gefahr er sich, als junger Arzt, befunden haben mußte.**[51]

The story ends with Franziska's unexplained disappearance, implicit only in her husband's casual reference to a new wife, and in the confusion of the old woman's thoughts. The two women never emerge from the discourses which constrain their interaction, but the multiple voices in the text coincide to reveal more to the reader than either is able to perceive.

Conclusion

The story 'Das Gebell' is the one most explicitly linked to the theme of Austria's fascist past and to the *Todesarten* trilogy, in which the cruel pathologization of Franziska by her psychoanalyst husband was to be one of the main story lines. In one of Bachmann's introductions to readings from *Das Buch Franza* she made explicit her conviction that the evil which had spawned National Socialism lived on in the everyday cruelties and inhumanity of post-war Austrian society:

> **Es ist mir, und wahrscheinlich auch Ihnen oft durch den Kopf gegangen, wohin das Virus Verbrechen gegangen ist—es kann doch nicht vor zwanzig Jahren**

[51] 'But she remained somewhat uneasy, because the old woman sometimes had such a convoluted way of saying things and yet not saying them, and she was then left confused, although she was suddenly filled with pride that someone in Leo's family had been through something so dreadful, and that Leo, in his tactful modesty, had never mentioned it to her, nor the danger which he must have been in, as a young doctor' (*S* 297–8).

> **plötzlich aus unserer Welt verschwunden sein, bloß weil hier Mord nicht mehr ausgezeichnet, verlangt, mit Orden bedacht und unterstützt wird. Die Massaker sind zwar vorbei, die Mörder noch unter uns . . . [Das Buch] versucht, mit etwas bekanntzumachen, etwas aufzusuchen, was nicht aus der Welt verschwunden ist. Denn es ist heute nur unendlich viel schwerer, Verbrechen zu begehen, und daher sind diese Verbrechen so sublim, daß wir sie kaum wahrnehmen und begreifen können, obwohl sie täglich in unserer Umgebung, in unsrer Nachbarschaft begangen werden.**[52]

This is clearly the context in which we must understand the damaged figures of Nadja, Elisabeth, and the old Frau Jordan, as also the self-preservation strategies of Beatrix and Miranda. Although the 'victims' might appear to be exclusively female, it is debatable whether Bachmann runs the risk of demonizing masculinity and reinforcing a polarized view of gender.[53] There is certainly evidence to suggest stereotypes of emotional, imaginative femininity versus goal-directed masculine rationality, as in Nadja's outburst against male bureaucracy in 'Simultan': 'ihr Männer seid eine gottverdammte Bande, immer müßt ihr etwas Gewöhnliches draus machen'.[54] There is also overt criticism of masculinity in 'Drei Wege zum See', where Elisabeth decides that, in the absence of the 'new man', it is better to renounce all intimate relationships with men. However, as we have seen, Bachmann's depiction of femininity is more complex than these examples suggest, her female characters more ambiguously complicit in their own marginalization.[55]

Indeed, one could argue that in 'Drei Wege zum See' Bachmann's central concern with the representation of suffering coincides with a reversal of gender stereotypes, Elisabeth being one of her least 'feminine' protagonists, her lovers almost feminized in contrast. While the men in the story represent the lost peoples of the Austro-Hungarian Empire (Trotta is the son of a great Habsburg family, Branco from Slovenia, and

[52] 'I have often wondered, as you probably have also, where the criminal virus has gone—it can't have suddenly disappeared from our world twenty years ago, simply because murder is no longer honoured here, no longer demanded, or promoted and rewarded with medals. The massacres may be over, the murderers are still among us . . . [This book] tries to make something known which has not disappeared from the world, to track it down. Because now, as it is infinitely more difficult to commit crimes, the crimes are so sublime we hardly notice or grasp them, although they are committed daily all around us, in our neighbourhood' (Pichl et al., *'Todesarten-Projekt'*, ii, 77–8).

[53] See Kurt Bartsch, '"Muß einer denken?" Zur Problematik der Geschlechterpoliarisierung im Werk der Ingeborg Bachmann', *Austriaca*, 43 (1996), 27–36, for a discussion of this issue.

[54] 'you men are a godforsaken bunch, you always have to turn things into something banal' (*S* 129).

[55] With the exception of Leo Jordan and Ludwig Frankel, none of the men in *Simultan* is particularly comfortable with his masculinity. As Elisabeth reflects of the men in her life, they tend to be weaklings and failures who need her support (*S* 402, 423–4).

Manes from Galicia), and Trotta himself is presented as an anachronism in the post-war world, he also has a positive influence on Elisabeth's attitude to journalism. He challenges her Enlightenment commitment to informing people about the atrocities in the world, alerting her to the desensitizing consequences of mass communication, and to the voyeurism encouraged by press reporting such as her own. She then becomes critical of newspaper reports from war zones around the world, and sensitive to the more widespread causes of human suffering: 'denn erschöpft waren die meisten nicht von den Ungeheuerlichkeiten, die in südamerikanischen oder asiatischen Ländern geschahen, sondern von ihrer eigenen Misere, der Teuerung, Übermüdungen und Depressionen, die sich natürlich neben den großen Verbrechen erbärmlich ausnahmen'.[56] When she accepts an assignment in Vietnam at the end of the story, the reader is left to surmise whether this is a 'suicide mission' or a sign of a renewed commitment to humanity. The last lines of the story resonate with Trotta's words, that his heart once belonged to Austria but now it just bleeds for what is lost, signalling the overarching theme of historical catastrophe and suffering which resonates throughout all of Bachmann's late prose.

[56] 'for most of them were exhausted, not from the atrocities occurring in South American or Asiatic countries, but from their own wretchedness, from the rising cost of living, their weariness and depression, which of course seemed pitiful in comparison with the major crimes' (*S* 398).

2 Elfriede Jelinek, *Die Liebhaberinnen* (1975)

Introduction

Elfriede Jelinek's novel *Die Liebhaberinnen* posed a considerable challenge to feminist readers when it appeared in 1975. Here was a text which seemed to address them directly, taking up many of the concerns of the second-wave women's movement, which was then in its infancy. It portrayed the dreary lives of two female protagonists who fall for their society's promise that they will achieve fulfilment through love and marriage; they pursue this ideal single-mindedly, only to remain at the end deeply unfulfilled. For Brigitte and Paula are shown to be at the mercy of the double-headed beast spawned by the alliance of patriarchy and capitalism: doubly oppressed, as workers and as women, they serve their employers and their menfolk, their bodies reduced to mere commodities in systems of value organized and controlled by men. The novel investigates issues which had previously been underrepresented in literature but were key concerns for the feminist movement of the 1970s, such as domestic violence, the relationship between women and work, and the lack of access of women to power. But in other respects the novel made surprisingly uncomfortable reading for its early feminist readers: female solidarity, the basis of feminist identity politics in the 1970s (one only has to think of consciousness-raising groups), is neither depicted among the characters nor explicitly courted in the female reader; quite the reverse is in fact the case. Jelinek's protagonists are not 'rounded' or autobiographically based characters with whom the reader is asked to empathize as she is asked to do in other feminist texts from this era (for example, Verena Stefan's *Häutungen*, 1975, and Brigitte Schwaiger's *Wie kommt das Salz ins Meer*, 1977), but one-dimensional, unsympathetic figures in a text which repeatedly draws attention to its own constructedness. Despite their designations as 'das gute beispiel brigitte' and 'das schlechte beispiel paula' ('the good example brigitte', 'the bad example paula', *L* 26), neither of them is exemplary: they do not resist oppression but actively pursue the goals which lead to their imprisonment. They have no insight, even at the end, into the causes of their own predicament, so hoodwinked are they by patriarchal capitalist ideology. Furthermore, the cold and mocking narrative tone seems designed positively to repel and alienate the reader. Finally, the ending is bleak in the extreme: Brigitte realizes her goals but is doomed to a loveless marriage and a life of labour, while Paula loses her children and ends up where Brigitte began, on the production line at the factory producing women's lingerie, that powerful symbol of patriarchal society's unbending will to shape women to its designs. No obvious means of escape from the deadly cycle of drudgery and violence is suggested, no possibility of collective action is shown. Any heightened awareness of the plight of women that the text effects in its readers seems undercut by its bleak and pessimistic outlook.

Clearly, then, the text was calling for a complex response from its readership and resists giving any easy answers to the questions it poses. This chapter will argue that the complexity arises from a basic three-way tension between the Marxist, feminist, and post-structuralist aspects of the text, a tension which continues to trouble and enrich Jelinek research nearly three decades later. Some critics are polarized. Marlies Janz, for example, argues against what she sees as the tendency to depoliticize the author; in her view Jelinek does not indulge in postmodern play with cultural forms, neither can she be claimed unambiguously for feminism; rather, Marxism is the key to understanding all of her texts, for '[d]er Primat von Ökonomie wird exponiert und in keiner Phase des Werks in Frage gestellt'.[1] Matthias Konzett, by contrast, argues that Jelinek tends towards a 'strikingly new version of a post-ideological form of writing', and that this was evident even in her earlier work.[2] He sees her as one of a group of Austrian writers who share, among other things, 'a radical non-affiliation or non-conformity with any collective interest; a nonredemptive vision of the function of art; and the histrionic exposure of art as a practice that serves purposes of cultural edification and emancipation'.[3] Others steer a middle course. Allyson Fiddler, for example, shows that while Jelinek remains in the tradition of the Enlightenment because of her adherence to certain meta-narratives, there is a kind of postmodernism, Hal Foster's 'postmodernism of resistance', which 'seeks to question rather than exploit cultural codes', with which this is compatible.[4] Also, by mixing her modes, Jelinek 'is being "playful" with postmodernism itself'.[5]

[1] 'the primacy of the economic is exposed and not placed in question at any stage of her work' (Janz, *Elfriede Jelinek* (Stuttgart: Metzler, 1995), pp. vii, viii).

[2] Konzett, *The Rhetoric of National Dissent in Thomas Bernhard, Peter Handke, and Elfriede Jelinek* (Rochester, NY: Camden House, 2000), 95, 118.

[3] Konzett, *The Rhetoric of National Dissent*, 21.

[4] Hal Foster, quoted in Allyson Fiddler, 'There Goes That Word Again, or Elfriede Jelinek and Postmodernism', in Jorun B. Johns and Katherine Arens (eds.), *Elfriede Jelinek: Framed by Language* (Riverside, Calif.: Ariadne, 1994), 128–49 (144). Jelinek's satirical postmodernism is also treated in John Pizer, 'Modern vs. Postmodern Satire: Karl Kraus and Elfriede Jelinek', *Monatshefte*, 86/4 (1994), 500–13.

[5] Fiddler, 'There Goes That Word Again', 144–5.

There is evidence in this text to support all three positions. Marxist aspects of *Die Liebhaberinnen* include not only the depiction of the workings of capitalism and the exploration of the function of ideology in producing subjectivity, but also the didactic frame whereby, in techniques adapted from Bertolt Brecht and also the structuralist work of Roland Barthes, ideology or false consciousness is unmasked as untruth. The feminist themes outlined above are compatible with the Marxist aspects in that capitalism and patriarchy are shown to feed off each other. However, implicit in the text is the question of whether altering the economic base (which is ultimately the driving force of any Marxist analysis) would lift women's oppression, or whether something much more fundamental might be required; that is, a reform or overthrow of the symbolic order. This particular tension was at the heart of what was memorably termed 'the unhappy marriage' of Marxism and feminism in the 1970s and 1980s.[6] Finally, the enlightening and teleological view characteristic of Marxism and indeed of liberal humanist forms of feminism, which tells us that we can see the truth about and work towards the ending of class and gender oppression, is itself thrown into doubt by the self-conscious nature of the narration and the constant undermining of the truth function of language. This opens the way for a post-structuralist, but still materialist and feminist, reading of the text.

Contexts and intertexts

To read *Die Liebhaberinnen* for a simple feminist message would be to do an injustice to what is a deeply intertextual text that is far more than simply a product of the women's movement.[7] By 'intertexts' is meant not only those literary and philosophical texts which are quoted from or referred to in the novel but also those whose form or content helped shape it. Jelinek borrows extensively from both 'high' literature and popular literature to produce an unsettling mixture of genres and registers. The opening words of *Die Liebhaberinnen*, which invoke the all-important theme of *Heimat*, 'kennen Sie dieses SCHÖNE land mit seinen tälern und hügeln?', for example, are adapted from Mignon's 'Italienlied' in Goethe's *Wilhelm Meisters Lehrjahre* and would be

[6] See Heidi Hartmann, 'The Unhappy Marriage of Marxism and Feminism: Towards a More Progressive Union', in Lydia Sargent (ed.), *The Unhappy Marriage of Marxism and Feminism: A Debate of Class and Patriarchy* (London: Pluto, 1981), 1–41.

[7] The elaboration of Jelinek's intertexts in this section is indebted to Allyson Fiddler, *Rewriting Reality: An Introduction to Elfriede Jelinek* (Oxford: Berg, 1994), 1–35.

familiar to a German readership.[8] The reference here signals a characteristic disrespect for a cultural tradition which has become clichéd through overuse and which is revealed as perpetuating the false myth of the idyllic Austrian rural scene: the beautiful valley is in fact the site of an ugly factory. The novel as a whole is, by contrast, set up to be a parody of a kind of 'Trivialliteratur', the romantic novel, following the familiar stages of women seeking and entering into marriage, while undermining at every turn the ethos of romantic love by showing the economic reasons for marriage and the brutal reality of sexual relations. But Jelinek does not just quote from other authors and parody their forms; here, as elsewhere in her works, intertextuality segues into montage, as she consciously constructs her narrative from fragments of contemporary discourses, in particular the language of the media, advertising, and the ideology of everyday life, in relation to which the narrative voice constantly shifts its attitude. To examine the texts and discourses on which she draws is not at all to detract from the originality of Jelinek's work but rather to analyse her text as a complex response to and reflection of contemporary stimuli.

Though Jelinek is an Austrian writer, she is more specifically a Viennese one. Her father was of Jewish descent and through him she feels an affinity with the Jewish tradition of cultural critique propagated by such writers as Hugo von Hofmannsthal, the Viennese satirist Karl Kraus, and Elias Canetti. Konzett points out that this is a melancholic inheritance, for Jewish life in Vienna was abruptly terminated under the Third Reich, though the memory of it lives on, and a new generation is resurrecting it.[9] Like her fellow Austrian Ingeborg Bachmann, who died in 1973, Jelinek is influenced by Ludwig Wittgenstein's philosophy, and in particular his statement that '*die Grenzen meiner Sprache* bedeuten die Grenzen meiner Welt'.[10] Their responses to this are very different, however: while Bachmann's work is marked by traumatic silence, Jelinek's texts are characterized by a polemical force which attempts to shatter taboos, particularly those concerning Austria's Nazi past.[11] Both, however, share an interest not so much in fascism as an historical phenomenon as in the continuation of the fascism of

[8] 'do you know this LOVELY land with its valleys and hills?' (*L* 5). See 'Kennst du das Land, wo die Zitronen blühn' (Johann Wolfgang Goethe, *Wilhelm Meisters Lehrjahre* (Munich: DTV, 1979), 155).

[9] Konzett, *The Rhetoric of National Dissent*, 96.

[10] '*The limits of my language* mean the limits of my world' (Wittgenstein, *Tractatus Logico-Philosophicus*, trans. C. K. Ogden (London: Routledge, 1986; 1st pub. 1922), 148–9; Wittgenstein's emphasis).

[11] See Beatrice Hanssen, 'Elfriede Jelinek's Language of Violence', *New German Critique*, 68 (1996), 79–112 (112).

everyday life.[12] Like her fellow contemporary Austrian writers Peter Handke and Thomas Bernhard, Jelinek has consistently placed herself in opposition to the official myths and traditions of Austrian culture, such as the powerful myth of the pure Austrian *Heimat*, which deny the reality of Austria's Nazi past.

Die Liebhaberinnen was one of Jelinek's earliest texts, and its partly experimental form, for example the lack of upper-case letters, betrays the influence of French Surrealism and of avant-garde writers' groups, the *Wiener Gruppe* of the 1950s and the *Grazer Gruppe* of the 1970s, of which she was a prominent member, and continues the aesthetic innovation she undertook in her earliest works, such as *Michael: Ein Jugendbuch für die Infantilgesellschaft* (1973). In other respects, however, the text represents a new departure for the author, being very tightly controlled in its structure, and, like her play *Was geschah, nachdem Nora ihren Mann verlassen hatte, oder, Stützen der Gesellschaften* (1980), taking up themes from the women's-liberation movement. Though she went on to write two disturbing novels on gender politics, namely *Die Klavierspielerin* (1983) and *Lust* (1989), it is generally the case that she stands out among women writers by giving a new slant to traditionally 'male' topics, such as politics (in the exposé of Austria's National Socialist past in *Burgtheater*, 1982), the environment (*Oh Wildnis, oh Schutz vor ihr*, 1985), and sport (*Ein Sportstück*, 1998), and by subverting 'male' genres such as pornography (*Lust*) and horror (*Die Kinder der Toten*, 1995). Her latest novel, *Gier* (2000), brings together several of these elements. She is also a rare example of a highly successful female playwright.

All of this is not to deny the influence of the women's movement on this text, but to stress that it is one influence among many. The women's movement occurred somewhat later in Austria than in West Germany and was never so vocal. As a socially and culturally conservative country, attitudes towards women's emancipation were then and remain now somewhat traditional.[13] In the German-speaking countries, as elsewhere in Western Europe, the women's movement was part of a general

[12] See Sabine Wilke, 'Kritik als Mimesis ans Verhärtete: Elfriede Jelineks Texte als Zerrspiegel imaginierter Weiblichkeit', in Wilke, *Dialektik und Geschlecht: Feministische Schreibpraxis in der Gegenwartsliteratur* (Tübingen: Stauffenburg, 1996), 87–122 (90–1). An interesting convergence occurred when Jelinek wrote the screenplay for the film of Bachmann's famous novel *Malina* (see Sigrid Schmid-Bortenschlager, 'Jelinek liest Bachmann: Verschiebungen', *Austriaca*, 43 (1996), 97–104, and Irene Heidelberger-Leonard, 'War es Doppelmord? Anmerkungen zu Elfriede Jelineks Bachmann-Rezeption und ihrem Filmbuch *Malina*', in Heinz Ludwig Arnold (ed.), *Elfriede Jelinek* (Munich: Text und Kritik, 1993), 78–85).

[13] See Allyson Fiddler, 'Post-war Austrian Women Writers', in Chris Weedon (ed.), *Post-War Women's Writing in German: Feminist Critical Approaches* (Oxford: Berghahn, 1997), 243–68.

politicization arising from the students' movement, which was heavily influenced by Marxist thinkers, in particular those of the Frankfurt School. A key text here was Max Horkheimer and Theodor Adorno's *Dialektik der Aufklärung* (*Dialectic of Enlightenment*) (1947), which examined the negative consequences of the originally highly optimistic philosophy of Enlightenment in the light of the disaster of German National Socialism, and commented on the links between fascism and patriarchy. The pessimism of much of Jelinek's work is also influenced by Adorno's concept of negative dialectics, which was a radical reworking of Marxist theories of historical materialism. While historical materialism is a teleological form of thought which sees human history as moving forward dialectically in a series of stages to a point where capitalism will inevitably be overthrown, negative dialectics perceives alienation to be not just a product of capitalism but all-pervasive in modern life; it has lost the hope of a better future that most Marxist theories offer, while still holding open the possibility of critique.

Prior to writing *Die Liebhaberinnen* Jelinek read with great interest Roland Barthes' *Mythologies* (1957), a work which playfully examines everyday cultural artefacts and reveals how they came to appear natural, and wrote a response in her essay, 'Die endlose Unschuldigkeit' (1970). But whereas Barthes revels in the fact that myths in the modern world have become empty form, Jelinek, influenced also by the German Marxist writer Bertolt Brecht, is more concerned to reveal the traces still left by the material causes behind the petrification of values, and thereby to enlighten her readers and challenge them to change the status quo.

Capitalism and patriarchy

Jelinek has always made clear her affiliation to Marxism and her desire for her works to have a political effect. In the split in the *Grazer Gruppe* in 1970, for example, she and Peter Scharang argued against Alfred Kolleritsch and Peter Handke for the political involvement of art.[14] She was a member of the *Kommunistische Partei Österreichs* (Austrian Communist Party) until 1991, and her political involvement remains intense: after the election of the coalition government between the *Österreichische Volkspartei* (Austrian People's Party) and Jörg Haider's *Freiheitliche Partei Österreichs* (Freedom Party of Austria) in 1999, for

[14] Fiddler, *Rewriting Reality*, 24.

example, she banned public performances of her plays at state theatres in Austria in protest. The focus on women and on the private sphere in *Die Liebhaberinnen* should not obscure the fact that the text highlights the world of work and the economic forces which, under capitalism, perpetuate women's oppression, but also that of all workers.

The employer–worker relations depicted are of a type prevailing in rural Austria in the 1970s, where many features had changed little since the nineteenth century. Work is scarce and competition for it fierce; the contract between worker and employer is not freely entered into. Working conditions for all workers are harsh, leading to daily exhaustion and debilitating illness: the metonyms 'bandscheiben' ('discs') and 'asthma' used to refer to Heinz's father and Erich's father respectively, for example, denote their objectification under the capitalist system and their reduction to more or less functional bodies: the former has a bad back as a result of his work as a long-distance lorry driver, a job he loses during the course of the novel (*L* 99), while the latter suffers from asthma as a result of his work on the railways (*L* 41). Working conditions also have a brutalizing effect, best seen in the cycle of violence in which Erich's family is caught up; nevertheless fear of unemployment is a major motivating factor. All profit disappears into the hands of invisible capitalists. The work that women do is less well paid and of lower status than that of the men, which is why women seek marriage as a way to improve their lot—thus, however, ensuring that men's control over them is maintained.

For the major locus for the exploitation of women is the family. Marriage is equated with death for both men and women (*L* 17–18), and family life is brutal in the extreme, the stress resulting from exploitation at work leading to domestic violence. Paid work thus oppresses and makes the male worker complicit in a hierarchical social system in which men have power over women. This, in addition to the deadly effects of women's unpaid work in the home which, in a Marxist-feminist analysis, contributes to the economy by servicing male workers and producing new workers,[15] means that life is one degree worse for the women than it is for the men. As Jelinek stated in interview: 'Wie man weiß, gibt es keinen Mann, der so arm, ausgebeutet und kaputt ist, daß er nicht noch jemanden hätte, der noch ärmer dran ist, nämlich seine Frau.'[16]

[15] See Michèle Barrett, *Women's Oppression Today: Problems in Marxist Feminist Analysis* (London: Verso, 1980), 208–26.

[16] 'As we know, there is no man who is so poor, exploited, and broken that he hasn't still got someone who is even worse off, namely his wife' (Jelinek in Josef-Hermann Sauter, 'Interviews mit Barbara Frischmuth, Elfriede Jelinek, Michael Scharang', *Weimarer Beiträge*, 27/6 (1981), 109–17 (109)).

Like Friedrich Engels before her, Jelinek believes in the importance of paid employment for women as a first stage in their emancipation: 'Arbeit ist eine Möglichkeit der Frau, zum Subjekt zu werden, indem sie ökonomische Unabhängigkeit vom Mann erwirbt.'[17] Nevertheless her female protagonists are blind to the liberatory potential of work, and seek marriage as a way to escape from its constraints. Paula briefly breaks out of the pattern of choice for local women between sales assistant or housewife, but then drops this for Erich. Brigitte marries Heinz in order to escape her work in the underwear factory and share in Heinz's earning power as a businessman, though her married life turns out to consist of monotony and work too (*L* 143). To understand their compliance it is necessary to examine them as subjects.

Subjection and power

It might seem perverse to consider Brigitte and Paula as subjects, as they are so clearly one-dimensional figures with whom the narrator plays. Susi, Brigitte's rival in the pursuit of Heinz, is the only female protagonist with anything approaching depth, and even this is revealed to be a self-delusion. But it is precisely their constructedness which is of interest. Jelinek has no time for psychology or 'character', which she considers outdated concepts. She focuses instead on the forces which create subjectivity and the lack of possibilities for the individual to act autonomously. The concern with the constructedness of the subject goes back to nineteenth-century determinism, in which individuals were seen to be products of their environment and of forces beyond their control (though they were still seen as unified), but also anticipates the post-structuralist notion that language is constitutive of subjectivity, a notion which Jelinek upholds.[18] The title of the novel was chosen to echo, or perhaps mimic, the title of D. H. Lawrence's novel *Sons and Lovers*, and thus raise the question of whether women, who in patriarchal capitalist societies are subjected to men's power and the power of capital, can be desiring subjects in their own right. The novel seems to answer this question in the negative: certainly Brigitte and Paula know what

[17] 'Work is a means by which a woman can become a subject by earning economic independence from her husband' ('Elfriede Jelinek im Gespräch mit Adolf-Ernst Meyer', in Elfriede Jelinek, Jutta Heinrich, Adolf-Ernst Meyer, *Sturm und Zwang: Schreiben als Geschlechterkampf* (Hamburg: Klein, 1995), 7–74 (57)).

[18] See Brenda L. Bethman, '"My Characters Live Only Insofar as They Speak": Interview with Elfriede Jelinek', *Women in German Yearbook*, 16 (2000), 61–72 (65).

they want and act in order to get it, pursuing the men whom they see as offering a way out of drudgery (in Brigitte's case) or as embodying the romantic ideal (in Paula's); nevertheless the reader is clearly shown that their desires correspond to what society wants for them. The question thereby raised, namely the paradoxical one of how subjects can desire what oppresses them, is, however, one that has been central to Marxist and post-structuralist feminism.

With a few notable exceptions, such as Friedrich Engels's *Der Ursprung der Familie, des Privateigenthums und des Staats* (*The Origin of the Family, Private Property and the State*) (1884), Marxism traditionally downplayed the inner life, the personal sphere, and questions of gender until socialist feminists began to fill in these important gaps in the 1970s and 1980s: one of the best known slogans of the women's movement was 'The personal is political'. The key text here in theorizing the internalization of power structures was Louis Althusser's essay, 'Ideology and Ideological State Apparatuses (Notes Towards an Investigation)' (1970), which examined the relationship between ideology and subjectivity. In common parlance the term ideology means a set of beliefs belonging to a class or interest group and is often used pejoratively to designate false consciousness. In Marxist discourse hitherto it had been used to designate the world-view of the capitalist class which obscured the real relations of production, which were based on exploitation. Althusser argued that the subject comes into being by being 'interpellated', or hailed, by ideology. Thus subjects are the product of ideology and cannot exist outside it. The importance of this theory for Marxism was that it showed that economic forces determine not only what people do but also who they are and why they are compliant. The reason for Paula's blindness to the forces which determine her existence is the fact that, to use Althusser's term, she has been successfully 'interpellated' by the ideology of love and marriage perpetuated by the media, which, in Althusser's scheme, comprise an 'ideological state apparatus'. In other words, the forces to which she is subject are not only exterior to but also internalized in her subjectivity. Thus Paula is described as being like a sponge which absorbs but cannot process material (*L* 32). When beaten up by her mother because of the shame her pregnancy brings, and fearing that her baby may be dead inside her, she is still responding to the call of the romantic happy ending, in complete denial of the reality of her situation:

> **in paula klingt ein lied, aber sehr schwach.**
> **statt der wunden ein bodenlanges weißes spitzenkleid samt schleier.**
> **keine seifenlauge, sondern eine schöne blumenhaube.**

> keine aborte, sondern eine gute hochzeitstorte.
> kein toter embryo klein, sondern ein guter braten vom schwein.[19]

The main problem with Althusser's theory for feminists, however, was that his structuralist model did not explain how resistance might be possible. Judith Butler has returned repeatedly to Althusser's essay in her works, adding insights from Michel Foucault's 1980s work on sexuality as a construction, a product of differing discourses that are themselves sites of power. For Butler, the subject 'is passionately attached to the law that both subjects and constitutes it' and 'exists in an ambivalent relation to power structures that it desires rather than not desiring at all'. Crucially, however, the subject can exceed that law, some of whose interpellative calls anyway fail as performative acts (that is, as speech acts which simultaneously perform an action).[20] Agency and resistance are therefore possible; for,

> that estrangement or division produced by the mesh of interpellating calls and the 'I' who is its site is not only violating, but enabling as well, what Gayatri Spivak refers to as 'an enabling violation'. The 'I' who would oppose its construction is always in some sense drawing from that construction to articulate its opposition; further, the 'I' draws what is called its 'agency' in part through being implicated in the very relations of power that it seeks to oppose. To be *implicated* in the relations of power, indeed, enabled by the relations of power that the 'I' opposes is not, as a consequence, to be reducible to their existing forms.[21]

The 'I's that are Paula, Brigitte, and Susi do not significantly oppose the relations of power that create them, and leave untested Butler's claim that agency is possible, but they are constituted by them in significantly different ways. Paula's subjectivity is composed of a mesh of at least three incompatible interpellating calls. First liberal humanism tells her that she is not an object but a human being of intrinsic worth (*L* 96). This encourages her to try to break out of the cycle by training as a seamstress, though this is unprecedented for a girl in her community (*L* 18–19). While the novel as a whole applauds her attempt to break out, her naive belief in her own worth is dealt with scathingly by the (here at least) assertively Marxist narrative voice: Paula, 'die dumme kuh' ('the stupid cow', *L* 71), is in fact nothing more than an object, and 'über den gegenstand paula bestimmt erich, über dessen körperkräfte wieder

[19] 'a song is heard in paula, but very feebly. | instead of the wounds a fabulous long white dress with veil. | no soapsuds, just a beautiful bunch of flowers. | no abortions, just a fine wedding cake. | no embryo small and dead, just some fine roast pig instead' (*L* 97).

[20] Sara Salih, *Judith Butler* (London: Routledge, 2002), 135.

[21] Judith Butler, *Bodies That Matter: On the Discursive Limits of 'Sex'* (New York: Routledge, 1993), 122–3 (Butler's emphasis).

andre bestimmen'.[22] Belief in her own worth is then quickly ousted when 'love', in the form of Erich, the second interpellative call, comes along, and Paula misrecognizes him as the romantic hero she has read about in the pages of magazines. But the culmination of romantic love and also the next stage after it is motherhood (the third interpellative call); that is, the production of a child who is 'die personifizierte liebe' ('love personified', *L* 68). The ideologies of love and motherhood are not compatible for Paula either, however: to protect her children from poverty arising from their father's drinking, and to overcome her loneliness, she prostitutes herself and is punished by losing her children.

Brigitte, by contrast, illustrates Butler's view that the subject's relation to power is ambivalent: from the start pragmatic and egocentric, she does not respond positively to the call of romance or of motherhood (those performative acts fail), and hard-headedly seeks the best deal for herself. Like Paula she desires what oppresses her (marriage and family life), but she desires this 'rather than not desiring at all':[23] there is no pleasure in that desire, apart from the pleasure of escaping poverty. In her own eyes Brigitte wins 'den kampf der geschlechter' ('the battle of the sexes', *L* 126), indicating that she responds, albeit negatively and with extreme cynicism, to the call of another contemporary discourse, that of a crude, man-hating feminism.

Susi is a product of more diverse, middle-class discourses and advantages and is therefore even more implicated in relations of power: sporty, educated, feminine, snobbish, but with a social conscience, she is able to reject Heinz and delay taking on the inevitable 'los der frau' ('lot of woman', *L* 143), though this will eventually happen, as Heinz observes to himself with a characteristically obscene turn of phrase: 'susi wird den schwanz fest in die möse und das familienleben fest in den kopf gepflanzt bekommen'.[24] Susi's superior position in the economic hierarchy buys her time, but that is all.

The exchange of women

Thus far, then, we see an exaggerated Marxist-feminist account of life under capitalism, in which men and women are both, but not equally,

[22] 'decisions about the object paula are made by erich, decisions about his physical labour are made by others again' (*L* 130).

[23] Salih, *Judith Butler*, 135.

[24] 'the cock will be firmly planted in susi's cunt and family life will be firmly planted in her head' (*L* 83).

exploited and alienated, and in which economic forces and the workings of ideology produce what are for the most part compliant subjects. But the text's persistent use of the language of commodities and markets to describe what is happening in Paula and Brigitte's search for husbands indicates that Jelinek is also concerned to expose exploitative economies which pre-date and exceed capitalism. At first it seems the women have their own 'capital' (that is, their bodies) to 'invest' in this market: 'brigitte hat einen körper zu bieten' ('brigitte has a body to offer', *L* 13), and she claims 'ownership' of Heinz (*L* 73). This already represents a brutal undercutting of the romantic ideal but gives at least the sense that the women are acting autonomously; soon, however, it becomes clear that their capital is judged according to an exterior system of value: 'brigitte hat brüste, schenkel, beine, hüften und eine möse. | das haben andre auch, manchmal sogar von besserer qualität'.[25] In this market women are interchangeable commodities; thus they have a 'marktwert' ('market value', *L* 30) and 'besitzer' ('owners', *L* 92), they are 'entwertet' ('devalued', *L* 70) when old, they suffer 'wertreduzierung' ('a reduction in value', *L* 120) when pregnant, and can be rejected if suspected of being already 'gebraucht' ('used', *L* 17); their loss of value when pregnant can even—and here we see a tragicomic use of the 'aesthetics of exaggeration' highlighted by Fiddler[26]—be measured in kilogrammes (*L* 100). Despite the jocularity here, there is something deadly serious in Jelinek's relentless use of this vocabulary.

Theories of value derive from Karl Marx, whose influence, Jacques Derrida commented, is still all-pervasive in western culture.[27] Value is a surprisingly flexible concept, as Gayatri Spivak points out; lacking in content and in itself simple, Marx used the term to rewrite

> **not mediation, but the possibility of the mediation that makes possible in its turn all exchange, all communication, sociality itself. Marx's especial concern is the appropriation of the human capacity to produce, not objects, nor anything tangible, but that simple contentless thing which is *not* pure form; the possibility of mediation (through coding) so that exchange and sociality can exist. Marx's point of entry is the economic coding of value, but the notion itself has a much more supple range.**[28]

[25] 'brigitte has breasts, thighs, legs, hips and a cunt. | others have got these too, sometimes even of better quality' (*L* 13).

[26] Fiddler, *Rewriting Reality*, 126.

[27] Jacques Derrida, 'In the Name of the Revolution', in Stuart Sim (ed.), *Post-Marxism: A Reader* (Edinburgh: Edinburgh University Press, 1998), 143–54 (144).

[28] Gayatri Chakravorti Spivak, 'Poststructuralism, Marginality, Postcoloniality and Value', in Peter Collier and Helga Geyer-Ryan (eds.), *Literary Theory Today* (Cambridge: Polity, 1990), 219–44 (226) (Spivak's emphasis).

In the same year that *Die Liebhaberinnen* was published the American anthropologist Gayle Rubin developed Claude Lévi-Strauss's application of the theory of value to social relations, and specifically his theory that the essence of kinship systems lies in the exchange of women between men. These systems are based on the gift, which creates a social link between the partners of an exchange, and the incest taboo. The importance of Rubin's theory is that it places the oppression of women within social systems rather than in biology, and shows how gender, obligatory heterosexuality, and the constraint of female sexuality underwrite social organization under patriarchy.[29]

The feminist philosopher Luce Irigaray places this exchange in a still wider context: not just within capitalism or societies based on kinship but within the symbolic order. Under patriarchy, which she defines as a 'hom(m)o-sexual economy' (that is, an economy of relations between men), women, like commodities, have no intrinsic or permanent value but have value only in that they can be exchanged. This places them in competition with each other, makes them anxious to speak to and confirm their value, denies them any right to their own pleasure, cuts off their access to the symbolic, and renders them liable to fetishization as a manifestation of the power of the phallus.[30] Examples of these effects of patriarchy abound in Jelinek's text. The competition between Brigitte and Susi for Heinz represents a systemic competition between women, and is symptomatic of the utter lack of solidarity between women, even between mothers and daughters, in the text. Rather, the women assert their legitimacy through their men, their only access to the power of the phallus: the women of the village talk of their men as 'MEINER' ('MINE') with a 'siegerlächeln' ('victorious smile', *L* 31); Brigitte desires Heinz's name for herself (*L* 10), becomes truly female when she marries him (*L* 134), and achieves the protection of the phallus when she can exchange her individual name for the designation 'mama' ('Mamma', *L* 149); Paula, always the unlucky one, hopes for a boy child (*L* 121–2) but is rewarded with a girl. That women have no right to their own pleasure is shown graphically through Brigitte's sexual encounters with Heinz, which fill her with disgust (*L* 55–6), and Paula's with Erich, which are physically painful and bear no relation to the amorous exchanges she has read about in magazines (*L* 91). That it is relations between men that matter is shown by the men's outrage not so much that Paula is unfaithful to her husband but that she consorts with an

[29] Gayle Rubin, 'The Traffic in Women: Notes on the "Political Economy" of Sex', in Rayna R. Reiter (ed.), *Towards an Anthropology of Women* (New York: Monthly Review, 1975), 157–210 (175).

[30] Luce Irigaray, 'Women on the Market', in Irigaray, *This Sex Which Is Not One*, trans. Catherine Porter with Carolyn Burke (Ithaca, NY: Cornell University Press, 1985), 170–91.

outsider: 'ein ortsfremder hat ihnen ins nest geschissen'.[31] Men's sexuality is symbolized positively, if ironically, in imagery of panthers (*L* 41), sunsets, and natural catastrophes (*L* 56). Women's desire, by contrast, is simply left unfigured. Similarly, the only supportive and positively symbolized relationships are those between males: between Erich and his companions in the pub, for example (*L* 119–20), or between Heinz's father and his son: 'der opa kann dir auch beibringen, was ein mann wissen muß, wie man auf bäume klettert . . . weil der opa auch ein mann ist, weißt du',[32] whereas supportive relations between women, even mothers and daughters, are impossible.

Jelinek takes a cautious interest in feminist theory but parts company from it when, as with some French feminist theory, it tends to privilege women's oppression. But Wilke points out that she is at her closest to these theorists in her later work where she shows that women's desire cannot be represented.[33] *Die Liebhaberinnen* prefigures this and illustrates Butler's statement that '[t]he relation of reciprocity established between men . . . is the condition of a relation of radical nonreciprocity between men and women and a relation, as it were, of nonrelation between women'.[34] It also illustrates the straitjacketing effects of identity being derived from the positioning of an individual in relation to the value-coding of a society: 'We cannot grasp values as such; it is a possibility for grasping, without content. But if we position ourselves *as identities* in terms of links in the chain of a value-coding as if they were persons and things, and go on to ground our practice on that positioning, we become part of the problem'.[35] In deriving their identities from their exchange value in a patriarchal economy Brigitte and Paula forfeit all hope of exerting agency. This way of theorizing their subject acquisition does not hold out any Butlerian hope of resistance through subversion.

The aesthetics of mimicry

The gloomy negativity so far analysed—Brigitte and Paula desiring the exploitative power structures which hail them and speaking to their

[31] 'a stranger has shat in their nest' (*L* 153).

[32] 'grandpa can teach you what a man must know, how to climb trees . . . because grandpa is a man too, you know' (*L* 142).

[33] Wilke, 'Kritik als Mimesis ans Verhärtete', 90.

[34] Judith Butler, *Gender Trouble: Feminism and the Subversion of Identity* (London: Routledge, 1990), 41.

[35] Spivak, 'Poststructuralism', 227 (Spivak's emphasis).

value-coding in a patriarchal economy—is relentless and seems far removed from the 'strikingly new version of a post-ideological form of writing' that Konzett perceives in Jelinek. But as a piece of writing, the text performs a balancing act between enlightening and unsettling its readers. It borrows from Brecht's array of alienation techniques, for instance, in employing a model structure that sets out the fates and implicitly criticizes the actions of the two main protagonists, culminating in the parallel wedding scene (*L* 136–9), and by constantly highlighting its own artificiality; for example, in calling the first chapter 'anfang' ('start', *L* 9) and referring to Paula as 'die titelheldin' ('the eponymous heroine', *L* 112). These techniques are used with didactic intent and signal an authorial position which is in possession of a truth which it seeks to convey. Like most of Jelinek's texts, *Die Liebhaberinnen* is set up to demythologize in a Barthesian sense; that is, to reveal that certain myths which appear natural—that the Austrian countryside is an idyll untouched by industry, that work confers dignity on those who perform it, that romance is the path to fulfilment, for example—are in fact ideological constructions which conceal the true interests at work. Jelinek sometimes chooses a country setting because there things can be set out experimentally, as in a Petri dish.[36] When she describes her work as realist, she means precisely that it does not reflect the surface 'reality' of things in a mimetic way in order to bring forth maximum recognition in the reader—which would be one kind of realism—but that, through exaggeration and excess, it shatters this surface to reveal the reality beneath.[37] This Marxist-feminist agenda of the text marks a difference from Barthes, who tends to revel in semiological play, but there is a productive tension between the enlightening intent and the novelistic aspects—namely, the strong and capricious narrative voice, the high degree of intertextuality/montage, and the intensive use of literary devices, which serve to make meaning less easy to tie down and the sources of power less easy to locate.

The narrative voice is as complex and unpredictable as the protagonists are one-dimensional and knowable. It repeatedly draws attention to its own power over its creations, boasting for example that 'wir das

[36] Jelinek, 'Elfriede Jelinek im Gespräch', 69.

[37] Riki Winter, 'Gespräch mit Elfriede Jelinek', in Kurt Bartsch and Günther Höfler (eds.), *Dossier, ii. Elfriede Jelinek* (Graz: Droschl, 1991), 9–19. See also Alexander von Bormann, who investigates Jelinek's use in *Die Liebhaberinnen* of allegory, 'eine entschieden nicht-realistische Form' ('a decidedly not-realistic form') in 'Dialektik ohne Trost: Zur Stilform im Roman *Die Liebhaberinnen*', in Christa Gürtler (ed.), *Gegen den schönen Schein: Texte zu Elfriede Jelinek* (Frankfurt am Main: Neue Kritik, 1990), 56–74. For a useful survey of the interplay between realism and satire in Jelinek see Konstanze Fliedl, '"Echt sind nur wir!": Realismus und Satire bei Elfriede Jelinek', in Bartsch and Höfler, *Dossier, ii*, 57–77.

schicksal brigittes in der hand halten',[38] and over the reader's experience, for example when it suddenly addresses the reader directly in a jokey or aggressive way (*L* 104, 127). It often reveals its own prejudices, for example its distaste for family life (*L* 87–8), and it wavers in relation to Paula, usually standing in judgement over her, but then at the end unambiguously seeking to elicit the reader's anger on Paula's behalf: 'aus dem hoffnungsvollen lehrmädchen der schneiderei im ersten lehrjahr ist eine zerbrochene frau mit ungenügenden schneidereikenntnissen geworden. | das ist zu wenig'.[39] More characteristic, however, is the use of language when describing Paula's shock and pain after having sex with Erich: 'gebrochen ist nichts, außer einem menschenkinde in der blüte seiner jahre'.[40] While this is on one level an attempt to gain sympathy for Paula, the use of clichéd language here casts doubt on the narrator's sincerity. For elsewhere the narrative voice wages war, albeit playfully, on cliché. Thus when we read that Brigitte's hair shines like polished chestnuts (*L* 21), or hear of 'die heilsamen schmerzen des kinderkriegens',[41] or meet Heinz's mother, 'die heinzmutter, von natur aus gutmütig'[42] and find her to be anything but good-natured, our attention is drawn to the petrification and consequent inauthenticity of language. Many of these examples concern gender stereotypes; for example, when experiencing 'love' Heinz and Brigitte 'erschrecken vor der größe dieses gefühls. brigitte erschrickt mehr als heinz, weil gefühle mehr weiblich sind'.[43] Elsewhere the narrative voice mimics sexist language in apparent attempts to invite the reader to become a voyeur ('susi ist kein kleines mädel mehr, sondern schon eine richtige frau, was man beim räkeln genau merkt'),[44] and to condone violence against women: 'sie braucht auch die schläge vom erich, sie braucht auch mal die starke hand von einem mann'.[45] The sense thereby generated that the narrative voice is not to be relied upon is strengthened when literary and cultural citations (for example the misquotation of Brecht[46]

[38] 'we hold brigitte's fate in our hand' (*L* 105).

[39] 'the hopeful young dressmaker's apprentice in her first year has become a broken woman with insufficient knowledge of dressmaking. | that is too little' (*L* 154).

[40] 'nothing was broken except a child in the flower of her youth' (*L* 91).

[41] 'the healing pains of childbirth' (*L* 28).

[42] 'the heinzmother, naturally good-natured' (*L* 33).

[43] 'are shocked by the enormity of this feeling. brigitte is more shocked than heinz because feelings are more feminine' (*L* 23).

[44] 'susi isn't a little girl any more but has become a real woman, which you can really see when she stretches' (*L* 65).

[45] 'she needs that erich's blows, she sometimes just needs the strong hand of a man' (*L* 128).

[46] 'die geschichte von b. und h. ist nicht etwas, das wird, sie ist etwas, das plötzlich da ist (blitz) und liebe heißt' ('the story of b. and h. is not something that evolves, it is something that is

and the popular song 'Muß i denn', *L* 140) are adapted. The frequent use of cliché and general playfulness of the narrative voice divert attention away from the enlightening framework of the novel to the production of meaning within language itself, and the consequent limitations of the truth-function of language. This is not mimicry in Luce Irigaray's feminist sense of speaking as a woman in order to dislodge patriarchal discourse and recover 'a possible operation of the feminine in language',[47] but in a post-structuralist sense of shifting positions and moving between, rather than into and out of, discourses. This does not mean postmodern play either, because Jelinek is showing the power of discourses and mobilizing them to effect change in the reader, using them strategically.

The text does not just deconstruct language, though, it also makes exaggerated and self-conscious use of literary devices which creates an intensification of meaning, often to comic effect or as a demonstration of the bravura of the narrative voice, but sometimes also to return to the didactic frame. These include repetition with variations, metaphor and metonymy, alliteration, syllepsis, bathos, personification, irony, wordplay, the use of the present tense, and anaphora.[48] Two examples must suffice here: the use of personification (of hope, the present, and the future (*L* 36), love (*L* 37), envy (*L* 51), even, comically, of dressmaking: 'die schneiderei packt gerade ihre koffer, sie will den letzten postautobus noch erreichen'[49]) serves to mock the pretentiousness of romantic fiction, while the complex wordplay on the words 'gut', 'geld', and 'gilt' in the following passage highlights Paula's exclusion from the financial, social, and moral economy, which are, of course, one and the same: 'überall auf der straße steht eine menge geld und gut herum. | paula hat kein geld und ist nicht gut gewesen. | paula gilt als werdende mutter, aber nicht als werdende hausfrau. | paula ist so gut wie tot'.[50]

suddenly there (lightning) and is called love', *L* 10). See 'Die Realität ist nicht nur alles, was ist, sondern alles, was wird' ('Reality is not just everything which is, but everything which evolves') (Bertolt Brecht, 'Realität als Prozeß', in Werner Hecht [et al.], *Werke: Große kommentierte Berliner und Frankfurter Ausgabe*, 22/1, *Schriften ii, Teil 1, Schriften 1933–1942* (Frankfurt am Main: Suhrkamp, 1993), 458).

[47] Luce Irigaray, *This Sex Which Is Not One*, quoted in Margaret Whitford, *Luce Irigaray: Philosophy in the Feminine* (London: Routledge, 1991), 71.

[48] For a close analysis of the language of the text see Michael Fischer, *Trivialmythen in Elfriede Jelineks Romanen 'Die Liebhaberinnen' und 'Die Klavierspielerin'* (St Ingbert: Röhrig, 1991), 21–43.

[49] 'dressmaking is just packing her bags, she wants to catch the last post bus' (*L* 105).

[50] 'everywhere on the street there is a heap of money and goods standing around. | paula has no money and has not been good. | paula counts as a mother to be but not as a housewife to be. | paula is as good as dead' (*L* 110).

Conclusion

Jelinek's attacks on language show that it is not enough to change capitalism. As she said in interview, 'man muß die Sprache foltern, damit sie die Wahrheit sagt'.[51] Her narrator does violence to the discourses that do violence to people, through ruthless mimicry, whether it be of the discourse of the idyllic Austrian *Heimat*, or of the human face of capitalism, the clichéd discourse of 'common sense', or the powerful discourse of romance which leads Paula astray. Margret Brügmann has argued that Jelinek's approach differs from Brecht's in that her narrator speaks from a position closer to her protagonists and deliberately refrains from stating the essence of what is being depicted, thus making the reader work harder and denying him/her the catharsis resulting from a clear analysis.[52] The constant shifting of narrative position in relation to the language used suggests that Jelinek is aware that truth, like ideology, is discursively constructed. Jelinek does not propose a way out of the impasse of women's role in symbolic exchange because an alternative is literally unimaginable. Paula and Brigitte are not simply excluded from economic power but are constructed by and subject to this exchange. Nevertheless the technique in *Die Liebhaberinnen*, while indebted to Brechtian and Barthesian uncoverings of myth as false consciousness, also has affinities with feminist and post-structuralist mimicry, which speaks from a position within ideology but still allows for resistance.

[51] 'one has to torture language to make it tell the truth' (Jelinek, 'Elfriede Jelinek im Gespräch', 73).

[52] Margret Brügmann, *Amazonen der Literatur: Studien zur deutschsprachigen Frauenliteratur der 70er Jahre* (Amsterdam: Rodopi, 1986), 156–7.

3 Anne Duden, 'Übergang' (1982)

Introduction

Anne Duden has been acclaimed as one of the most innovative writers of her generation, her distinctive poetic voice combining political engagement with experimental form. When her first major publications appeared in the 1980s the appeal of her writing to a feminist readership was readily understood. The linked themes of violence against women, the horror of the Holocaust, and fears of ecological catastrophe reflected a wider cultural pessimism which resonated with many women readers. In terms of feminine aesthetics, her poetic prose style could be described as *écriture féminine*, its rhythmic patterns and play with ambiguity pointing beyond the symbolic dimension of language. Given the relentless and often disturbing focus on the body in her work, Duden's writing also lends itself to postmodern readings concerned with sexual difference and embodiment. In fact, the reception of Duden's first prose collection *Übergang* can be seen as a barometer of recent developments in feminist theory in Europe and the USA. In particular the debate between Sigrid Weigel and Leslie Adelson (1987–8) threw into sharp focus the different consequences of taking gender as a privileged category of analysis as opposed to seeing it in relation to race, ethnicity, and class. This chapter will chart some of these developments in relation to the title story 'Übergang', incorporating a biographical reading of the text as literature of trauma, and a comparative discussion of different psychoanalytical approaches; finally, it will consider how recent feminist ontology opens up fresh and productive possibilities for appreciating Duden's work.

Literature of trauma

Anne Duden's lectures on poetics 'Zungengewahrsam: Erkundungen einer Schreibexistenz' afford biographical insights into her genesis as a writer which offer useful background to her prose debut *Übergang*.[1]

[1] Published as Anne Duden, *Zungengewahrsam: Kleine Schriften zur Poetik und zur Kunst* (Cologne: Kiepenheuer & Witsch, 1999), 11–62. These lectures were first delivered in 1995 when Duden was a visiting lecturer at the University of Paderborn.

Born in 1942, Duden's early childhood was spent in Berlin and Ilsenburg in the Harz, but in 1953 her mother fled the GDR with her two children, settling finally in Oldenburg. This flight via West Berlin, which was still ravaged by world war and was by then the centre of the cold war, is recalled as an early experience of the after-effects of trauma. Duden vividly evokes the incomprehensible experience of denazification, dismissed as 'propaganda' by the adults, while growing up surrounded by the unspoken knowledge of the Holocaust and the normalization of violence in everyday life. Germany was both a visible country in the present and an invisible legacy which had to be repressed: 'Eine unsichtbare Hinterlassenschaft, ein ungreifbares Erbe, das nur durch eins einzuholen sein würde, einzuklagen, einzuheimsen, einzufordern: durch Schreiben. Ich war elf Jahre alt und an Schreiben war gar nicht zu denken. Also wurde zunächst gesammelt, geschluckt. Schreiben war Schlucken. Schluckgebot. Eines Gebietes, unter einem gestaltlosen Gebieter, einem Fehlwirt, Fehlvater.'[2] This personal history re-emerges in italicized passages in 'Übergang', the autobiographically informed story of a violent attack in which the young female protagonist's face is badly damaged and of the equally violent experience of medical reconstruction of her jaw and mouth. The physical damage she suffers has the effect of releasing memories which link the violence against women to the legacy of National Socialism and render her personal experience representative of that of a generation of Germans growing up in the aftermath of the war. While 'Übergang' may be seen as Duden's most autobiographical text, the impact of the trauma it depicts can be seen also elsewhere in the volume *Übergang*: 'Herz und Mund' (*Ü* 44–9) evokes in horrific detail the experience of inarticulable, unbearable pain as a result of facial injury; 'Chemische Reaktion' (*Ü* 50–8) expresses hypersensitivity to everyday violence; 'Tag und Nacht' (*Ü* 107–16) treats the drastic transitions between consciousness and unconsciousness.

Indeed, it is tempting to read much of this volume and Duden's subsequent work as a reworking of trauma, if trauma is understood as the response to an event too horrific to be integrated and so recuperable as normal memory, yet indelibly imprinted to return with the shocking immediacy of flashback, and unplaced within any narrative of the self. It is neither consciously remembered nor unconsciously repressed.

[2] 'An invisible legacy, an intangible inheritance, which only one thing would be capable of hauling in, suing for, raking in, demanding: writing. I was eleven years old and writing was out of the question. So for the time being I collected, swallowed. Writing was swallowing. The command to swallow. From a territory, under a formless master, a false landlord, a false father' (Duden, *Zungengewahrsam*, 28).

Contemporary trauma studies are divided as to the comparability of different forms of trauma,[3] but there is a general consensus as to its characteristic symptoms: flashbacks and dreams which assault the psyche with images it has not been able to assimilate; hyperarousal and persecution anxieties; feelings of numbness and defencelessness. The absence of pain immediately after the attack in 'Übergang' is conveyed in the detached, third-person narration of the event itself, and sustained even when a first-person narrator takes over and notes: 'Die Schmerzen, die der Arzt fürsorgend über meinen Kopf hinweg ausgesprochen hatte, kamen bei mir nicht vor.'[4] While undergoing treatment, however, the protagonist is in a state of constant alert verging on panic, especially when encountering black people whom she implicates in a murderous conspiracy with the black GIs who attacked her (*Ü* 71, 86). The intrusion of horrific dreams into the narrative is a feature of this and other texts by Duden, their literalness betraying their status not as encoded contents of the unconscious but as traumatic knowledge against which the psyche has no defences. Of the two generally recognized types of writing about trauma, the immediate eyewitness account and the trauma narrative, which attempts to historicize the event by integrating it into autobiography, 'Übergang' could be said to belong in the latter category. There does seem to be an attempt to locate the traumatic experience in a life story which emerges gradually in the italicized passages in the text. The fragmentary nature of the narrative itself, however, is testimony to the power of the trauma, and its outcome cannot be understood as a 'recovery'. The protagonist feels no relief when the restraining wires are removed from her jaw, and the end of the text is marked by anxiety mixed with despair. However, the childhood memories also offer insights into the gendered nature of subject-formation, a dimension which trauma theory tends to neglect, and which other psychoanalytical perspectives can illuminate to greater effect.

Psychoanalytical readings

Psychoanalysis has most frequently been used to locate Duden's writing within a modernist aesthetic tradition or to read it as an indictment

[3] Cathy Caruth (ed.), *Trauma: Explorations in Memory* (Baltimore, Md.: Johns Hopkins University Press, 1995) contains essays arguing both for and against a more inclusive definition of trauma.

[4] 'The pain which the doctor thoughtfully mentioned [to the porter] over my head did not occur for me' (*Ü* 67).

of a patriarchal symbolic order. The former, not necessarily gender-specific, reading draws on the writings of Freud and Kristeva, while the latter is more specifically indebted to Lacan and Irigaray. Hubert Winkels's 1988 study of German literature of the 1980s reads 'Übergang' with reference to Freud's *Beyond the Pleasure Principle* (1920), seeing the mouth as the organ which articulates the loss of the primary love object, and thereby compensates for that loss.[5] The damage to the mouth deprives the subject of symbolic compensation for the loss of the (real) object; thus what the text attempts to express are the chaotic intensities experienced in the body. Jürgen Nieraad locates Duden's work in the tradition of European surrealism and the avant-garde, relating it to Julia Kristeva's notion of textsemiosis.[6] The textual consequences of allowing the semiotic forces in the body to dominate the writing process include a privileging of form over content, the exploitation of the materiality of language, the loosening of the link between signifier and signified, and the uncensored assertion of the violence and horror which our culture represses. The increasingly poetic nature of Duden's writing, combined with the relentless focus on violence and suffering, would certainly seem to vindicate locating her within such a modernist tradition. *Das Judasschaf* (1985) depicts the perceptions of a hypersensitive female protagonist in the cities of Berlin, Venice, and New York, but is scarcely linked by enough narrative to be called a novel, and her publications of the 1990s tend to dispense with a narrative subject altogether, in particular the poem cycles *Steinschlag* (1993) and *Hingegend* (1999). Increasingly the materiality of language and the endless potential for meaning to be subverted and deferred are foregrounded in her recent work.

However, as feminist critics such as Rita Felski have pointed out, the European aesthetic avant-garde has most often been associated with notions of sovereign, autonomous creativity and transgressive masculinity. So perhaps it is not surprising that both Nieraad and Winkels present a gender-blind reading of Duden's work, despite their recourse to Kristeva's account of avant-garde literature.[7] Ambivalent though Kristeva's relationship to feminist politics may be, her work has certainly been mobilized in the service of feminism, as she explicitly associates

[5] Hubert Winkels, 'Mundtot: Die leibhaftige Prosa Anne Dudens', in Winkels, *Einschnitte: Zur Literatur der 80er Jahre* (Cologne: Kiepenheuer & Witsch, 1988), 42–58.

[6] Jürgen Nieraad, *Die Spur der Gewalt: Zur Geschichte des Schrecklichen in der Literatur und ihrer Theorie* (Lüneburg: zu Klampen, 1994), 131.

[7] When gender does enter into their analyses, it is used as a criticism, such as where Winkels accuses Duden of a crude 1970s feminist agenda (p. 54) and Nieraad suggests that she fails to sustain her radical impulse, falling into mysticism. Winkels also notes: 'Die Märtyrerin wird Mystikerin' ('the martyr turns into a mystic', p. 58), thus unwittingly associating Duden with an acknowledged site of subversive female discourse, that of mysticism.

the movements of the semiotic with the maternal body, thus linking the feminine (in writing by men and women) with the forces that destabilize symbolic meaning. While she resists according any specificity to female subjectivity, insisting on the sexual differentiation within *all* subjects, Kristeva also identifies pregnancy and the maternal body as important figures of 'alterity within', which make women the embodiment of a challenge to dominant forms of unitary identity.[8]

The problematic relationship of women to the symbolic also underlies Sigrid Weigel's influential Lacanian reading of 'Übergang' as a critique of patriarchal constructions of femininity.[9] She interprets the text as an articulation of the feminine excess which can never be entirely represented in the symbolic. In order to follow this and other feminist readings of Duden's work, a grasp of some of Lacan's fundamental ideas is necessary. According to Lacan the subject comes into being as a result of the traumatic encounter with the Other's desire, experienced as a primordial, overwhelming experience of pleasure/pain which is termed *jouissance*.[10] In order to overcome its fixation on this experience and become a social being, the subject has to go through a process of development which involves renunciation of the mother–child bond, and alienation in language. The child's ego is formed first from identification with ideal images, and then by the assumption of a place in language which splits the subject into ego and unconscious. In this process a third term is introduced into the mother–infant dyad, which Freud termed the Reality Principle and Lacan infamously dubbed the Name of the Father, the signifier that substitutes for the mother's desire. It is the rift in the bond with the mother which creates the logical space for a subject to come into being, but this also entails the renunciation of the *jouissance* of plenitude associated with the immediacy of this bond. Something of this *jouissance* is then refound in language, or, as Bruce Fink puts it: 'it is only insofar as we alienate ourselves in the Other and enlist ourselves in support of the Other's discourse that we can share some of the jouissance circulating in the Other'.[11] In psychosis the barrier

[8] See Julia Kristeva, 'A New Type of Intellectual: The Dissident' (1st pub. 1977), in Toril Moi (ed.), *The Kristeva Reader* (Oxford: Blackwell, 1986), 292–300 (297).

[9] Sigrid Weigel, *Die Stimme der Medusa: Schreibweisen in der Gegenwartsliteratur von Frauen* (Reinbek: Rowohlt, 1989; 1st pub. 1987), esp. 124.

[10] What tends to sound improbably like an 'event' or 'stage' which the subject has to pass through in Lacan's model is probably better understood as part of a continuing process of subjectification, in which the child must submit to what is other-than-it. Thus the Other as language must be assimilated if the child is not to become psychotic. The Other as desire refers to the desires of others which precede the child's birth, and of which the child is not the sole object. Coming to terms with this is, for Lacan, a protracted and painful process.

[11] Fink, *The Lacanian Subject: Between Language and Jouissance* (Princeton, NJ: Princeton University Press, 1995), 99.

between mother and child offered by the Name of the Father is not sufficiently solid: 'the signifier is not able to neutralize the child's jouissance, and that jouissance irrupts into his or her life, overwhelming and invading him or her'.[12]

So far reference has been made only to the sexually undifferentiated subject, and much criticism of Lacan rests on the assumption that the subject in his writings is normatively male and that he rules out the potential of a female subject position in language, constructing femininity as no more than the object of male desire. If this were, indeed, the case, it would seem inconceivable that so much feminist psychoanalysis would take its cue from Lacan's work. In Bruce Fink's exposition of the Lacanian subject he offers a corrective to this view, claiming only that Lacan posits a different (and incompatible) structure for male and female desire. In this account Lacan proposes a male structure (which need not map on to biological males) as one of complete alienation in language and avoidance of the real, with pleasure limited to that in the play of the signifier ('phallic pleasure'). Female structure, in contrast, is not wholly subject to the symbolic order, affording the potential of both phallic pleasure and another form of *jouissance* which is unsymbolizable. This is Irigaray's point of departure when she explores the potential of mystical and hysterical discourse for the articulation of a specifically female form of desire in 'La Mystérique'.[13] It is also important for Kristeva's discussion of abjection and 'borderline subjects' who have never completely entered the symbolic. These are prone to sublimating discourses (aesthetic or religious), which are also characteristic of Lacan's female structure of desire.[14]

The Lacanian view of subject-formation as a traumatic process is the starting point for most psychoanalytical readings of 'Übergang', which posit this as the underlying violence for which the physical damage depicted in the text may be seen as little more than a metaphor. Thus the protagonist reflects on her injuries in terms which suggest that they mirror the state of her psyche:

> **Dabei konnte ich doch von Glück sagen, daß nun endlich auch meine Anatomie einen Knacks bekommen hatte, daß der Körper aufzuholen beginnen konnte, was bis dahin allein meinem Gehirnkopf vorbehalten war, nämlich dem grenzenlosen Chaos der Welt auf allen Schleichwegen und überallhin zu folgen, wo es sich bemerkbar machte, es also auch**

[12] Fink, *The Lacanian Subject*, 74.

[13] Luce Irigaray, *Speculum of the Other Woman*, trans. Gillian C. Gill (Ithaca, NY: Cornell University Press, 1985), 191–202.

[14] Fink, *The Lacanian Subject*, 114–15.

in mich einbrechen und in mir wüten zu lassen. Im Grunde war ich erleichtert.[15]

The cause of the protagonist's relief appears to be that the violent attack has dislodged her subjective anchoring in the symbolic, enabling her to confront the violence which has been repressed in her unconscious. The notion of being invaded and inhabited by external forces implies Lacan's view of the unconscious as the internalized discourse, knowledge, aspirations, and desires of other people. Instead of something personal to us, it is a foreign body within, in this case containing the knowledge of the Holocaust, which is never openly discussed.

The development of a female ego-ideal in the past is recalled in the italicized memories liberated by the attack in the narrative present. The woman remembers the despair she once felt on seeing a film starring Audrey Hepburn, and the growing preoccupation with clothes, hair, and her appearance: 'Ich schminkte mich bald schon täglich.'[16] The alienation involved in becoming a socially acceptable female subject is made explicit with a literary reference: 'werde, die du nicht bist'.[17] After the attack she regards her mirror image with horror and occasional wry humour (*Ü* 86), and is alarmed at the doctor's confident assurance that her face will be restored to its former appearance. This reflects Duden's critique of what she sees as society's tolerance of only one kind of body, 'den Körper als Ausstellungsgegenstand',[18] which amounts to a repression of the body's actual materiality and mortality. Hence in this text the damaged female body reflects both a rejection of the 'Leben in Schönheit—des Körpers und des Verstandes'[19] and a visible testimony to the violence of repression.

From the earliest physical sensations of being lifted out of bed in night-time air raids, to the incomprehensible confrontations with Soviet troops, and later the exposure to unexplained denazification

[15] 'I could count myself lucky that now at last my anatomy had sprung a crack, that my body could begin to catch up with what had so far been reserved for my brain-head; that is, to follow the boundless chaos of the world on all its illicit paths and wherever it made itself felt, even to let it break into me and rage within me. Basically, I was relieved' (*Ü* 67).

[16] 'Soon I was using make-up every day' (*Ü* 81).

[17] 'Become who you are not' (*Ü* 88). The intertextual reference is to Hedwig Dohm's 1894 novella *Werde, die du bist*. Dohm (1831–1919) was a feminist writer and campaigner for equal rights and economic independence for women.

[18] 'The body as exhibition object' (interview with Claudia Kramatschek, 'In den Faltungen der Sprache', *Neue deutsche literatur*, 48/2 (2000), 32–44 (35)). In this interview Duden also expresses her admiration for modernists such as Bataille and Artaud for their uncompromising opposition to the repression of death and the body.

[19] 'Life in beauty—of the body and of the mind' (*Ü* 68).

films at school, the girl's body becomes a repository for the knowledge of war and death:

> **Ich schluckte ganze Schlachten weg, Leichenberge von Besiegten ... Ich tat es nur, ich hätte nichts darüber sagen können, da die Sprache ja das Gegessene und Verschluckte selber war. Und ich war wie eine Tafel, auf der ununterbrochen geschrieben wird, aber nie ein einziger Buchstabe stehen bleibt und nachzulesen ist: der Körper das unbeschriebene Blatt. Beweis für das Verschwinden von Kriegen.**[20]

This aporia or apparent contradiction condenses two Lacanian ideas, that of the body 'written with signifiers' as a result of entry into the symbolic, and the idea that the unconscious is itself made up of language, of signifiers which resist symbolization and can cause intense distress, without having any 'meaning'.[21] Their existence in the unconscious is also permanent in the life of an individual, as Duden's protagonist gradually understands: 'Es wurde langsam manifest, daß alle einzeln niedergerungenen und abgetriebenen Momente meines Lebens heimlich in meinem Körper geblieben waren . . . Kein einziger Bruchteil hatte mich je verlassen.'[22] The permanence of unconscious contents is also suggested later in the text, in the image of countless road-kills on the motorway, heaped up in the child's body and turning her into 'ein einziges großes Massengrab' ('one great big mass grave', *Ü* 94).

However crucial it is for the protection of the subject in the Lacanian schema that repression take place, more important still in 'Übergang' is the violence with which language cuts us off finally from the real, substituting for what remains of our instinctual being. This is re-enacted in the narrative, which begins in the detached, matter-of-fact third person, only changing to first person when the doctor names what has happened to the protagonist, and the effect of symbolization is devastating:

> **Mit einem unblutigen, präzisen Schnitt trennte der Arzt mich ab von dem, was war. Ein Überfall also. Hinter dem zentralen Wort sackte alles weg. Es setzte sich augenblicklich an die Stelle dieses Gemisches aus Sequenzen, Wirbeln und Stillständen, aus hohler Dunkelheit und diffuser Beleuchtung, angespannt ruhig verharrenden und abrupt agierenden**

[20] 'I swallowed whole battles down, mountains of corpses of the defeated... I just did it, I couldn't have said anything about it, because language was the very thing I was swallowing. And I was like a blackboard on which someone was continuously writing, but not a single letter remained to be read: the body, the blank page. Proof of the disappearance of wars' (*Ü* 77).

[21] The notion that signifiers have a more than significatory role, effects other than meaning effects, is crucial to Lacan's view of trauma and *jouissance*, both of which can be understood as the result of confrontation with the residue of the unsymbolizable real (see Fink, *The Lacanian Subject*, 119).

[22] 'It gradually became clear that every individually forced down and expelled moment of my life had remained secretly in my body... Not one fragment had ever left me' (*Ü* 88).

Körperteilen, Gesichtsarealen und Mauerkanten, aus diesiger Feuchtigkeit und glänzendem Asphalt. Es verschluckte und verdaute zur selben Zeit und sonderte sogleich auch das Produkt, den fertigen Überrest, ab.[23]

This implies a radical version of the Lacanian view that the process of symbolic representation is a 'killing' off of lived experience, replacing it with nothing but the signifier.[24] The protagonist's indignation indicates that the violence perpetrated by her attackers is only a continuation of the violence underlying the process of symbolic subjectification. As she recovers from anaesthesia in hospital, the attempts of those around her to rouse her from her oblivion are perceived as violent; their words 'hailing' her as the subject they know penetrate her like gunshot fire (*Ü* 74). She is also repeatedly alienated by the language of the hospital staff which seeks to normalize her condition. When confronted with the horror of a mouth X-ray which she experiences as a violation akin to rape, the nurse's cheerful 'Geht das so' elicits the (silent) response: 'Als ob überhaupt irgendetwas ginge . . . Heben—Strecken. Sie schien nicht zu wissen, was los war.'[25] Her release from the 'terror' of the symbolic regime is greeted with relief: 'Der Terror würde nachlassen in dem Maße, wie das Kaputte nicht zu flicken und die Unversehrtheit nicht wiederherzustellen war. Ein Gefühl wie vor Antritt ewiger Ferien breitete sich in mir aus.'[26] Thus the loss of both ego-ideal and of a subject position in language in 'Übergang' can be seen as a welcome renunciation of symbolic identity, this body identifying more with the status of corpse than with the 'sportlicher Typ' ('athletic sort') addressed dismissively by the doctor (*Ü* 93). This would seem to vindicate Sigrid Weigel's view of 'Übergang' as the radical reversal of the process of subject-formation, and a positive articulation of the inexpressible otherness of woman.[27]

[23] 'With a bloodless, precise cut the doctor separated me off from what was. An attack then. Behind the central word everything fell away. In a moment it stood in for that mixture of sequences, whirling and standstills, of hollow darkness and diffuse lighting, of tense, quiet waiting then abruptly acting body parts, planes of faces and edges of walls, of hazy dampness and shining asphalt. It swallowed and digested simultaneously, and discharged at once also the product, the finished remains' (*Ü* 66).

[24] Bruce Fink describes this as follows: 'The body is subdued; "the letter kills" the body. The "living being" (*le vivant*)—our animal nature—dies, language coming to life in its place and living us. The body is rewritten, in a manner of speaking, physiology giving way to the signifier, and our bodily pleasures all come to imply/involve a relationship to the Other' (Fink, *The Lacanian Subject*, 12).

[25] 'Is that all right?'; 'As if anything at all was all right . . . Lift—stretch. She didn't seem to know what was going on' (*Ü* 82).

[26] 'The terror would ease to the extent that what was broken could not be mended, the intactness could not be restored. A feeling spread over me as at the start of an eternal holiday' (*Ü* 68).

[27] Weigel, *Die Stimme der Medusa*, 128.

One of the most persistent features of Duden's writing from *Übergang* on is the foregrounding of the body, of damaged flesh and intense physical sensation. This has led several critics to make a connection with Kristeva's notion of the abject, as a lasting legacy of the violence of subject-formation. Where Lacan stresses the necessity to substitute desire (which sustains the subject) for *jouissance* (which endangers it), Julia Kristeva's essay *Powers of Horror* (1980) focuses on the expulsion of the maternal body as the prerequisite for subject-formation. All that is 'abject' causes inexplicably violent revulsion, being a reminder of our corporeal beginnings, and a potential threat to subjective integrity. Body fluids and excreta are neither wholly part of nor wholly separate from us, only sources of disgust because once such an intimate part of us, yet they have to be expelled from the body in order for the autonomous, Oedipalized subject to exist. The abject also preserves an archaic memory of birth, that first and violent separation. Its significance for Kristeva is that it reveals the cost of subjectivity and the fragility of the symbolic: 'The abject is the violence of mourning for an "object" that has always already been lost. The abject shatters the wall of repression and its judgments. It takes the ego back to its source on the abominable limits from which, in order to be, the ego has broken away—it assigns it a source in the non-ego, drive, and death.'[28] Elizabeth Grosz has made more explicit still the significance of the abject for feminism, stating that body fluids are not in themselves threatening, but are only so in as much as they disrupt a symbolic system based on solidity and the priority of active mind over inert matter: 'Body fluids flow, they seep, they infiltrate; their control is a matter of vigilance, never guaranteed. In this sense, they betray a certain irreducible materiality; they assert the priority of the body over subjectivity; they demonstrate the limits of subjectivity in the body, the irreducible specificity of particular bodies.'[29] Grosz's emphasis on the materiality of the abject will be discussed further in due course, as it offers a link to postmodern notions of embodiment which go beyond Kristeva's account.

For Kristeva the dead body is a figure of abjection, as a residue of the unsymbolized real, not signifying anything we can comprehend, and thus unbearable to confront.[30] Understood in this way, the image of the corpse in 'Übergang' can be seen as just one instance of the text's

[28] Julia Kristeva, *Powers of Horror: An Essay on Abjection*, trans. Leon S. Roudiez (New York: University of Columbia Press, 1982; 1st pub. 1980), 15.

[29] Elizabeth Grosz, *Volatile Bodies: Toward a Corporeal Feminism* (Bloomington and Indianapolis, Ind.: Indiana University Press, 1994), 194.

[30] Kristeva, *Powers of Horror*, 3.

circling around the horror of abjection, the uncontrollable seeping of the body suggesting an irreversible dissolution of the subject, succumbing, it would seem at the end of the text, to the stasis of the death drive. The repeated references to the urge to vomit can be interpreted as a reference to the violent reassertion of the subject's space, which the very treatment (the wiring of the jaw) seems calculated to block. In a horrific description of coming round from anaesthetic, urged by those around her to respond to their presence, the protagonist's vomit explicitly 'lives on' after it leaves her body, in a grotesque demonstration of the in-between status of the abject and its challenge to subjective boundaries:

> **Erinnerung—Anstrengung—Identität. Das Geschoß hatte einen inneren, zentral gelegenen Sack durchschlagen, eine bis dahin sicher abgekapselte Blase. Mit unwiderstehlichem Druck drängte ihr Inhalt aufwärts . . . riß den bandagierten Höllenrachen, der nichts als geschlossen und bewegungslos sein wollte, mit wüster Kraft und Gewalt auf, so daß ein Stechen, Ziehen, Rucken und Schneiden die hintersten Winkel des Gehirns durchfetzte, und wälzte sich dann als schleimig schwarz-rote Substanz wie Rotwein mit darunter geschlagenem Ei in eine Wanne. In der Nierenschale schwappte er eine Weile hin und her, eine Masse noch lebenden Aufruhrs.[31]**

When her jaws are immobilized the urge to vomit is associated with a repressed scream, which becomes a recurrent trope in Duden's work. It can be interpreted as a cry of pain in empathy for the suffering in the world,[32] but also as another gesture of expulsion which finds no outlet, as in a horrific dream of burial alive: 'die Luft ist so eng, daß der Schrei, der die ganze Zeit schon aus mir herauswill, zwischen den Lippen steckenbleibt und da weder vor noch zurück kann.'[33] The experience of the wiring of her jaw is associated with the humiliation of abjection, as she reflects on her own sweat, unwashed hair, and food residue in her mouth. The doctor's flirting with his assistant while working on his patient indicates the extent to which the abject body forfeits its subject

[31] 'Memory—effort—identity. The shot had hit through an inner, centrally located sack, a bubble which had until then been safely isolated. With irresistible pressure its contents surged upwards . . . tore open the bandaged jaws of hell, which wanted nothing more than to remain closed and motionless, with a wild strength and violence, so that a pricking, pulling, jarring and cutting tore through the farthest corners of the brain, and then rolled around in a bowl as a slimy, reddish-black substance, like red wine with an egg beaten into it. In the kidney dish it lapped about for a while, a mass of still living turmoil' (*Ü* 75).

[32] See Margaret Littler, 'Diverging Trends in Feminist Aesthetics: Anne Duden and Brigitte Kronauer', in Arthur Williams, Stuart Parkes, Julian Preece (eds.), *Contemporary German Writers, Their Aesthetics and Their Language* (Berne: Lang, 1996), 161–80.

[33] 'the air is so tight that the scream which is trying to get out of me the whole time gets stuck between my teeth, unable to go out or in' (*Ü* 93).

status. The end of the text suggests a debilitating despair and paranoid anticipation of the next assault.[34]

The horror of these and similar passages makes identification with this female subject uncomfortable, as it implies a retreat into psychosis rather than a defiant disruption of symbolic subjectivity. The problem of reader identification is a central issue in Stephanie Bird's interpretation of Duden's *Das Judasschaf*, as is what she considers the almost indulgent focus on violence and mutilation in her work more generally, suggesting a more complex Lacanian reading than any so far discussed. Bird is circumspect about feminist criticism which is predicated on the reader's identifying with female protagonists, and claims that Duden herself problematizes the role of identification in subject-formation, by depicting female subjects whose identity depends on the contemplation of violence and identification with victimhood. This is not to cast doubt on the suffering of the protagonist, but to suggest that there is also a dimension to suffering that is *jouissance*, not enjoyment but excitement, even in the depiction of horrific scenes.[35] There is certainly less cruelty and dismemberment in 'Übergang' than in Duden's subsequent work, but the descriptions of the wired-up jaw and the casual brutality of the medical professionals could be seen *both* as a criticism of everyday violence *and* as the beginning of a fascination with the role of violence in the assertion of identity.[36] Temporary relief from suffering is afforded by the contemplation of paintings in *Das Judasschaf*, whereas in 'Übergang' respite is found in listening to music, which offers a release from subjecthood dependent on visual recognition.

The protagonist's implication in the inexorable process of extermination denounced in 'Übergang' is most clearly suggested when she refers to her membership both of the German nation and of the human race: 'Die Spezies, zu der ich gehörte, kam zu allerletzt dran; es war zugleich die Spezies der Verantwortlichen.'[37] This permits a wider-ranging understanding of the cultural critique in 'Übergang'. It concerns not only the German responsibility for the extermination of the Jews, but also mankind's destructive urge which will ultimately be turned against

[34] This makes it difficult to support wholeheartedly Sigrid Weigel's assertion that the destruction of the jaw in 'Übergang' represents the 'Möglichkeit eines Neubeginns' ('possibility of a new beginning') (Weigel, *Die Stimme der Medusa*, 123).

[35] Stephanie Bird, 'Desire and Complicity in Anne Duden's *Das Judasschaf*', *Modern Language Review*, 93/3 (1998), 741–53 (748).

[36] Bird quotes Lacan's view of the ego as a kind of Hegelian 'schöne Seele' ('beautiful soul') who does not recognize 'his very own *raison d'être* in the disorder that he denounces in the world' (Bird, 'Desire and Complicity', 751).

[37] 'The species to which I belonged was the last in line; it was at the same time the species which bore responsibility' (*Ü* 68).

itself. This would account for the otherwise unexplained image of a caged lizard, a symbol of all other endangered species, also for the dead animals on the motorway (*Ü* 94), and for the suggestion at the end of the text that only vestiges of humanity remain on an otherwise deserted earth. This reading, which deprives Duden's female protagonist of unambiguous victim status, perhaps does greater justice to the complexity of the writing than those which identify unquestioningly with her moral stance.

Positionality and fleshy bodies: postmodern approaches

In contrast to the almost universally positive reception of Duden's work in Europe, in 1986 North American critic Leslie Adelson took feminist interpretations of 'Übergang' as an opportunity to criticize 'the racist abuses and implications of some aspects of feminist aesthetics'.[38] Adelson argued that the 'core image' of 'Übergang' (the black GIs) was racist, because not historically located in relation to its 1970s Berlin setting or the white German protagonist. Furthermore, the appropriation of images of darkness and blackness connoted as 'feminine' does not compensate for the fact that the blacks are not accorded any historically located subjectivity in the text. Sigrid Weigel defended Duden's text on the basis that the black GIs have a symbolic, not a realist, function, and argued that it would be inverse racism to claim that no black perpetrators may be depicted in literature.[39] In view of the text's status as a trauma narrative, it is perhaps not surprising that a full account of the positionality of the perpetrators is not given, but the debate which ensued between Weigel's West German feminist view and Adelson's North American Jewish perspective tells us as much about the positionalities of the critics themselves as it does about Duden's text.[40] It shows the difference between the psychoanalytical focus on the gendered subject's relationship to language and desire and the postmodern emphasis on positionality and the subject's relationship to knowledge and power.

[38] Leslie Adelson, *Making Bodies, Making History: Feminism and German Identity* (Lincoln, Nebr.: University of Nebraska Press, 1993), 37–55 (38). Adelson's criticism was first presented to the third conference of 'Frauen in der Literaturwissenschaft' as 'Rassismus und feministische Ästhetik in Anne Duden's "Übergang"', in Hamburg, 1986. It was then published as 'Racism and Feminist Aesthetics: The Provocation of Anne Duden's *Opening of the Mouth*', *Signs*, 13/2 (1988), 234–52.

[39] Weigel, *Die Stimme der Medusa*, 128–9.

[40] See Annette Meusinger, 'The Wired Mouth: On the Positionality of Perception in Anne Duden's *Opening of the Mouth* and *Das Judasschaf*', *Women in German Yearbook*, 13 (1997), 189–203, for a summary of the debate.

The latter is dependent on multiple factors including race, class, ethnicity, religion, and sexuality, sexual difference not occupying a privileged place among them. From such a particularist, postmodern perspective, Weigel's interpretation implies a too universalizing view of 'woman', and a too willing acceptance of her exclusion from the symbolic.

Adelson challenges the representation of woman as either victim of history or allegorical emblem of the nation, proposing instead an understanding of female subjectivity as a site of contested and heterogeneous identities. She gives Duden credit for allowing no neat distinctions between her protagonist's femaleness, Germanness, and whiteness, but criticizes the text for its undifferentiated representation of blacks. She analyses the different functions of blackness in the text in order 'to explore how it is that a racist image becomes the pivot on which a text that aspires to feminist aesthetics comes to turn'.[41] She takes issue with feminist readings which can only see in 'Übergang' an expression of 'universal' female experience because they ignore the racism implicit in the text. For Adelson the black GIs represent 'indiscriminate evil' and are an 'affirmation of the racist stereotype that black men pose an inherent danger to white people and to white women in particular'.[42] Whether or not one agrees with Adelson's view that this is not mitigated by other aspects of the text (such as the sympathetic black anaesthetist, or the nightmare vision of menacing blond neo-Nazis), her argument highlights important issues about the danger of confusing negativity as an oppositional stance with negativity as mere absence or silence, which has been the place conventionally accorded to women by patriarchy. She points out that blackness is associated with the protagonist's exclusion from the symbolic order of signification, but that it is also experienced as positive in this and other texts in the volume. Darkness, once seen as a threat, also appears as liberation, which is the basis of positive feminist readings (such as Weigel's) which Adelson accuses of mystifying and dehistoricizing femininity. The protagonist was *not* 'everywoman', but a white, German, non-Jewish woman whose victim status is relativized by her identification with the perpetrators of German history. Furthermore, according to Adelson, the violence of the GIs has to be seen against the political and historical background of the National Socialist past, the allied occupation of West Germany, and the presence of guest-workers, all of which provide a context of racial tension which is elided in the apparent arbitrariness of the attack: 'the racist image of the GIs points a finger at a sociocultural context that the text itself does not

[41] Adelson, *Making Bodies*, 38.
[42] Ibid. 39.

elaborate.'[43] While this may appear excessively prescriptive as a critique of a literary text, it does point up some of the potential problems with feminist aesthetics based on a psychoanalytical notion of 'the feminine' which has no necessary connection with historically located women.

It is this aspect present even in much postmodern feminist theory that concerns the philosopher Christine Battersby in her recent work on feminist ontology. She detects an epistemological bias in feminist theory which militates against female agency, stemming from the influence of 'the two Jacques', Derrida and Lacan, 'who both place the "*féminin*" outside the bounds of the knowable, instead of emphasizing woman's potential to transform the actual'.[44] She finds a notion of essence necessary to theorize the conflict between the real (experience) and the discursive (which mediates experience). Lacan's model of subjectivity is too firmly based on Kantian metaphysics to allow of any serious engagement with the body as anything but a discursive site. Kant's system requires a firm inside/outside distinction, and a notion of permanent, inert matter as the self's necessary 'other'. The transcendental self is constituted by its relation to not-self, matter which is subject to the imposition of form by the mind.[45] Matter is even gendered similarly by Kant and Lacan, the feminine occupying a position on the horizon of the phenomenal/the symbolic, excluded from it. Battersby sees Irigaray as the only one of the French feminist theorists to challenge the implicit Kantian model in Lacan's thought, positing a porous boundary between self and not-self: 'Irigaray begins to open up an ontological alternative to a metaphysics of substance and a metaphysics of presence as she maps identities that emerge from flesh and from flux.'[46]

Unlike Irigaray, however, Battersby finds alternatives to this Kantian metaphysics within the western philosophical tradition, which Irigaray tends to dismiss as uniformly characterized by an 'economy of the same'.[47] She points to the existence (already at the time when Irigaray's early work was published) of the new scientific discourses of dissipative systems and chaos theory, which offer alternatives to the hylomorphism of western culture; that is, the view that active form imposes itself on inert matter. This is essential for her project of 'thinking a new subject

[43] Ibid. 54.

[44] Christine Battersby, *The Phenomenal Woman: Feminist Metaphysics and Patterns of Identity* (New York: Routledge, 1998), 13.

[45] This is what differentiates Kant's understanding of selfhood from Descartes's rational *cogito*, which is self-contained, knowing itself by pure introspection, independent of any outside world (Battersby, *The Phenomenal Woman*, 70).

[46] Ibid. 101.

[47] Battersby draws on ideas from Adorno, Kierkegaard, Foucault, and Deleuze, to name but a few.

that can exist in a world in which bodies are fleshy and matter can birth'.[48] Instead of theorizing subjectivity as dependent on a 'cut' from the other, and the body as 'container' of the mind, she posits identity emerging gradually out of a play of unequal relationships, persisting through time but embodied and capable of radical change. This perhaps gives a new angle from which to regard the 'abject body' in Duden's text; the abject is not simply a signifier of 'the feminine', but demonstrates to us how libidinally invested the body is. We do not 'have' bodies in the same way that we have other objects, and there is an 'incompleteness' in the human infant, whose instincts are insufficient to support its needs, making it dependent on the good will of others.[49] Both the irreducible materiality of the body and its dependence on others are crucial for Battersby's notion of the emergence of the subject.

Battersby enumerates five features of the female subject position as commonly experienced in patriarchal cultures, using these as starting points from which to think subjectivity differently: natality, or the capacity to give birth; power inequalities and dependence; a lack of sharp self/other distinction; embodiment; and monstrosity, deriving mainly from the capacity to give birth, which is 'abnormal' in a male-dominated symbolic. We have already seen the importance of the body in Duden's work, as locus of cultural memory, or as abject and unsettling to the containment and integrity of the subject. The question is whether the body can also be seen as matter which has the capacity to change, and, if so, whether a Lacanian framework is adequate to account for the positive moment in her writing. This may be found in the striking link between embodiment and monstrosity, most manifest in Duden's treatment of images of dragon-slaying.[50] These texts emphasize the dragon's profligate body, defying sexual categorization, and its organic fleshiness as opposed to the armoured containment of the conquering saint. Most depictions of dragon-slaying show the victim being killed by penetration of the mouth, rendering the creature *mundtot* (silenced).[51] This resonates with the protagonist's experience in 'Übergang', in which the damaged female body shares something of the monstrosity of the

[48] Battersby, *The Phenomenal Woman*, 97.

[49] Grosz, *Volatile Bodies*, 54–5.

[50] Most of these are found in Anne Duden, *Der wunde Punkt im Alphabet* (Reinbek: Rowohlt, 1995). See especially 'Der wunde Punkt im Alphabet', 77–84; 'O dolorosa Sorte: Über die Musik Carlo Gesualdos (1560–1613)', 7–12; and 'Gegenstrebige Fügung', 119–25. Teresa Ludden's as yet unpublished Ph.D. thesis, '"Das Undarstellbare darstellen": *Kulturkritik* and the Representation of Difference in the Work of Anne Duden' (University of Warwick) provides detailed analysis of these texts.

[51] Duden, *Der wunde Punkt*, 77.

dragon, in terms of its deviation from the norms of socially acceptable embodiment. For Christine Battersby the existence of a body that can birth is '"monstrous" in terms of those modes of "common sense" that regard the self as a substance that persists unaltered through change'.[52] In 'Übergang', therefore, one can perhaps detect a priority accorded to matter which has eluded the psychoanalytical readings so far discussed. Analysis of the subject–object relationship in the text, and of the role of music in their construction, generates a reading which points beyond the impasse of trauma and abjection.

Teresa Ludden provides just such a reading of Duden's work, taking as her starting point the description of the damaged body in 'Herz und Mund' as 'der Klumpen im Rollstuhl' ('the lump in the wheelchair'), entirely 'entmündigt' by her injuries.[53] Inwardly pleading with the hospital staff to treat her agonized body more carefully, she realizes that, from their point of view, she has been reduced to pure 'matter': 'Material ist stumm. Wo kämen wir hin, wenn wir auch noch aufs Material hören würden.'[54] Ludden reads both irony and a serious proposition into this statement, seeing the silencing of the body (as 'matter') in western culture as the central target of Duden's critique. Her analysis of subject–object relations in Duden's work challenges the idea that dissolution of the self is traumatic, because there is no clear-cut stability in the first place. Subject and object are not discrete entities, yet they never entirely merge, and matter has the capacity for movement immanent to itself. Thus in 'Übergang' the heartbeat, breath, and mouth have their own movements, independent of the subject's will: 'Ein rhythmisch hastiges und dumpfes Schlagen im Brustkorb wollte noch ganz schnell einen Ausgang finden, kam aber nur bis zur Kehle. Die Atemzüge wollten gleichmäßig weitermachen. Luft holen, ausatmen, Luft holen. Der Mund wollte sagen: Noch nicht. Nein. Aber er dachte es nur halb und erstickte schon an dem Gedanken.'[55] The narrator's legs seem to develop a life of their own (*Ü* 78) as she struggles to find a comfortable position, and the pain of the metal wires in her mouth collapses

[52] Battersby, *The Phenomenal Woman*, 205.

[53] *Ü* 47. 'Entmündigt', meaning to be deprived of the right of decision, evokes also the literal meaning of being deprived of one's mouth (see Teresa Ludden, 'Material Movements in Texts by Anne Duden', in Heike Bartel and Elizabeth Boa (eds.), *Anne Duden: A Revolution of Words. Approaches to her Fiction, Poetry, and Essays* (Amsterdam: Rodopi, 2003), 72–87).

[54] 'Material is mute. Where would we end up if we were to listen to matter on top of everything else?' (*Ü* 49).

[55] 'A rhythmically hasty and dull beating in the ribcage was urgently looking for a way out, but only got as far as the throat. The breaths tried to carry on regularly. Breathe in, breathe out, breathe in. The mouth wanted to say: Not yet. No. But it only half thought it and suffocated at the very thought' (*Ü* 71).

the distinction between self and other: 'Ich wußte auch nicht, ob es schmerzte oder ob ich nicht eigentlich selber das Messer war, das immerzu ins Fleisch schnitt.'[56] At times the description of intense pain appears detached from any recognizable subject, in particular after the horrific experience of the mouth X-ray: 'Die Wundheit im oberen Bereich, ihre wütenden Spitzen und messerscharfen Kanten verhüllten sich allmählich und tauchten dann in etwas Weicheres ein. Ein paar folgende Bewegungen und weit entfernte Erschütterungen fanden ein wohltuendes, langausgestrecktes, vollkommen erschöpftes und erlöstes Ende, aus dem mich eine plötzliche Kühle und ein Stich am Oberschenkel wieder herausholten.'[57] While these examples certainly indicate that matter is anything but inert, it is nevertheless difficult to see the experience of such pain purely as affirmation of the flesh and a challenge to the dominance of reason. Battersby makes a distinction which may be useful here, between the philosophical cynicism of Adorno's critique of instrumental reason and the celebratory 'kynicism' advocated by Peter Sloterdijk. Whereas Adorno laments the corruption of reason to a tool of domination in modernity and opposes to it a negative critique, Sloterdijk proposes a celebration of the ridiculous (including the body and its wastes) 'as a way of mocking the pretensions of reason'.[58] Sloterdijk accuses Adorno of taking a kind of pleasure in his despair, a stance which one might also identify in Duden's insistent focus on pain and the damaged body in 'Übergang'. This would reinforce the view that her writing probes the darker corners of the human psyche in ways which make reader-identification uncomfortable. It is perhaps easier in her later, less narrative texts, those in which the subject is increasingly elided, to see the 'movements of matter' in a more positive light.

Ludden makes a strong case, however, for the interpretation of aural experience in Duden's work as challenging the opposition of disembodied self to inert material other. As Battersby puts it, whereas sight contri-

[56] 'I didn't know either if it was hurting or if I was really myself the knife, cutting constantly into my flesh' (*Ü* 96).

[57] 'The soreness in the upper region, its angry spikes and knife-sharp edges were gradually shrouded and plunged into something softer. A few further movements and far distant tremors came to a soothing, long-drawn-out, perfectly exhausted and redeemed end, out of which a sudden chill and a prick in my upper thigh retrieved me again' (*Ü* 83).

[58] Battersby, *The Phenomenal Woman*, 143. Peter Sloterdijk's *Kritik der zynischen Vernunft* (Frankfurt am Main: Suhrkamp, 1983), trans. Michael Eldred as *Critique of Cynical Reason* (Minneapolis, Minn.: University of Minnesota Press, 1987) refers directly to Immanuel Kant's *Kritik der reinen Vernunft* (1781; *Critique of Pure Reason*) and is a reflection on the possibility of Enlightenment in the postmodern age. Of particular interest to contemporary feminism is Sloterdijk's commitment to embodied thought, as opposed to the disembodied rationality characteristic of much of the tradition of Enlightenment.

butes to our sense of distanced 'mastery' over the world, our more passive relationship to sound may help us to think of the self differently; a self which has control and direction, without the necessity of a 'cut' from the other: 'Hearing involves a dynamic response to novelty in a non-episodic continuum. Indeed the "I" constitutes itself through taking the "other" within the self.'[59] She points to the importance of the notion of the 'refrain' in Gilles Deleuze and Felix Guattari's *A Thousand Plateaus*, as offering the possibility of continuity and progress, without proceeding in a linear fashion by linking individual notes. Music is multilinear, a becoming which links past and present, and whose patterns of repeated sound provide a model for belonging together in ways other than as subject and object. In Duden's work late medieval polyphonic music offers just such an experience of enabling something new, unexpected, and transient to emerge:

> **Ihre Fähigkeit ... polyphon, pansonant, dissonant und harmonisch sich zu Gebilden zusammenzuschließen, rhythmisch gegliedert, die einen ungeahnten Bewegungsradius erhalten und dabei transparent und vergänglich bleiben, die aufrührerisch und verführerisch Räume öffnen, Räume aller Art, und dann die Öffnung im Raum stehenlassen, während sie schon wieder vergangen und verklungen sind, sich als Gebilde in Nichts aufgelöst haben.**[60]

As in this example, music is repeatedly associated by Duden with the opening up of new spaces, presenting a challenge to the notion of permanent objects in a homogenized, Kantian space-time.[61] In the text 'Das Landhaus' the narrator recalls the effect of a sixteenth-century motet as being that of opening up a series of rooms, each larger than the last, finally sweeping her up on a 'Luftwoge, die einen schließlich mitnahm ins Offene und einen dort ruhig und gleichmäßig beatmete'.[62] Here, the subject of the breathing is the air itself, not the human subject, suggesting

[59] Battersby, *The Phenomenal Woman*, 180.

[60] 'Its [music's] capacity ... to come together in structures which are polyphonous, sounding from everywhere, dissonant and harmonious, rhythmically structured and attaining an unexpected radius of motion, while remaining transparent and ephemeral, rebelliously and seductively opening up spaces, spaces of all sorts, and then leaving the opening in space to stand, when they have already died away again, having dissolved themselves as a shape into nothingness' (Duden, *Zungengewahrsam*, 58).

[61] Kant dismissed music because it involved a bodily response rather than a judgemental one: 'The "unity" of music is primarily bodily, and not imposed by the mind in the manner of the "synthesis" of sight' (Battersby, *The Phenomenal Woman*, 181). As Battersby points out, this is precisely the value of music to feminist music aesthetics.

[62] 'wave of air which finally took one with it into the open and breathed air into one peacefully and evenly' (*Ü* 23).

the interpenetration of self and other, without a dissolution of self. In 'Übergang' the only relief experienced by the protagonist comes in the form of music, which had always had the effect of dislodging all fixity, allowing her to be porous, so that the outside/inside distinction is suspended: 'Wie ein Sturmwind brachte sie etwas in Bewegung, zerschlug blitzschnell alles Feste und Schwere und gab mir ein Gefühl von Durchlässigkeit, wo das Innen genauso viel galt wie das Außen. Die Musik ging einfach hindurch, durch Mauern und Wände, durch die Haut.'[63] In hospital she acquires a small tape recorder and subsequently relies on music to take her into 'ein vollkommen neues Linien- und Flächensystem, in dem alles Ausdruck finden, also in Bewegung kommen konnte, ohne je an etwas anzustoßen, ohne aber auch je in Bereiche zu verschwinden, in die ich nicht mitgegangen wäre'.[64] This suggests music as an alternative to language as a form of expression, one in which nothing is repressed. But rather than posing a threat to the subject, it creates a force field in which the subject can persist.[65] In this respect, music could indeed be seen as offering a model for the subject's emerging through movement and 'the temporary equilibrium of force-fields', while avoiding 'positing underlying "substances" that remain unaltered through change'.[66] Ludden sees in such evocations of polyphony and multidimensionality a '[u]topian realm of difference, openness and freedom for Duden', in which the collapse of binary oppositions does not involve the collapse of subjectivity itself. With her focus on 'intensities' (which are always positive), in preference to the ambivalence of *jouissance,* Ludden plays down the potentially disturbing and even disabling impact of extreme experience. While her reading certainly accounts for the positive moments in Duden's work, it risks neglecting the real historical suffering and individual trauma from which there is only ever temporary and fleeting relief.

[63] 'Like a gale it made something move, smashed all that was solid and heavy and instantly made me feel porous, the inside exactly equivalent to the outside. The music simply went through, through walls and partitions, through the skin' (*Ü* 74).

[64] 'A completely new system of lines and planes, in which everything could be expressed and could start moving without ever colliding with anything else, but also without ever disappearing into realms into which I was not prepared to follow' (*Ü* 90).

[65] Johanna Bossinade points out that the involuntary perception of sound can also be traumatic in Duden's work, threatening the collapse of existential space. However, the space-creating effects of music have epistemological rather than ontological significance for Bossinade, functioning mainly to unsettle meaning (see Bossinade, 'Original Differentiation: The Poetics of Anne Duden', in Chris Weedon (ed.), *Post-War Women's Writing in German: Feminist Critical Approaches* (Oxford: Berghahn, 1997), 131–51).

[66] Battersby, *The Phenomenal Woman*, 12.

Conclusion

We have seen that the elision of the narrative 'I' almost to the point of disappearance in Duden's work is open to contrasting interpretations. It can be seen as the effect of trauma so overwhelming and ubiquitous that no recovery of the damaged psyche is possible. It could signal a modernist gesture, as posited by Kristeva, whereby the theme of horror and the poetic disruption of syntax threaten the stability of the symbolic order. Alternatively, it could be a postmodern gesture, challenging the subject–object binary but allowing a subjective presence to persist. Here, the subject exists in relation not only to the symbolic but also to the material world which has an agency of its own. In terms of the viability of the subject that emerges, one could argue that there is little to choose between them, as suggested by Duden herself in a recent interview: '*Übergang* ist somit mein Versuch gewesen—und ich glaube, ich arbeite weiter daran—eine unmögliche Daseinsmöglichkeit auszudrücken, und das geht für mich nur durch und in Sprache, über Schrift.'[67] Paradoxically, this points up the dilemma of the *literary* artist attempting to express embodied subjectivity in which matter is not inert: it is only possible through the medium of language. The problem of representing the real is at the heart of both Duden's writing and its critical interpretation. However, there is a productive tension between psychoanalytical readings in which the only encounter with the real is through *jouissance*, and postmodern attempts to recuperate matter and accord it an active place in the construction of gendered subjects. It is only through an incorporation of multiple theoretical perspectives that justice can be done to both the critical and the creative moments in Duden's work.

[67] '*Übergang* was thus my attempt—one in which I believe I'm still engaged—to express an impossible mode of being, and for me this is only possible through and in language, by means of writing' (interview with Kramatschek, 'In den Faltungen der Sprache', 33).

4 Christa Wolf, *Kassandra* (1983)

Introduction

It is not surprising that Christa Wolf's 1983 reinterpretation of the myth of Cassandra should have resonated with feminists the world over and reached the widest international audience of all her works until then. For in the tradition which began with Homer's *Iliad* and Aeschylus' *Oresteia*, Cassandra's role as a prophetess whose fate was to speak the truth but not be believed made her, in the eyes of many, iconic of the position of women in patriarchal societies. Wolf sought, however, to defy the tradition and, via the strength of her Kassandra's voice and the power of her witness, make herself heard.[1] The work's main message —that perverted structures of thought in western culture, which lead inevitably to war, must be changed—was recognizably urgent in the early 1980s because escalating tensions in the cold war were making war on European soil seem an imminent danger. Thus the work appealed not just to feminists but also to critical thinkers and all who were anxious to avoid war. It could be read as Wolf's contribution to *Kulturkritik* (critiques of culture), a tradition stretching back at least as far as the 'hermeneutics of suspicion'[2] of Karl Marx, Friedrich Nietzsche, and Sigmund Freud, and a response to two of its most influential recent interventions: Max Horkheimer and Theodor Adorno's critique of instrumental reason *Dialektik der Aufklärung* (*Dialectic of Enlightenment*) (1947) and Ernst Bloch's assertion of the continuing importance of utopian thinking in *Das Prinzip Hoffnung* (*The Principle of Hope*) (1959). Specifically, Wolf's text warned that, through its engagement in the arms race, the socialist camp—that is, the eastern bloc—was fast becoming

[1] English names, for example Cassandra, are used throughout to refer to the figures from myth, while German names, for example Kassandra, denote Wolf's fictional re-creations. Place names are given throughout in English.

[2] Paul Ricœur's phrase, quoted in Andrew Bowie, 'Critiques of Culture', in Eva Kolinsky and Wilfried van der Will (eds.), *The Cambridge Companion to Modern German Culture* (Cambridge: Cambridge University Press, 1998), 132–52 (140). Bowie explains the phrase thus: 'For these thinkers the surface meaning of cultural phenomena is suspect because its genesis is "overdetermined" by motivational factors which are not immediately accessible to the producers of that meaning. These factors need not, though, be excluded from eventually becoming rationally accessible, for example through "ideology critique" or psychoanalysis'.

indistinguishable from the capitalist West, its ideological opponent. Within the GDR, and for all those with prior knowledge of Wolf and her country, a further dimension to the Cassandra theme was immediately apparent, for the novel begged to be unlocked as a *Schlüsselerzählung* (*roman-à-clef*) about the GDR,[3] the corruption of its original ideals, and Wolf's own positioning within its power structures: Kassandra, in other words, was a thin disguise for Wolf herself. (The censoring of the GDR edition of the accompanying lectures—though not of the novel—as well as the attack on Wolf by the critic Wilhelm Girnus on the charge of portraying history as the struggle between the sexes instead of as class struggle did nothing to dispel this view.[4]) This approach complicates any feminist reading; for Wolf's Kassandra, while objectively a victim at the hands of individual men and of a patriarchal society, is a perpetrator as well: she becomes aware, far too late, of her own deep complicity in the regime she serves. The text thus raises vital questions not just about deadly power structures but also about women's apparent inability to think themselves free of them.

The novel takes the form of a monologue by Kassandra at the gates of Mycenae just before her death. After the fall of Troy the Trojan princess and priestess has been taken prisoner by the Greek king, Agamemnon. Kassandra knows, though Agamemnon does not, that both of them are about to be murdered by his queen, Klytaimnestra, who has ruled Mycenae for ten years in his absence. In a stream-of-consciousness narrative, Kassandra looks back on the long build-up to the Trojan Wars in which, as a member of the Trojan elite, she was heavily implicated. She did not, for example, reveal to the Trojan population that the war was ostensibly fought over a phantom: the veiled woman paraded as Helena by Kassandra's brother Paris is no such person. Kassandra only realizes her guilt in perpetuating this tissue of lies when, towards the end of the war, she joins an alternative, harmonious community living in caves

[3] Wolf herself referred to the novel thus at the time (*K* 152), and in a letter to Günter Grass in 1993 she wrote, 'Ich habe dieses Land [the GDR] geliebt. Daß es am Ende war, wußte ich, weil es die besten Leute nicht mehr integrieren konnte, weil es Menschenopfer forderte. Ich habe das in *Kassandra* beschrieben, die Zensur stocherte in den 'Vorlesungen' herum; ich wartete gespannt, ob sie es wagen würden, die Botschaft der Erzählung zu verstehen, nämlich, daß Troja untergehen muß. Sie haben es nicht gewagt und die Erzählung ungekürzt gedruckt. Die Leser in der DDR verstanden sie'. 'I loved this country [the GDR]. I knew it was finished because it could no longer integrate the best people, because it was demanding human sacrifices. I described this in *Kassandra*, the censors poked around in the "lectures"; I waited with bated breath to see if they would dare to understand the message of the tale, namely that Troy must fall. They did not dare and published the tale uncut. The readers in the GDR understood' (*Auf dem Weg nach Tabou: Texte 1990–1994* (Cologne: Kiepenheuer und Witsch, 1994), 262–3).

[4] For details of both see Sonja Hilzinger, 'Nachwort' and 'Entstehung, Veröffentlichung und Rezeption', in *K* 419–28, 429–46.

by the banks of the Scamander river outside Troy. She makes a stand against her father's war plan—by refusing to play a part in the plot to trap Achill using her beloved sister Polyxena as bait—too late to make a difference. The war is long, exceedingly bloody, and brutal; it polarizes gender roles, systematically forcing men, such as Kassandra's unwilling brother Hektor, to become aggressors, and both excluding women from decision-making and reducing them to objects. Kassandra's first intimation of the horrific reality of war is when 'Achill das Vieh' ('Achilles the brute'), who in Homer is the epitome of the noble Greek hero, defiles Apoll's temple, where her beloved brother Troilus has sought sanctuary, by entering and murdering him there. This is only the first of many traumatic events: Penthesilea, the fearless Amazon queen, is killed in battle and her body desecrated by the monstrous Achill; in revenge for this act, Panthoos, the Greek priest who serves the Trojans, is beaten to death by a mob of Amazon and Trojan women; the weakened Troy is eventually overrun by cunning—by means of the wooden horse; the cave community is swept away; Polyxena goes mad and is murdered; Kassandra herself, passing up the option to leave with her lover Aineias, is raped and taken prisoner. Her monologue is her testament and ends when she hears the guards coming to lead her to her death.

The critique of propaganda as an instrument of control and the harrowing depiction of war as the end result of rationality gone mad are devastating, but critics have highlighted a central tension between the 'weakness' of Wolf's solutions to the problem of instrumental reason on the one hand and the 'strength' of her central figure and the 'closure' of her narrative on the other.[5] Wolf's sketch of a utopian community in the caves, however tenderly depicted, remains just that, a sketch, and the group itself is open to parody as a kind of hippy commune. The community is fragile and is swept away the moment the ruthless Greeks finally conquer Troy. Nothing has changed by the end of the novel: Kassandra opts not to join her lover Aineias in founding a new community because she knows it will repeat the mistakes of the past and that she will be unable to love him once he is forced to adopt the role of hero. Kassandra's choice is potentially problematic for feminism, for in settling for death and becoming a tragic heroine she accepts the sacrificial logic of western culture. Her final achievement of self-awareness is also problematic,

[5] These positions are set out, for example, in Leslie Adelson, 'The Bomb and I: Peter Sloterdijk, Botho Strauß, and Christa Wolf', *Monatshefte* 78/4 (1986), 500–13; Ricarda Schmidt, 'Über gesellschaftliche Ohnmacht und Utopie in Christa Wolfs *Kassandra*', *Oxford German Studies*, 16 (1985), 109–21; and Sigrid Weigel, 'Vom Sehen zur Seherin: Christa Wolfs Umdeutung des Mythos und die Spur der Bachmann-Rezeption in ihrer Literatur', in Angela Drescher (ed.), *Christa Wolf: Ein Arbeitsbuch* (Luchterhand: Frankfurt am Main, 1990), 169–203.

as it renders her text on first reading somewhat didactic. And just as Kassandra sees no way out, Wolf too, her penetrating critique notwithstanding, appears to have failed to break free of the western intellectual tradition and its aesthetics which she condemned as deadly, remaining instead deeply in their thrall. For Kassandra's highly dramatic monologue, while epic in scope, obeys the unities of time, action, and place, and proceeds, with a mounting sense of inevitability, towards the destruction of Troy and her own death, which impending event gives structure to the whole narrative. This formal perfection and reliance on death, together with Wolf's extraordinary power to evoke pity and fear in the reader, apparently invoke rather than repudiate the tradition of ancient Greek tragedy and claim a direct line of descent from it. This chapter probes these issues anew in the context of Wolf's changing aesthetics and of her intervention in modernist and postmodernist debates about myth; in particular parallels will be drawn with the work of the Italian feminist philosopher Adriana Cavarero, who also 'steals' female figures from mythology with political intent.

Politics and aesthetics

The aesthetic closure of the novel and the self-assurance of the central figure represented a new departure for Wolf, whose major works to date, *Nachdenken über Christa T.* (1968) and *Kindheitsmuster* (1976), were characterized by three traits: 'subjective authenticity', a style of writing in which the author's reflections on the writing process were incorporated into her narrative; 'epistemological scepticism', a thematization of the difficulty of knowing; and the difficulty of saying 'I'. The adoption of these features, which may broadly be described as modernist, is commonly interpreted as a reaction against the GDR's prescriptive aesthetic mode, socialist realism, to which Wolf had herself conformed in her earliest texts, *Moskauer Novelle* (1961) and *Der geteilte Himmel* (1963). Socialist realism depicts positive heroes who work for the common good, whereas in *Nachdenken über Christa T.*, one of the most influential works of GDR literature, Wolf had implied criticism of the regime by thematizing the destructive effects of the pressure to conform on the individual. In *Kindheitsmuster* she had probed the erasure of the Nazi period from the discourses of the GDR through a complex narrative which mixed autobiography with elements of the novel. Wolf's disillusionment with the regime that, as a young woman in 1949, she had firmly supported for its strong anti-fascist stance reached a new level of intensity in 1976 after the expulsion of the singer/songwriter Wolf Biermann and the repressive measures brought against those intellectuals, including Wolf, who had supported him. Her next novel, *Kein Ort: Nirgends* (1979), gave expression to this sense of crisis by moving back in time to the Romantic era. Through the inability of the central figures, Heinrich von Kleist and Karoline von Günderrode, to flourish, or even survive in the repressive and authoritarian period after the turn of the nineteenth century, Wolf articulated in code the sense her generation felt of being out of tune with their time. The aesthetic and the view of subjectivity had shifted, however: the novel's construction as a montage of marked and unmarked quotations suggested the textual construction of subjectivity, while paradoxically, as Sara Friedrichsmeyer points out, there is also 'the ghost of an idealist subject lurking behind these splits, for the implication is that, given a saner society, both writers would flourish'.[6]

If *Kassandra*—which, with its mythological setting, continues the move back in time begun in *Kein Ort: Nirgends*—also continues the return to autonomous selfhood begun there (Kassandra has no difficulty saying 'I'), it is, Friedrichsmeyer argues, for political reasons: '[t]he more important it seemed to offer meaningful alternatives to her country's repressive system, the more vital it became to identify the individual as the locus of reason and potential source of meaningful change'.[7] Interestingly, this parallels a move in recent feminist theory away from textual constructions of subjectivity to more materialist, embodied theories of self which allow for agency: those who have traditionally been denied subject status are less willing to deconstruct the subject.[8] The same trends are continued in Wolf's first post-reunification novel, *Medea: Stimmen* (1996), which can be read as her response to the *Literaturstreit* (literary dispute), in which, as the most prominent representative of the GDR intelligentsia, she was vilified in the West German press after the publication of her short text *Was bleibt* (1990).[9] Despite its apparently polyvocal structure, *Medea: Stimmen* tells a singular tale, reinterpreting the mythological figure of Medea—notorious as a monstrous mother

[6] Sara Friedrichsmeyer, 'On Multiple Selves and Dialogics: Christa Wolf's Challenge to the "Enlightened" Faust', in W. Daniel Wilson and Robert C. Holub (eds.), *Impure Reason: Dialectic of Enlightenment in Germany* (Detroit, Mich.: Wayne State University Press, 1993), 65–86 (74).

[7] Friedrichsmeyer, 'On Multiple Selves and Dialogics', 73.

[8] See e.g. Christine Battersby, *The Phenomenal Woman: Feminist Metaphysics and the Patterns of Identity* (New York: Routledge, 1998).

[9] See Thomas Anz (ed.), *Es geht nicht um Christa Wolf: Der Literaturstreit im vereinten Deutschland* (Frankfurt: Fischer, 1995) and Karl Deiritz and Hannes Krauss, *Der deutsch–deutsche Literaturstreit oder 'Freunde, es spricht sich schlecht mit gebundener Zunge'* (Hamburg: Luchterhand, 1991).

who murdered her own children—as a woman falsely accused and used as a scapegoat.

The sense that the novel *Kassandra* is less radical in form than Wolf's earlier work can, however, be challenged by pointing out that it does not stand, and should not be read, alone. The text's first incarnation was as the fifth of five lectures on poetics given by Wolf in Frankfurt in 1982, and though novel and lectures were published separately in 1983 they are now reunited in the new Luchterhand critical edition, together with the first draft of the novel, reconstructed with the help of a sound recording made at the time. The project itself had begun with Wolf's trip to Greece with her husband in March and April 1980, during which she visited Athens, her host's village in the countryside, several classical sites such as Mycenae, and Crete, home of the ancient and mysterious Minoan civilization. The first two lectures in *Voraussetzungen einer Erzählung: Kassandra* are travel reports about her trip, the third a work diary written after her return home, and the fourth a letter. Wolf describes as a turning point in her life hearing the voice of Cassandra speaking to her across the centuries from Aeschylus' text. The identification was intense: 'Kassandra. Ich sah sie gleich. Sie, die Gefangene, nahm mich gefangen, sie, selbst Objekt fremder Zwecke, besetzte mich . . . Ihr glaubte ich jedes Wort, das gab es noch, bedingungsloses Vertrauen. Dreitausend Jahre—weggeschmolzen.'[10] From that point the lectures chart Wolf's fascination with the figure and her efforts to research the history and archaeology of the pre-Hellenic period with a view to retelling Cassandra's story; the reader is invited to read the novel against the story of its own genesis. W. E. McDonald argues that Kassandra and Wolf thus become protagonists in parallel *Bildungsromane* (novels of education),[11] and Laurie Melissa Vogelsang points out that Wolf confronts the dichotomy fundamental to all western discourse, namely that of subject over object, and asks whether one can have a literary object not dominated by the author.[12] But much more is also included: the lectures contain unsystematic musings on, among other things, literature ancient and modern, philosophy, archaeology, women's writing, contemporary events, as well as undigested recordings of daily life in Greece

[10] 'Cassandra. I saw her straight away. She, the captive, took me captive, she, herself the object of others' use, occupied me . . . I believed every word she spoke, it still existed, unconditional trust. Three thousand years—melted away' (*K* 15–16).

[11] W. E. McDonald, 'Who's Afraid of Wolf's Cassandra—or Cassandra's Wolf?: Male Tradition and Women's Knowledge in *Cassandra*', *Journal of Narrative Technique*, 20/3 (1990), 267–83 (273).

[12] Laurie Melissa Vogelsang, 'Killa's Tertium: Christa Wolf and Cassandra', in Marilyn Sibley Fries (ed.), *Responses to Christa Wolf: Critical Essays* (Detroit, Mich.: Wayne State University Press, 1989), 367–77 (369).

(from an outsider's perspective) and (from an intimate perspective) at Wolf's country cottage in Meteln in the GDR. Included also are references to the legacy of the Second World War, in particular memories of the Holocaust and the aftermath of the dropping of the atomic bomb on the Japanese city of Hiroshima, and to contemporary international politics: modern-day Greece, the Iran–Iraq War (1980–8), the apartheid regime in South Africa, and the progress of arms negotiations in the cold war, for example. The reader is invited to make his or her own connections, and the consequent openness of form (Judith Ryan calls this a kind of 'performativer Poetik'[13]), the lack of authorial direction, and the choice of traditionally feminine genres such as the letter stand in stark contrast to the closure of the novel and relativize the aesthetic decisions taken there.

Wolf claims in the introduction to the lectures that she has no poetics, but then immediately undermines this by proposing the image of the 'Gewebe' ('fabric', *K* 12) which cannot be taken in at a glance, has loose ends, and from which a single strand cannot be extracted without damaging the whole (*K* 176). Elsewhere she reformulates this as a 'Grammatik der vielfachen gleichzeitigen Bezüge';[14] it is preferable to the monologic course customarily taken by western culture, where philosophy and literature have made the same mistake. She has the feeling that

> **das strikte einwegbesessene Vorgehn, das Herauspräparieren eines 'Stranges' zu Erzähl- und Untersuchungszwecken das ganze Gewebe und auch diesen 'Strang' beschädigt. Aber eben diesen Weg ist doch, vereinfacht gesagt, das abendländische Denken gegangen, den Weg der Sonderung, der Analyse, des Verzichts auf die Mannigfaltigkeit der Erscheinungen zugunsten des Dualismus, des Monismus, zugunsten der Geschlossenheit von Weltbildern und Systemen; des Verzichts auf Subjektivität zugunsten gesicherter 'Objektivität'.**[15]

What Wolf admires about Ingeborg Bachmann, a discussion of whose works occupies much of the fourth lecture, is her ability to renounce her attachment to the distance conferred by aesthetic forms (*K* 191),

[13] 'performative poetics' (Ryan, 'Poetik als Experiment: Christa Wolf, *Voraussetzungen einer Erzählung. Kassandra*', in Paul Michael Lützeler (ed.), *Poetik der Autoren* (Frankfurt am Main: Fischer, 1994), 80–94 (85)).

[14] 'grammar of multiple, simultaneous connections' (*K* 164).

[15] 'the strict, obsessively utilitarian way of proceeding, the taking out and preservation of one "skein" for the purposes of narration and examination damages the whole fabric and also this "skein". But, put simply, western thought has taken just this path, the path of selection, of analysis, of giving up the multiplicity of appearances in favour of dualism, monism, in favour of the closure of world-views and systems; of giving up subjectivity in favour of secure "objectivity"' (*K* 176).

whereas it could be said that in imitating the closure of western aesthetic forms in the novel but embedding that material, over which she has achieved 'Souveränität' ('sovereignty') (*K* 12), within a corpus over which she has not, Wolf is trying to have her cake and eat it. But she is disarmingly frank about the impasse to which she has come: 'Empfinde die geschlossene Form der Kassandra-Erzählung als Widerspruch zu der fragmentarischen Struktur, aus der sie sich für mich eigentlich zusammensetzt. Der Widerspruch kann nicht gelöst, nur benannt werden.'[16] Another way of approaching the dilemma is to examine her choice of myth as a medium of expression.

Women, myth, and modernity

Inge Stephan has noted a boom in the use of myth in literature after 1945 and in the GDR of the seventies and eighties.[17] As part of this second moment, Wolf's return to mythological themes with the Kassandra project was triggered by what Paul Ricœur, borrowing from Karl Jaspers, calls a 'boundary situation', as was her later recourse to myth in *Medea: Stimmen*. At times of crisis such as impending war (or indeed the collapse of a state) a community will return to 'the very roots of its identity; to that mythical nucleus which ultimately grounds and determines it. The solution to the immediate crisis is no longer a purely political or technical matter but demands that we ask ourselves the ultimate questions concerning our origins and ends: Where do we come from: Where do we go?'[18] Myth's suitability for handling big questions—'Im Mythos denkt man die Weltgeschichte noch einmal ganz'[19]—and its consequent refusal to die in the modern and postmodern world derive from a central paradox: it is 'false', unlike history or science, but also 'true', in that it gets to the heart of the matter.[20] It used to be supposed that western culture is based on the defeat of myth, for ever since Plato threw the poets out of his Republic philosophy (*logos*) has considered itself superior

[16] '[I] find the closed form of the Kassandra tale a contradiction to the fragmentary structure from which I think it is actually composed. The contradiction cannot be solved, only named' (*K* 154).

[17] Inge Stephan, *Musen und Medusen: Mythos und Geschlecht in der Literatur des 20. Jahrhunderts* (Cologne: Böhlau, 1997), 9–10, 214. See also Heinz-Peter Preußer, *Mythos als Sinnkonstruktion: Die Antikenprojekte von Christa Wolf, Heiner Müller, Stefan Schütz und Volker Braun* (Cologne: Böhlau, 2000).

[18] Paul Ricœur, 'Myth as the Bearer of Possible Worlds', in Mario J. Valdés (ed.), *A Ricœur Reader: Reflection and Imagination* (New York: Harvester Wheatsheaf, 1991), 482–90 (484).

[19] 'In myth one thinks world history again in its entirety' (Preußer, *Mythos als Sinnkonstruktion*, 3).

[20] Ken Dowden, *The Uses of Greek Mythology* (London: Routledge, 1992), 3.

to literature (*mythos*): the repudiation of poetry was a condition upon which philosophical enquiry, which searches for timeless truths and proceeds by way of rational argument, could begin.[21] Within modernity there is a common perception of a teleological progression in human history from a time when mythological knowledge held sway to a time (whether it be located at the birth of philosophy with the Greeks or later with the rise of science in the seventeenth century) when objective scientific enquiry was launched and took its place centre stage; myth, now discredited as the prime means of access to truth, lives on, displaced into political ideologies, music, and literature.[22] This is broadly the view of human history as 'an ongoing process of emancipation'.[23] But this is a grand Eurocentric narrative and collapses, as Gianni Vattimo points out, when both the idea of history and the idea of progress are challenged as myths themselves; with this, the postmodern age begins. Thus if modernity can be seen as the age of demythologization, of the primacy of *logos* over *mythos*, the postmodern can be seen as the age of the demythologization of demythologization, or a return to myth.

But this western trajectory applies only obliquely to culture in the eastern-bloc states. Wolfgang Emmerich argued in 1988 that, as a result of cultural policy, the literature of the GDR had *at the same time* mostly pre-modern and to a lesser extent modernist and postmodern traits, and the Kassandra project bears this out.[24] Wolf's approach to myth may be broadly described as being both mythographic and mythopoeic;[25] that is, as interrogating the tradition of myth as it has come down to us, but also and at the same time engaging with it because of a heightened sense of cultural continuity in the GDR, and from a pragmatic wish to evade censorship. But her feminist positioning—that is, her awareness, like that of other women writers who have rewritten myth, such as Margaret Atwood in *The Handmaid's Tale* (1986), that women have been marginalized and objectified by myth, philosophy, and science alike—also affects her perception. On the one hand she provides a feminist critique of the Homeric tradition that celebrates the exploits of heroes and simultaneously silences and objectifies women; on the other she rewrites the story of the Trojan Wars from the perspective

[21] Adriana Cavarero, *Relating Narratives: Storytelling and Selfhood*, trans. Paul A. Kottman (London: Routledge, 2000), 95.

[22] Gianni Vattimo, *The Transparent Society*, trans. David Webb (Cambridge: Polity, 1992), 28–30.

[23] Vattimo, *The Transparent Society*, 2.

[24] Emmerich, referred to in Hannes Krauss, 'Rückzug in die Moderne: Christa Wolf und Virginia Woolf', in Robert Atkins and Martin Kane (eds.), *Retrospect and Review: Aspects of the Literature of the GDR 1976–1990* (Amsterdam: Rodopi, 1997), 164–75 (164) (emphasis added).

[25] Terms taken from Laurence Coupe, *Myth* (London: Routledge, 1997), 18.

of one of those silenced and objectified women, thus reinventing the myth for the twentieth and indeed the twenty-first century. The joint approach produces a creative tension, for the mythographic side of the project adopts a detached, analytic, albeit angry, perspective, while mythopoeia, or the reinvention of myth, relies on imagination, identification, and the power of narration.

Vattimo offers a broad typology of three contemporary attitudes to myth, which he terms archaism, cultural relativism, and limited rationality, which may help us to place Wolf's project. Archaism springs from a 'mistrust of Western techno-scientific culture as a way of life that violates and destroys our authentic relation to ourselves and to nature, and which is also inextricably bound to the system of capitalist exploitation and its imperialistic tendencies'.[26] It seeks renewed contact with myth, which it sees as a more authentic form of knowledge. It tends to idealize the time of origins, and is politically dangerous.[27] Wolf's project is certainly based on a mistrust of western techno-scientific culture. In this it develops the critique of instrumental reason begun by Horkheimer and Adorno, who, responding to the catastrophe of the Third Reich and the Holocaust, set out to address the question 'warum die Menschheit, anstatt in einen wahrhaft menschlichen Zustand einzutreten, in eine neue Art von Barbarei versinkt'.[28] They concluded that the goal of the Enlightenment—to free mankind from servitude—while still worthy in itself, had become misdirected so that Enlightenment itself had become totalitarian.[29] Wolf's novel illustrates instrumental reason by charting how war, propagated for economic and strategic reasons (access to the Dardanelles), dehumanizes, subverts truth, polarizes gender roles, and wreaks terrible death and destruction. (Arguably, in the polarized and, in the case of Achill, extreme presentation of men the novel takes this critique too far: the male figures tend to be either idealized, like Troilus, the wise Anchises, and his son Aineias, Kassandra's lover, or weak in some way, like Kassandra's father Priamos, her brothers Hektor and Paris, and Kalchas, the seer.) In searching for the moment where western culture took a wrong turning, Wolf confesses to having been tempted to idealize both Trojan society before the war (calling it 'ein Modell für eine Art von Utopie'[30]) and ancient Minoan culture, the traces of which, particularly

[26] Vattimo, *The Transparent Society*, 31.

[27] Ibid. 33.

[28] 'why mankind, instead of entering into a truly human state, is sinking into a new kind of barbarism' (Max Horkheimer and Theodor W. Adorno, *Dialektik der Aufklärung: Philosophische Fragmente* (Amsterdam: Querido, 1947), 5).

[29] Horkheimer and Adorno, *Dialektik der Aufklärung*, 16.

[30] 'a model for a kind of utopia' (*K* 107).

the cult of matriarchal goddesses, are to be seen in the utopian community by the Scamander river.[31] She resists idealizing the time of origins on both counts, however: Troy's downfall does not spring from being corrupted by the warmongering Greeks, rather Troy is shown to contain all the seeds of corruption within itself;[32] it is an important part of Kassandra's process of coming to an understanding of the past that she sees her nostalgia for the past for what it is. Also Wolf observes that the eagerness of the American feminists she meets in Crete to prove that Minoan culture was a matriarchy reveals more about women's present plight than it does about antiquity (*K* 74). She herself muses on the possible perfection of Minoan culture but then notes that Minoans had slaves (*K* 81).[33]

Vattimo's second approach, cultural relativism, is a postmodern position in that it claims that there is no outside perspective from which to judge truth claims. Even scientific rationality is 'ultimately a myth, a shared belief on the basis of which our culture is organized'.[34] Cultural relativism does not privilege either mythical knowledge or scientific knowledge (but runs into difficulties when it cannot locate its own place of articulation). Wolf's project cannot be situated here for, like the philosopher Jürgen Habermas and the Marxist critic Fredric Jameson, she remains attached to Enlightenment ideals and broadly sees the project of modernity as unfinished. She makes truth claims, she is attached to the *logos*: '[d]ie Zentrierung um den Logos, das Wort als Fetisch—vielleicht der tiefste Aberglaube des Abendlands, jedenfalls der, dem ich inbrünstig anhänge'.[35] The systematic exposure of the lies used as justification for war—the story of the 'Drei Schiffe' ('Three Ships') and of Helena—for example, places Wolf within a tradition of demythologization, or exposure of myth as false ideology, which owes much to Bertolt Brecht and to Roland Barthes's *Mythologies*, a fact of which she is aware (*K* 134).

[31] Wolf confesses to her fascination with theories of matriarchy. She describes herself as 'eine . . . Autorin, die nicht umhin konnte und kann, jeden Gang in die Tiefe der Zeit als einen Gang zu den Müttern zu unternehmen' ('an author who could not and cannot resist undertaking every trip into the depths of time as a trip to the mothers') ('Von Kassandra zu Medea', in *Hierzulande: Andernorts* (Munich: Luchterhand, 1999), 158–68 (161)).

[32] Karin Eysel points out, for example, that the Trojans had built their national identity on enmity to the other (Eysel, 'Christa Wolf's *Kassandra*: Refashioning National Imagination Beyond the Nation', in *Women in German Yearbook*, 9 (1994), 163–81 (175)). W. E. McDonald also points out that a society founded on child sacrifice—witness the fate of Paris—cannot be termed utopian ('Who's Afraid of Wolf's Cassandra', 276).

[33] In the ancient world, myths of matriarchy functioned didactically, representing primitive disorder or that which was beyond the pale (see Dowden, *The Uses of Greek Mythology*, 153–4).

[34] Vattimo, *The Transparent Society*, 34.

[35] 'the centering on the logos, the word as fetish—perhaps the deepest superstition of the West, at any rate the one to which I fervently subscribe' (*K* 35).

Wolf does not reject rationality *per se*—Kassandra prizes her own ability to think rationally—merely what it has become, represented in its most extreme form by the binary logic of the Greeks:

> **Für die Griechen gibt es nur entweder Wahrheit oder Lüge, richtig oder falsch, Sieg oder Niederlage, Freund oder Feind, Leben oder Tod. Sie denken anders. Was nicht sichtbar, riechbar, hörbar, tastbar ist, ist nicht vorhanden. Es ist das andere, das sie zwischen ihren scharfen Unterscheidungen zerquetschen, das Dritte, das es nach ihrer Meinung überhaupt nicht gibt, das lächelnde Lebendige, das imstande ist, sich immer wieder aus sich selbst hervorzubringen, das Ungetrennte, Geist im Leben, Leben im Geist.**[36]

But the highest degree of correspondence in Wolf is with Vattimo's third approach, limited rationality, which has a more specific understanding of mythical knowledge, which, it reminds us, has a structure of its own, that of narrative, and which it sees as 'a form of thought better suited to certain regions of experience'.[37] This is based on the view that 'certain fields of experience are not susceptible to demonstrative reason or scientific method, and require instead another type of understanding that can only be described as mythical'.[38] Wolf was seeking a way out of instrumental reason and alternatives to western aesthetic forms. Myth offers the possibility to break out of conventional ways of thinking, and it was this which attracted her to it:

> **Den Mythos lesen lernen ist ein Abenteuer eigner Art; eine allmähliche eigne Verwandlung setzt diese Kunst voraus, eine Bereitschaft, der scheinbar leichten Verknüpfung von phantastischen Tatsachen, von dem Bedürfnis der jeweiligen Gruppe angepaßten Überlieferungen, Wünschen und Hoffnungen, Erfahrungen und Techniken der Magie—kurz, einem anderen Inhalt des Begriffs 'Wirklichkeit' sich hinzugeben.**[39]

Wolf described the encounter with the figure of Cassandra as a liberating experience which brought new connections and altered her way of seeing (*K* 166). Myth gives this flexibility to thought because of its formal qualities. Traditional myths have no authors, are essentially plural,

[36] 'For the Greeks there is only either truth or lie, right or wrong, victory or defeat, friend or foe, life or death. They think differently. What cannot be seen, smelled, heard or touched is not there. It is the other, which they squash between their sharp distinctions, the third, which in their opinion does not exist at all, the smiling living thing which is able to reproduce itself time and again, the undivided, spirit in life, life in spirit' (*K* 349).

[37] Vattimo, *The Transparent Society*, 35.

[38] Ibid. 36–7.

[39] 'To learn to read myth is an adventure of a particular kind; this art requires that one transform gradually, it requires a readiness to submit to the seemingly easy connecting of fantastic facts, of traditions, desires and hopes, experiences and techniques of magic suited to the need of the relevant group—in short to the concept "reality" having another content' (*K* 74–5).

and work with paradigms, or archetypal characters and situations.[40] Though their historical origins are closely associated with the rituals and belief systems of specific communities, it is this paradigmatic quality, or shared horizon, which makes them partly translatable into different cultures.[41] Thus the classicist Stephanie West proceeds too literally when she argues that despite her pretensions to researching meticulously the historical coordinates of the Cassandra myth Wolf has presented us with a late-twentieth-century Cassandra, who, because she is '[d]emythologized, secularized, sexually experienced, neither troubled nor comforted by religious belief . . . has moved as far from her classical forerunners as she could without becoming completely unrecognizable'.[42] For by drawing on the paradigmatic quality of myth Wolf is able to suggest continuities—her Kassandra is fully traditional in being marginalized by and excluded from the dominant culture when she speaks against it—while also invoking precise modern coordinates: Kassandra's encounter with the propaganda and surveillance of Eumelos and his men locates her also recognizably within the daily reality of GDR life, for example.

As narratives, myths always strive towards closure and perfection, which of course brings inherent dangers when political mythologies are involved.[43] But this does not invalidate the form: Wolf quotes Thomas Mann approvingly when he calls for myth—read through psychology—to be returned to a humane function and rescued from the fascists who have brought it into disrepute (*K* 133). But the third dimension of myth is, according to Ricœur, the most productive. Myth speaks of possible worlds and always exceeds the contexts of its articulation. Interpreted as a poetics of the possible, Ricœur sees myth as a genuine dimension of modern thought. He does not advocate a naive return to myth, for that would lead to archaism. Rather, he suggests something like Friedrich Nietzsche's 'Es ist ein Traum! Ich will ihn weiter träumen.'[44] To quote from Vattimo again: '[w]hen demythologization itself is revealed as myth, myth regains its legitimacy, but only within the frame of a generally "weakened" experience of truth'.[45] The new legitimacy of the

[40] The terms 'paradigm', 'perfection', and 'possibility' are taken from Coupe, *Myth*, 1–9.

[41] Ricœur, 'Myth as the Bearer of Possible Worlds', 488.

[42] West, 'Christa Wolf's *Kassandra*: A Classical Perspective', *Oxford German Studies*, 20, 21 (1991–2), 164–85 (184).

[43] '[S]everal of its recurrent forms have become deviant and dangerous, e.g., the myth of absolute power (fascism) and the myth of the sacrificial scapegoat (anti-Semitism and racism)' (Ricœur, 'Myth as the Bearer of Possible Worlds', 485).

[44] 'It is a dream! I wish to carry on dreaming it' (Nietzsche, *Die Geburt der Tragödie oder Griechentum und Pessimismus*, i, in Karl Schlechta (ed.) *Werke*, i (Frankfurt: Ullstein, 1976), 23).

[45] Vattimo, *The Transparent Society*, 42.

mythic imaginary 'resides in the very acknowledgement of the *limits* of myth—its inherent modesty and *faiblesse* as an experience of truth. The weakness of myth is its strength.'[46] The chance for a weakened form of myth, as narrative, and as limited rationality, to speak of possible worlds is one which Wolf takes up, in common with the Italian feminist philosopher Adriana Cavarero.

Diane Purkiss comments that for feminists the rewriting of myth denotes 'the struggle to alter gender asymmetries agreed upon for centuries by myth's disseminators'.[47] Cavarero, whom Wolf quotes in *Medea: Stimmen*,[48] is involved in a similar examination and appropriation of myth for feminist ends. In *In Spite of Plato* (1995) Cavarero 'steals' marginal female figures from Greek myth (the weaver Penelope, the nameless maidservant from Thrace who laughs at the philosopher Thales when he falls into a well, the mother figure Demeter, and the wise woman Diotima) and explores their stories from a female point of view.[49] Cavarero's motivation is political, her 'enterprise of theft is inspired by women's present needs'.[50] Like Wolf, she is reliant on the inherited metaphysical tradition which she deconstructs as upholding patriarchy, while simultaneously seeking to destabilize this tradition from within by reading through the grid of sexual difference, and usurping the inexhaustible power of myth to speak both new and old truths. She mounts a critique of the western intellectual tradition to the effect that it is founded on symbolic matricide as a result of male envy of maternal power, that it separates mind from body, devaluing the latter, and is obsessed with death. Drawing on the work of the political philosopher Hannah Arendt, she attempts to glimpse a new order based on 'a *two*, not a *one*',[51] which pays due attention to the fact that each individual is always embodied, and, unlike the abstraction 'Man', which 'is never born and never lives',[52] enters life through birth. The new order will require a new politics, for the symbolic order takes people away from embodiedness into a politics which gives them a gendered function[53] (nowhere more clearly shown than in the polarization of gender roles in the build-up to war in *Kassandra*). A focus on birth—on the concrete

[46] Richard Kearney, quoted in Coupe, *Myth*, 196.

[47] Purkiss, 'Women's Rewriting of Myth', in Carolyne Larrington (ed.), *The Feminist Companion to Mythology* (London: Pandora, 1992), 441–57 (441).

[48] Wolf, *Medea: Stimmen* (Munich: DTV, 1996), 215.

[49] Cavarero, *In Spite of Plato: A Feminist Rewriting of Ancient Philosophy*, trans. Serena Anderlini-D'Onofrio and Áine O'Healy (Cambridge: Polity, 1995).

[50] Cavarero, *In Spite of Plato*, 9.

[51] Ibid. 6 (Cavarero's emphasis).

[52] Ibid. 59.

[53] Ibid. 81.

embodied uniqueness of each individual—will bring a movement away from political abstractions and a narrowing of the societal sphere: 'This sets limits on both legislation and the political symbolic order, which must divest itself of its totalizing and evangelizing aims, allowing the meaning of human life to exist outside the confines of the *polis*'.[54]

Caverero's *Relating Narratives: Storytelling and Selfhood* (2000) further develops this new politics which does not rely on universal concepts but consists of interaction between individuals, or, as she calls them, 'unique existents'. Cavarero seeks to theorize the uniqueness of individual identity in order to rescue it from the suspicion shown by postmodernists, particularly feminist postmodernists, who are apt to confuse uniqueness with traditional conceptions of the individual as autonomous and sovereign. Uniqueness does not, for her, involve 'interiority, psychology, agency, self-presence, mastery',[55] but, rather, is 'exposed, relational, altruistic', and thus '*external*'.[56] To cite one illuminating example: while Freud stresses the universals in the story of Oedipus (everyman as Oedipus), Oedipus himself desires to know his unique embodied identity—in other words, who his mother was—which he can only learn from the narration of others. Narration is crucial to Cavarero, for while philosophy speaks of universals, asking '*what* is Man?', narration speaks of uniqueness, asking instead of someone '*who* he or she is'.[57] She calls for a new philosophy of narration, which she sees as a feminine art, since women have been excluded from the discourse of the universal: 'the tragedy of the original scission between the universal Man and the uniqueness of the self, between the abstraction of the subject and the concreteness of the uniqueness—in a word, between the discursive order of philosophy and that of narration—is an entirely masculine tragedy'.[58] Narration, by contrast, 'reveals the meaning without committing the error of defining it'.[59] She illustrates this with the example, taken from Karen Blixen, of a stork: a man runs around in the dark plugging a leak in a dyke, then sees in the morning that his footprints have traced the figure of a stork on the ground. Blixen asked: 'When the design of my life is complete, will I see, or will others see a stork?'[60] Cavarero adds this gloss: 'The figural unity of the design, the unifying meaning of the story, can only be posed, by the one who lives it, in the form of a

[54] Cavarero, *In Spite of Plato*, 84.
[55] Paul A. Cottman, translator's introduction, in Cavarero, *Relating Narratives*, pp. vii–xxxi (p. x).
[56] Cavarero, *Relating Narratives*, 89 (Cavarero's emphasis).
[57] Ibid. 13 (Cavarero's emphasis).
[58] Ibid. 52.
[59] Hannah Arendt, quoted in Cavarero, *Relating Narratives*, 3.
[60] Cavarero, *Relating Narratives*, 1.

question. Or, perhaps, in the form of a desire.'[61] To draw out the relevance of Cavarero's work for the Kassandra project we need to look more closely at the figure of Kassandra and at the cave community, Wolf's new political scene.

Identity, narration, knowledge

It was perhaps unfortunate that, as Helga Geyer-Ryan points out, Luchterhand's original choice of 'the most naked representation' of Cassandra's rape from an Attic bowl from the fifth century BC for the cover of the lectures perpetuated one of the ways she had traditionally appeared: as either a voice in text or a body in pictures. Whether as voice or image, she has always been 'within the bounds of male appropriation and control. The voice is fragmented, the body shot through with sexuality to appeal to male eyes and hands.'[62] Wolf's reconstruction of the figure, by contrast, gives us 'the first successful attempt in the history of the Cassandra myth to gather the fragmented pieces of her body and her speech together and make her whole again'.[63] The wholeness is, however, for the reader to discern rather than for Kassandra herself to possess (though this is what she desires), or even to access, except fleetingly as a stork, for the unified, self-aware, rational subject she thinks she has become is based on self-deception:[64] Kassandra acknowledges only reluctantly, though the text clearly demonstrates, the importance for her continuing identity-formation of her unconscious, of her body as a source of knowledge, and of the input of others.

Wolf was initially attracted to the figure of Cassandra because of her self-knowledge: the prophetess struck her as the only person in the *Oresteia* who knew herself (*K* 16). Wolf is also, however, drawn to the damaged figure of Franza, from Bachmann's novel *Der Fall Franza*, precisely because she is not able to get a grip on her life and tell her own story (*K* 191). The two positions are not incompatible. Wolf's Kassandra certainly seeks self-knowledge—a search endorsed by Wolf in the lectures (*K* 184)—and feels she has found it: there is even something self-congratulatory about her statement, 'Das Glück, ich selbst zu werden und

[61] Ibid. 2.

[62] Geyer-Ryan, 'The Castration of Cassandra', in Geyer-Ryan, *Fables of Desire: Studies in the Ethics of Art and Gender* (Cambridge: Polity, 1994), 69–81 (76).

[63] Ibid. 80.

[64] See Hilzinger, 'Nachwort', 424.

dadurch den andern nützlicher—ich hab es noch erlebt.'[65] She feels in possession of a hard-won truth which she wishes to convey to future generations (*K* 319). The text presents her—as the Cassandra paradigm requires—as superior, in that she is in possession of a knowledge which others cannot or will not acquire. But this does not necessarily make her a figure of identification for the reader, for the arrogance and lack of humility learned as the king's daughter remain with her to the end, even after she has admitted her culpability. That she has blind spots of her own has been argued convincingly by Eva Ludwiga Szalay: Kassandra is unable to live the third way proposed by the cave women because she has internalized patriarchal power structures in her unconscious. The fact that she goes to her death can be interpreted as 'a qualified acknowledgement of the reiterative performance of dominant power in constituting (feminine) identity';[66] she has internalized 'the palace optic'.[67] Kassandra cannot rid herself of her strong identification with her father Priamos, and, by extension, with patriarchal power, and cannot step outside binary thinking, as the dream where she is asked to choose whether the sun or the moon shines brighter indicates: she cannot see, though Arisbe can, that the question itself is faulty (*K* 326–7).

Kassandra also reproduces the western tradition's valorizing of mind over body: 'Jetzt kann ich brauchen, was ich lebenslang geübt, meine Gefühle durch Denken besiegen.'[68] That she should distance herself from her body is not surprising in view of the fact that it has been appropriated by others from an early age, culminating in enforced marriage, rape, and bondage: '[s]ie erlernt Abtötungstechniken'.[69] Yet time and again the text highlights the body as a source of knowledge, demonstrating Leonardo da Vinci's maxim, referred to in the lectures, that '[d]ie Erkenntnis, die nicht durch die Sinne gegangen ist, kann keine andere Wahrheit erzeugen als die schädliche'.[70] When Kassandra was upholding the official rhetoric on the war against the evidence of her senses, for example, her body would react with fits and seizures, heralding bouts of 'madness' (*K* 275–6, 295–7, 304–5); when Arisbe interprets the sun and moon dream for her, her relief is a physical one: 'Ein Atemholen war es, ein Lockern der Gelenke, ein Aufblühn des

[65] 'The happiness of becoming myself and thereby more useful to others—I experienced it' (*K* 238).

[66] Szalay, '"I, the seeress, was owned by the palace.": The Dynamics of Feminine Collusion in Christa Wolf's *Cassandra*', *Women in German Yearbook*, 16 (2000), 167–89 (184).

[67] Adelson, 'The Bomb and I', 511.

[68] 'Now I can use what I have practised my whole life, conquering my emotions through thought' (*K* 233).

[69] 'she acquires techniques to deaden the pain' (*K* 114).

[70] 'knowledge that has not passed through the senses can produce none other than damaging truth' (*K* 156).

Fleisches';[71] she learns from the mountain women, not through words but by watching them (*K* 317); she knows of her brother Hektor's death through empathy;[72] her present reassessment of her life is possible only because she admits her fear (*K* 265). She has come to the point where she defines being alive as not being afraid to alter one's self-image (*K* 248). The ultimate sign of her lack of control over her own body is her pregnancy, resulting from her marriage of convenience to Eurypylos, which at first deepens her alienation from her body. Christine Battersby has argued that rethinking philosophy from the starting point of a body that is capable of birthing (of producing the other from itself) and of the reality of birth (that matter is active and capable of spontaneous transformation) would overcome one of the central blind spots in our culture.[73] Kassandra's pregnancy forces her to confront this particular blind spot in herself. She compares her reluctant acknowledgement of the twins' independent movements in her body to her awareness of unconscious knowledge appearing through dreams, and it is a moment which moves her to tears: the barrier preventing her from loving 'd[ie] Kinder eines aufgezwungenen Vaters'[74] is opened. The twins, now detached from the agency of their father, gain a status of their own. All of this points to the fact that, through the totality of the figure of Kassandra, Wolf is mounting a critique of the mind/body split that has bedevilled western metaphysics, and contributing to a feminist ontology which, like Cavarero's Penelope, attempts to weave together once again the body and soul that were separated with the birth of philosophy.[75]

The Kassandra project also presents identity as essentially relational. A leitmotiv of the travelogues—Wolf is at first a timorous and irritable traveller—is a fear of exile as a state of utter isolation (*K* 36). In becoming a priestess Kassandra was seeking a solitary life away from the normal lot of women, but comes to see that as a member of the elite she was serving the prevailing interests and had no actual autonomy; isolation within the community is not possible and to seek it is to evade responsibility. She has enough self-knowledge to admit that she resents other people's insight into her (*K* 298). It becomes clear, though, that, like Oedipus, she only learns who, rather than what, she is because of the input of others. Arisbe is one of those others, as we have seen; she analyses Kassandra's recourse to madness as springing from self-pity (*K* 297). Panthoos also conveys uncomfortable truths to her, while

[71] 'It was like catching my breath, a loosening of my limbs, a blossoming of my flesh' (*K* 327).

[72] 'Ich war Hektor' ('I was Hector') (*K* 355).

[73] Battersby, *The Phenomenal Woman*, 1–15.

[74] 'the children of a father who was forced upon me' (*K* 316).

[75] Cavarero, *In Spite of Plato*, 29.

Penthesilea's perception of her compromised positioning with regard to power—'Gerade du: Nicht Fisch, nicht Fleisch!'[76]—is the cruellest cut of all: Kassandra's insight into the hopelessness of the Amazon queen's pursuit of death in battle does not invalidate Penthesilea's own penetrating analysis of her. It is only by absorbing what these and other people have to say and by recognizing them as 'narratable selves'[77] that Kassandra can begin to construct the narrative of her life and fulfil her desire to see the design it will leave. Memory and the evidence of her senses are not enough.

Finally, Kassandra's insight, so hard-won, is narrative in nature; it is, in Blixen's and Cavarero's terms, a stork. This is consonant with Wolf's —and Cavarero's—defence of narrative as a form. Wolf is at pains to argue that, though the epic arose from conflict (*K* 186), followed a male line of action (*K* 117), and has served to reinforce patriarchy (*K* 186), storytelling itself is humane (*K* 49).

A new political scene

In the precarious community by the Scamander river we can see the germ of Cavarero's new political scene in action, based not on abstract oppositions but on the local interaction of unique existents. The community is disorientating:[78] the usual coordinates are missing. Though provisionally located in the caves by the Scamander river, it is not associated with a sense of place: when Penthesilea, the Amazon queen, is invited to join the community by, significantly, a slave girl, it is in these terms: 'Komm zu uns . . . Ins Gebirge. In den Wald. In die Höhlen am Skamander.'[79] The community has no script, though storytelling and dance are very important, and it slips out of linear time, thus subverting teleological thought: 'Es gibt Zeichenlöcher. Dies ist so eines, hier und jetzt. Wir dürfen es nicht ungenutzt vergehen lassen.'[80] The community is not hierarchical, though due consideration is given to the age

[76] 'You of all people: neither fish nor fowl' (*K* 363).

[77] 'Precisely because it [the existent] is exposable, it is also narratable. Indeed, we are talking about the unrepeatable uniqueness of each human being' (Cavarero, *Relating Narratives*, 33).

[78] 'Emancipation, here [the end of modernity], consists in *disorientation*, which is at the same time also the liberation of differences, of local elements, of what could generally be called dialect' (Vattimo, *The Transparent Society*, 8; Vattimo's emphasis).

[79] 'Come to us...To the mountains. Into the forest. Into the caves by the Scamander' (*K* 362–3).

[80] 'There are gaps in time. This is one, here and now. We must not let it pass unused' (*K* 369).

and experience of Anchises and Arisbe. It is not divided along gender lines, nor based on any sense of nationality, for, though it is founded by women, wounded soldiers from both camps are taken in. Karin Eysel has commented that in *Kassandra* 'Wolf uncovers the antagonism, the fantasy of the enemy, which held together the nation state', and argued that her narrative 'gestures towards imagined communities beyond national, gender, and class divisions—communities in which nationality no longer constitutes citizenship'.[81] When Kassandra painfully learns and is allowed the right to say 'wir', it is not the value-laden 'we' that Cavarero discerns as being typical of the 'morality of pronouns' that revolutionary movements have in common ('we women', 'we workers'), but rather is based on 'an altruistic ethics of relation' that 'desires a *you* that is truly an other, in her uniqueness and distinction'.[82] In other words, Wolf posits a community based on the recognition of the uniqueness of individuals and what Vattimo would call the 'liberation of differences and dialects',[83] though it also owes much to Enlightenment values.[84] This is consonant with Cavarero's careful rejection of empathy in favour of altruism. Empathy, so often the error of feminism, 'risks producing a substance. Put simply, *who* I am and *who* you are seem to surrender to the urgency of the question of *what* Woman is'.[85] Altruism, by contrast, is 'the foundational principle of a self that knows itself to be constituted by another: *the necessary other*'.[86]

That the gods they worship are female deities from a previous era need not be interpreted as archaism on Wolf's part, but can be read as an attempt to overcome the symbolic matricide upon which western culture rests.[87] As Cavarero and Wolf demonstrate in their different ways, the political symbolic order denies individuals the possibility of exploring their embodied uniqueness by confining them in a politics based on abstractions which gives them a gendered function. It is therefore an urgent matter to redefine politics, starting with the individual's relations with the other. This is what Wolf modestly attempts to do.

[81] Eysel, 'Christa Wolf's *Kassandra*: Refashioning the National Imagination Beyond the Nation', *Women in German Yearbook*, 9 (1994), 163–81 (176).

[82] Cavarero, *Relating Narratives*, 90–2 (Cavarero's emphasis).

[83] Vattimo, *The Transparent Society*, 9.

[84] Friedrichsmeyer has argued that Wolf's 'concept of openness and diversity...owes more to Enlightenment "tolerance" than to postmodern *différance*' (Friedrichsmeyer, 'On Multiple Selves and Dialogics', 81).

[85] Cavarero, *Relating Narratives*, 60 (Cavarero's emphasis).

[86] Ibid. 84 (Cavarero's emphasis).

[87] Cavarero, *In Spite of Plato*, 57–90.

Conclusion

Just because women are now more aware than previously of their colonization by and entrapment within dominant power structures does not necessarily make their task of reforming those structures any easier. But myth can help here because it warns us to resist the perfectionism that leads to intolerance and because it speaks not just of past paradigms but also of present realities, and future possibilities. If Wolf's Kassandra project is viewed as mythography and mythopoeia within a framework of limited rationality that does not privilege either *logos* or *mythos*, then the binary opposition *logos/mythos* can be loosened and Wolf's 'weak' solutions and her simultaneous positioning inside and outside the western metaphysical and aesthetic traditions will seem appropriate after all. Anchises' injunction to dream with both feet on the ground (*K* 381), a paraphrase of Bloch's 'dreaming with one's eyes open',[88] expresses Wolf's commitment to imagining and working towards a better future from the flawed present. Wolf's lifelong critique of dominant power structures—on a global and a local scale—her search for communal ways of living which allow the individual to flourish, and her stress on the ethical responsibility of the individual may have become somewhat unfashionable, but they have never been more timely. War, the concrete outcome of the failure of politics, continues, as does women's particular vulnerability at times of war: though Kassandra—like the victims of the Bosnian rape camps—knew, in the fullest sense of the term (that is, with her mind and her body), that rape is a war crime, international law has only recently acknowledged and codified it as such. The political need to find solutions to the questions that troubled Wolf remains as pressing as ever it was, though perhaps some lessons have been learned: at the time of writing, Germany and France, so often mortal enemies in the past, are together facing the displeasure of the USA for their principled opposition to the second Gulf War.

[88] See Anna Kuhn, 'Cassandra: Myth, Matriarchy, and the Canon', in Kuhn, *Christa Wolf's Utopian Vision: From Marxism to Feminism* (Cambridge: Cambridge University Press, 1988), 178–209 (206).

5 Herta Müller, *Reisende auf einem Bein* (1989)

Introduction

Reisende auf einem Bein stands out among Herta Müller's works in that the main events are not set in the author's native Romania, or a thinly disguised version of it. Germans, or more accurately Swabians, had been living in the part of Romania called the Banat for nearly two hundred years when Müller was born there in a small village in 1953, and had preserved a strong sense of a distinct identity. Many Banat Germans of Müller's parents' generation had supported Hitler during the Second World War. After the war Romania changed from a fascist to a communist state, ruled over from 1966 until its fall in the winter of 1989 by the particularly brutal and oppressive regime of Nicolae Ceauşescu. Most of the ethnic Germans left the country in the course of the 1980s and 1990s. Müller herself left for West Berlin in 1987 after she and her writer friends had been persecuted by the *Securitate*, the notorious Romanian secret service, to the extent that at least two of them died in suspicious circumstances. The moribund German community is evoked in Müller's first published works, written when she was still resident in Romania, *Niederungen* (1982) and *Der Mensch ist ein großer Fasan auf der Welt* (1986). These demonstrated in poetic prose how the unvoiced crimes of the Nazi period continued to haunt the rural German community and how the pervasive intimidation and corruption of the Romanian state led to terror. Her more recent works, such as *Der Fuchs war damals schon der Jäger* (1992), *Herztier* (1994), and *Heute wär ich mir lieber nicht begegnet* (1997), all written from the relative safety of Germany, reflect her adult experiences in Romania and continue to give expression to the trauma produced by living in a dictatorship. Indeed, they have expressed this in ever more direct terms: while *Herztier* deals in a highly elliptical and heavily patterned style with the persecution of intellectuals in Romania, *Heute wär ich mir lieber nicht begegnet* provides more transparent fictional reworkings of the interrogations to which Müller herself was subjected.

Müller's works are thus 'autofictional',[1] that is creative reworkings of the author's experience, and *Reisende auf einem Bein* is no exception: Irene, its main protagonist, like Müller, left what she terms 'das andere Land' ('the other country') but is clearly based on Romania, in the late 1980s for West Berlin. However, the novel forms an exception in Müller's œuvre in that, apart from the first three chapters, it is set in West Berlin and presents a fictionalized account not of the author's Romanian experience but of her arrival in the West. Though we know that Irene thinks of her homeland often (*R* 51, 78), the narrative mainly records her observations of her present surroundings. Like Müller, Irene both does and does not belong in the Federal Republic: as an ethnic German she speaks the language and has an automatic right to citizenship; her cultural baggage, however, renders her alien—the German she speaks corresponds to a different reality to the one she finds here, and the multiple sensory impressions of western consumerist city life are as bewildering to her as the motivations of the people she meets. The novel charts her first few weeks and months, detailing Irene's wanderings through the city, her observation of the minutiae of daily life, and her interaction with people and with the intimate and large spaces of the city, up to the point where she opts to stay.

Irene is not a blank sheet, however: this chapter will argue that her encounter with Berlin is in large part shaped by her past, so that the Romanian experience, while not directly represented, is implicitly present throughout in the gaps and silences in the text and in the subjectivity and behaviour of the protagonist, which are all marked by trauma. It will explore how the relative freedoms afforded by western city life enable Irene to embrace her *Fremdheit* (alienation/foreignness/strangeness) without relinquishing her past. Trauma theory and Rosi Braidotti's projection of a 'nomadic subject' will be employed to show how the novel challenges conventional notions of bounded subjectivity and categories of perception while also pinpointing precisely an historical moment of flux in Europe. Trauma theory, which explains clinical symptoms as a belated reaction to shock, is essentially a gender-blind approach, equally applicable to male and female subjects, while Braidotti's nomadic subject is embodied and female. This dual approach is fruitful; for Müller, while accepting the gendered nature of experience, is dismissive of what she suspects as the tendency within feminism to privilege women's

[1] This is Müller's preferred term; it is borrowed from Georges Arthur Goldschmidt (see Brigid Haines and Margaret Littler, 'Gespräch mit Herta Müller', in Haines (ed.), *Herta Müller* (Cardiff: University of Wales Press, 1998), 14–24 (14)). This mode of writing presents difficulties for the critic, who must pay due attention to the autobiographical aspects while not overplaying their importance in the interpretative process.

oppression and thereby efface women's complicity. That she should think this is not surprising: women in Romania were subject to sexual oppression as a part of widespread corruption and of the state's barbaric family policy, which required them to produce at least five children and subjected them to compulsory gynaecological examinations. However, the doctors were frequently female, as were many party functionaries, and Elena Ceauşescu, the high-profile wife of the dictator, was prominent in the regime.[2] Firmly rejecting the label 'feminist', Müller prefers to declare simply: 'Ich bin vielleicht eine Individualistin, und ich bin eine Frau.'[3] The preoccupation with giving expression to the trauma engendered by abuses of power is primary in her work.

'Der fremde Blick' ('the alien gaze')

Reisende auf einem Bein was published at the historically significant moment of the autumn of 1989, two years after Müller's own arrival in West Berlin. This was a time of instability in and exodus from eastern-bloc countries as their regimes were beginning to crumble. It was timely for a novel set in the last days of the divided city to appear just as the barriers were about to be torn down. German reviewers, apparently expecting that its outsider perspective would reflect official images of Berlin and of the Federal Republic based on the crude binary oppositions of the cold war, found the picture actually presented in this city novel drawn 'vom Rand' ('from the margins')[4] unsettling.[5] Since the end of the Second World War West Berlin had functioned as a powerful symbol of western defiance in the cold war, with certain key moments (the airlift of 1948, the building of the Berlin Wall which cemented the division of the city in 1961, and John F. Kennedy's visit in June 1963) becoming iconic. It was also strongly marked by the radicalism of the

[2] See Müller, 'Hunger und Seide: Männer und Frauen im Alltag', in *Hunger und Seide* (Reinbek bei Hamburg: Rowohlt, 1995), 65–87.

[3] 'I am perhaps an individualist, and I am a woman' (Haines and Littler, 'Gespräch mit Herta Müller', 19).

[4] Antje Harnisch, '"Ausländerin im Ausland": Herta Müllers *Reisende auf einem Bein*', *Monatshefte*, 89/4 (1997), 507–20 (518).

[5] For a summary of the press reception see Norbert Otto Eke, 'Herta Müllers Werke im Spiegel der Kritik (1982–1990)', in Eke (ed.), *Die erfundene Wahrnehmung: Annäherung an Herta Müller* (Paderborn: Igel, 1991), 107–30. The most extreme reaction was from Christian Huther, who claimed that the Federal Republic was unrecognizable in Müller's text (quoted in Bernhard Doppler, 'Die Heimat ist das Exil: Eine Entwicklungsgestalt ohne Entwicklung: Zu *Reisende auf einem Bein*', in Eke (ed.), *Die erfundene Wahrnehmung*, 9–106 (98)).

student movement in 1968 and remained a centre of alternative culture and lifestyles. By the 1980s West Berlin liked to project an image of liberalism, hectic consumerism, and prosperity, in opposition to the political repression and economic stagnation of the GDR. These modern myths tended to erase the earlier history of the city, deny what was common to both halves of the city and of Germany, and present the success story of West Berlin as the whole story, though homegrown writers like Peter Schneider had long critiqued them from within.[6] Irene, coming from outside, seems to know nothing of all this, but gives an intimate picture nonetheless: she is aware of historical continuities, sees similarities with life in the country she has left, and registers the unglamorous underside of contemporary West Berlin life.

Germany is experienced by Irene as cold, both literally—the novel takes place over the course of one winter and spring—and culturally: 'KALTES LAND KALTE HERZEN RUF DOCH MAL AN JENS',[7] a piece of soliciting grafitti, makes her realize she is not alone in seeking human warmth. While she registers many visible differences from 'das andere Land', for example advertising and neon signs, she does not know what these signify; crucially, she also registers many similarities. She patrols the back streets, the U-Bahn and S-Bahn, the flea markets, and second-hand shops. The groups she moves among are asylum seekers, the urban poor, and workers from Eastern Europe. The people she observes in the street seem alienated and aimless. Her flat is far from the bustling shopping streets, being located in one of the quiet back courtyards characteristic of old Berlin housing. Though at one point Irene is on the famous shopping street, the Kürfürstendamm, it is not named; what she notices are the 'Gedächtniskirche', the preserved shell of a church which was bombed in the war, a reminder of a traumatic moment in Germany's past, and some street traders trying unsuccessfully to sell Christmas candleholders (*R* 34–5). Even the coats in the second-hand shop have seen wars (*R* 52). She is drawn to the Berlin Wall, symbol of the division of Germany and of Berlin, and visits it several times (*R* 30, 122). As she watches a cloud pass over, she is aware that the wall represents an arbitrary and new division (*R* 30).

In her explorations of West Berlin she is also very aware of past violence—'In den schönsten Häusern ist jemand gefoltert worden'[8]—present violence, for example when she hears the news that two women have been raped at knifepoint (*R* 90) and hears the sirens of a police

[6] See e.g. Peter Schneider's satirical take on the politics of the Berlin Wall, *Der Mauerspringer* (Darmstadt: Luchterhand, 1984).

[7] 'COLD COUNTRY COLD HEARTS GIVE ME A CALL JENS' (*R* 91).

[8] 'In the most beautiful houses somebody has been tortured' (*R* 162).

car (*R* 37), and of the possibility of future violence, should the days of the Nazi dictatorship return (*R* 49). She is horrified by the realization that the wife of 'der Diktator' (a reference to the hated Elena Ceauşescu) bears a striking resemblance to Rosa Luxemburg, the communist writer and politician who was murdered in 1919, and is drawn to the canal where her body was dumped (*R* 65, 159). The unexpected link between perpetrator and victim fascinates and appals Irene and is another example of the breaking down of boundaries arising from her unusual perspective.

The negative, or at least unfamiliar, view of West Berlin was initially read as an outsider's critique of western materialist life. But there is no sustained critique, for Irene does not understand the forces which govern life here, though she does connect on an emotional level with the suffering she perceives: 'In dem anderen Land, sagte Irene, hab ich verstanden, was die Menschen so kaputtmacht. Die Gründe lagen auf der Hand. Es hat sehr weh getan, täglich die Gründe zu sehn . . . Und hier, sagte Irene. Ich weiß, es gibt Gründe. Ich kann sie nicht sehn. Es tut weh, täglich die Gründe nicht zu sehn.'[9] Irene's fragmentary perceptions are reflected in the novel's aesthetic, which privileges unconnected details and presents these to the reader to process. The laconic third-person narrative voice refuses to provide an interpretative framework, and reproduces in short, open-ended sentences, which are often not integrated into paragraphs, surface snapshots of what Irene sees and does. The avoidance of signifying systems, resistance to plot, and focus on the detail are typical of Müller's work, though they are taken further here, for in her other novels, particularly *Herztier*, the details observed tend to recur as they are built up into metonymic patterns.[10]

Müller's positive valorizing of the detail—she once issued the injunction, borrowed from Eugène Ionesco, her fellow Romanian exile, 'Leben wir also. Aber man läßt uns nicht leben. Leben wir also im Detail'[11]—is to be read as a political but also a poetic manifesto, but in any case as a reaction against totalizing systems, whether literary or political, which stifle the individual and erase difference.[12] She maintains that this reaction was instinctive and first occurred at an early age. In her essay *Der Fremde Blick oder Das Leben ist ein Furz in der Laterne* she argues that

[9] 'In the other country, said Irene, I understood what it was that wrecked people. The reasons were obvious. It was painful to see the reasons all the time . . . And here, said Irene. I know there are reasons. I can't see them. It's painful not to be able to see the reasons all the time' (*R* 130).

[10] See Ricarda Schmidt, 'Metapher, Metonymie und Moral: Herta Müllers *Herztier*', in Haines (ed.) *Herta Müller*, 57–74.

[11] 'So let's live. But they don't allow us to. So let's live in the detail' ('Zehn Finger werden keine Utopie', in Müller, *Hunger und Seide*, 50–61 (61)).

[12] See Brigid Haines, '"Leben wir im Detail": Herta Müller's Micro-Politics of Resistance', in Haines (ed.), *Herta Muller*, 109–25.

'der fremde Blick' was formed as a result of the traumatic effects of state surveillance long before she made the move to the West.[13] Far from being a conscious aesthetic choice, then, 'der fremde Blick' is, she claims, an habitual mode of seeing not adopted by but forced on the individual by powers that are beyond his or her comprehension. Her work, she argues, thus crosses the 'literary' divide to provide strong links with the disturbed ways of seeing common to all victims of trauma. In this she consciously places her works in the tradition of other twentieth-century writers, such as Primo Levi, Paul Celan, Imre Kertész, Jorge Semprun, Ruth Klüger, and Alexander Solzhenitsyn (frequently cited by her as her own favoured reading), who survived the Nazi concentration camps or Stalin's Gulags in the Soviet Union.[14] The sense of personal powerlessness in the face of overwhelming force (the basic structure of trauma) provides the crucial link.

The traces of trauma

That trauma should have a particular resonance in our time is hardly surprising in view of the common perception of the twentieth century as 'd[as] blutigste[] Jahrhundert der Geschichte' ('the bloodiest century in history').[15] The discourse of trauma is also a product of the twentieth century: it emerged from the work of Charcot and Freud and was progressively refined when events proved its usefulness (in explaining the symptoms of survivors of the trenches and of the Holocaust, of Vietnam veterans, of victims of domestic abuse, for example). It has expanded its domain rapidly from the pages of psychoanalytic journals via various academic disciplines to the point where it has become a ubiquitous cultural phenomenon with a firm hold in the popular imagination.[16] Viewed ahistorically, trauma promises tantalizing connections between cultures and between disciplines.[17] It has become a powerful metonym for the unrepresentable and the unspeakable, particularly in the context

[13] Herta Müller, *Der Fremde Blick oder Das Leben ist ein Furz in der Laterne* (Göttingen: Wallstein, 1999).

[14] See Haines and Littler, 'Gespräch mit Herta Müller', 14.

[15] Elie Wiesel, in Jorge Semprun and Elie Wiesel, *Schweigen ist unmöglich*, trans. (from French) Wolfram Bayer (Frankfurt am Main: Suhrkamp, 1997), 26.

[16] Brief histories of trauma are to be found in Judith Lewis Herman, *Trauma and Recovery: From Domestic Abuse to Political Terror* (New York: Basic Books, 1992), 7–32, and Ruth Leys, *Trauma: A Genealogy* (Chicago, Ill.: University of Chigaco Press, 2000), 1–17.

[17] Birgit R. Erdle, 'Die Verführung der Parallelen: Zu Übertragungsverhältnissen zwischen Ereignis, Ort und Zitat', in Elisabeth Bronfen, Birgit R. Erdle, and Sigrid Weigel (eds.), *Trauma: Zwischen Psychoanalyse und kulturellem Deutungsmuster* (Cologne: Böhlau, 1999), 27–50 (30).

of German reflections on the Holocaust, the horror of that event being too great to allow for its representation.[18] Elisabeth Bronfen, Birgit R. Erdle, and Sigrid Weigel have also argued that trauma can be used to found 'ein neues Deutungsmuster für Moderne und Modernität allgemein',[19] because it offers a way of making visible the uniqueness and specificity of individual experience which cannot be integrated into historical knowledge. In their view trauma offers the possibility of referring to authentic experience in those gaps and aporias of understanding and representation which post-structuralism has highlighted. They see trauma as a way of linking post-structuralist thinking with politics and ethics, as does the influential literary critic Cathy Caruth.[20]

The core meaning of trauma is an individual pathology which results from the indelible imprint left on a patient's psyche by the sudden intrusion of events that defy his or her comprehension. The traumatized individual cannot grasp what has happened, does not possess the memory of the traumatic moment, but is possessed by it as it intrudes periodically upon consciousness in the form of flashbacks.[21] Trauma shatters pre-existing belief systems and assumptions of trust, leading to disorientation, a loss of control, and feelings of alienation, numbness, and detachment. The victim often experiences hyperarousal, a state of permanent alert which reflects 'the persistent expectation of danger'; intrusion, which reflects 'the indelible imprint of the traumatic moment'; and constriction, which reflects 'the numbing response of surrender';[22] and may either avoid or seek out replicas of the traumatic situation.[23]

The two kinds of literature commonly associated with trauma are testimony, or the eyewitness account of a traumatic event, and trauma narrative, in which the survivor attempts to come to terms with what has happened by placing the traumatic events within a larger framework. But, even were it possible, the traumatized individual often resists seizing the memory and transforming it into narrative—thus potentially opening the way towards recovery—for fear of diluting the experience[24]

[18] See Erdle, 'Die Verführung der Parallelen', 33.

[19] 'a new interpretative model for the modern world and modernity in general' (foreword to Bronfen, Erdle, and Weigel (eds.), *Trauma*, pp. vii–viii (p. vii)).

[20] Caruth, *Unclaimed Experience: Trauma, Narrative, and History* (Baltimore, Md.: Johns Hopkins University Press, 1996).

[21] See Cathy Caruth, introd. to pt. 1 and introd. to pt. 2 of Caruth (ed.), *Trauma: Explorations in Memory* (Baltimore, Md.: Johns Hopkins University Press, 1995), 3–12 , 151–7.

[22] Herman, *Trauma and Recovery*, 35.

[23] Bessel A. van der Kolk and Onno van der Hart, 'The Intrusive Past: The Flexibility of Memory and the Engraving of Trauma', in Caruth (ed.), *Trauma*, 158–82 (174).

[24] See Caruth: 'To cure oneself—whether by drugs or the telling of one's story or both—seems to many survivors to imply the giving-up of an important reality, or the dilution of a special truth' (preface to Caruth (ed.), *Trauma*, pp. vii–ix (p. vii)).

and betraying those others who may not have survived. Thus a third kind of literature could be termed literature *of* trauma: this does not attempt to represent or contextualize the trauma at all but lets it speak through the gaps and silences in the text. It is these gaps and silences—on which Müller's text is founded—which Jean-François Lyotard theorizes in his discussion of the impossibility yet necessity of writing about the Holocaust:

> Whenever one represents, one inscribes in memory, and this might seem a good defense against forgetting. It is, I believe, just the opposite. Only that which has been inscribed can, in the current sense of the term, be forgotten, because it could be effaced. But what is not inscribed, through lack of inscribable surface, of duration and place for the inscription to be situated, what has no place in the space nor in the time of domination, in the geography and the diachrony of the self-assured spirit, because it is not synthesizable . . . cannot be forgotten, does not offer a hold to forgetting, and remains present 'only' as an affection that one cannot even qualify, like a state of death in the life of the spirit. One *must*, certainly, inscribe in words, in images. One cannot escape the necessity of representing. It would be sin itself to believe oneself safe and sound. But it is one thing to do it in view of saving the memory, and quite another to try to preserve the remainder, the unforgettable forgotten, in writing.[25]

Lyn Marven has argued that Müller's entire creative output, which includes not only novels but also political and journalistic essays, as well as collages which combine image and word, is an expression of trauma. Further, she has demonstrated that the works show a continuing separation into prose, such as *Heute wär ich mir lieber nicht begegnet*, which testifies increasingly directly to the horrors of the Ceauşescu regime, collages which codify an aesthetics of fragmentation, and journalistic work, such as her essays in the volume *Hunger und Seide*, which directly expresses outrage at abuses of power.[26] *Reisende auf einem Bein* lies towards the beginning of this trajectory: though it does not depict what caused Irene to flee to the West or express outrage directly, it shows traces of trauma in her subjectivity and behaviour, and in the fragmented narrative structure; it also thematizes fragmentation in that Irene herself creates collages as a way of exploring the fluidity of her identity and her interaction with the world around her.

[25] Jean-François Lyotard, *Heidegger and 'the jews'*, trans. Andreas Michel and Mark S. Roberts (Minneapolis, Minn.: University of Minnesota Press, 1990), 26.

[26] Lyn Marven, '"Daß dies der Osten ist Was im Kopf nicht aufhört": Representations of the Body and Narrative Strategies in the Works of Herta Müller, Libuše Moníková, and Kerstin Hensel', D.Phil. thesis (Oxford, 2001), 134.

Irene behaves like a traumatized subject, a survivor; her life resembles that described by Alexander García Düttmann:

> **Das von einem Trauma ferngesteuerte Leben muß als ein Überleben betrachtet werden, als ein Leben, das von einer Zäsur im Lebenszusammenhang bestimmt wird, von einer Aussetzung, einer Durchlöcherung, einem Tod, an den widersprüchliche Verdoppelungen und die von ihnen gestiftete Zusammenhanglosigkeit erinnern. Das Überleben ist kein Leben mehr und dennoch das einzig mögliche Leben.**[27]

Irene's habitual emotional state for most of the novel is one of hyperarousal, which she sees as symptomatic of a widespread trauma in her country: she had hung over her bed a sign stolen from a building site depicting a man upside down: 'Auf dem Schild stand: Gefahr ins Leere zu stürzen . . . Sie hatte die Warnung auf ihr Leben bezogen. Und auf das Leben aller, die sie kannte.'[28] Feelings of constriction can be seen for example when she anticipates being wrongly accused of shoplifting and fears that she would not be able to deny the charge (*R* 54), or when the sensation of the beads from her broken necklace falling down her back give the impression that her backbone itself has dissolved (*R* 55). To herself she appears split, signalled by her inability to identify with her own image in photographs (*R* 18, 50). Her disorientation and lack of control force her into the role of observer and deprive her of agency and the ability to interact with her surroundings: 'In diesen Augenblicken wußte Irene, daß ihr Leben zu Beobachtungen geronnen war. Die Beobachtungen machten sie handlungsunfähig. | Wenn sich Irene zu Handlungen zwang, waren es keine . . . | So lebte Irene nicht in den Dingen, sondern in ihren Folgen.'[29]

One might expect a traumatized individual to experience stress on thinking of the past. Irene's memories of home arouse no emotion, however, as she is able quite coolly to compartmentalize and 'administer' them (*R* 78–9). But a distinction needs to be made here between narrative memory, those memories which are integrated into prior schemes of the mind, and traumatic memories, which cannot be recalled at will

[27] 'The life which is steered from afar by trauma must be regarded as a survival, as a life conditioned by a caesura in what gives a life coherence, by an exposure, a complete undermining, a death, of which contradictory doublings and the lack of connection they generate remind one. Survival is no longer a life, yet it is the only possible life' (Düttmann, 'Flugsimulator: Notizen zum Trauma', in Bronfen, Erdle, and Weigel (eds.), *Trauma*, 207–22 (217–18)).

[28] 'On the sign it said: Danger! Don't fall into the void! She had applied this warning to her life. And to the lives of all those she knew' (*R* 84).

[29] 'In these moments Irene knew that her life had run to observations. The observations made her unable to act. | When Irene forced herself to commit acts, they weren't acts . . . | So Irene did not live in things, but in their consequences' (*R* 139).

but are triggered by outside stimuli or intrude unbidden on the mind, apparently at random.[30] And that Irene is plagued by traumatic memories soon becomes clear. As she intimates to the photographer who takes her passport photograph, violent or troubling images intrude on her consciousness (*R* 17). Consonant with their traumatic origin, they are surprisingly literal.[31] Several concern the figure of 'der Diktator', whom the reader must take to be Ceauşescu himself, who, for example, appears in a dream in her room when she is preparing to leave, and, with an act of casual violence, steps on the light summer blouses she is packing (*R* 19). Other images intrude when Irene is observing life in her new city, West Berlin, with apparent detachment; for example, parked cars look to her like graves (*R* 85) and the decorations on Christmas trees remind her of entrails (*R* 35).

The triggering mechanism and the associated fear are nowhere more vividly described than on the two occasions when Irene is interviewed by the *Bundesnachrichtendienst* (Federal Intelligence Agency). Unlike the asylum seekers with whom she lives temporarily, she does not have to prove her case, for she has an automatic right to citizenship. But she refuses simply to be classified as an ethnic German immigrant, wanting but failing to convey to the official who interviews her the reality of the persecution she has suffered. Her behaviour strikes the reader, and indeed the official, as odd, for she is needlessly uncooperative and taciturn, not to say rude. But the interview situation transports her mentally back into unwished-for confrontations with authority in 'das andere Land'. Everything seems familiar to her—the look of the office, the official's suit, his bodily appearance—and instead of complying with his requests for information she provokes him by telling him so. The official cannot understand why she does not distinguish sharply between the two countries (*R* 51); it seems, though, that she is reacting automatically to a set of stimuli that she recognizes. And though her status, in comparison to similar situations at home, is privileged, and though the official remains courteous even under provocation, she interprets the situation as one of powerlessness in the face of power structures that seek to control. She refuses to be categorized as a dissident either, claiming that she had not wanted to topple the government back home (*R* 28), and that the secret services had made her an object of interest rather than her having any business with them (*R* 26). She cannot answer the official's questions concerning the daily reality of surveillance in 'das

[30] See van der Kolk and van der Hart, 'The Intrusive Past', in Caruth (ed.), *Trauma*, 158–82.

[31] Modern analysts have remarked on 'the surprising *literality* and nonsymbolic nature of traumatic dreams and flashbacks' (Caruth, intr. to pt. 1 of Caruth (ed.), *Trauma*, 5 (Caruth's emphasis)).

andere Land', for she was and is possessed by it, she is not in possession of it: 'Was wußte er, der mit den Blicken zielte, von leise am Randstein parkenden Autos, vom Echo der Brücken in der Stadt, vom Fingern der Blätter im Park.'[32]

If the first interview contributes to Irene's perception of her sense of identity dissolving (*R* 28), the second arouses terror as she imagines a finger under the tongue of the official's open mouth (*R* 52). This horrific image is reminiscent of the incident in *Heute wär ich mir lieber nicht begegnet* where the interrogator plants an amputated human finger in a matchbox for the protagonist to find; an action made more chilling by the fact that he never subsequently refers to it.[33] This and other incidents return to Irene in a nightmare (*R* 95–6).

Consonant with their traumatic origin, the actual causes of Irene's trauma elude representation. The reader must piece together clues from the evidence in the first two chapters and Irene's behaviour; in this, the autobiographical nature of the experience depicted is an aid to interpretation. The radar screens, patrolling soldiers, hotels reserved for foreigners, packs of marauding village children, and officious bureaucrats mentioned in the opening two chapters, as well as the continuing references to 'der Diktator' and his hated wife, indicate that Romania is the model for 'das andere Land'. Irene seems to fear that she is not safe from the security forces of 'das andere Land' in Berlin, finding evidence that her flat has been entered in her absence (*R* 112), and then setting the unseen intruders a trap (*R* 164). Irene's letters from home are censored (*R* 78) and bring bad news of 'suicides' (*R* 157). Many of her friends are dead as a result of political persecution (*R* 158). This is presumably why Irene is so touched and shocked by the suspicious death of a young politician (*R* 48, 68, 100), a figure clearly based on Uwe Barschel of the CDU, who was found dead in his bath in a hotel in Geneva in October 1987, with poison in his body. It is still not known whether his death was the result of suicide or murder; conspiracy theories link his death to the Stasi, the CIA, even Mossad.

Irene is drawn to the figure of the politician as she is to sites in the West which provide links with the trauma she has experienced. We have seen that Irene views Berlin through its past, present, and potential future traumas. And that she is perceptive in not placing her suffering (and the political oppression which caused it) in her past but to sense instead the omnipresence of trauma in the contemporary world

[32] 'What did he know, he who aimed with his gaze, of the cars parking quietly by the curb, of the echo of the bridges in the town, of the fingering of the leaves in the park' (*R* 27).

[33] Müller, *Heute wär ich mir lieber nicht begegnet* (Reinbek bei Hamburg: Rowohlt, 1997), 160.

is shown by her West German friend Stefan's trip to the Palestinian town of Ramallah on the occupied West Bank, which makes him understand for the first time her sentence 'daß die Luft Augen hat, wenn alles überwacht ist'.[34]

The city nomad

But West Berlin in the late 1980s is quite different from the oppressive Romania and the West Bank, and the experience of living there cannot be encapsulated by its turbulent past or its (then) current status as half of a divided city. Its other aspects—as a vibrant, multicultural, postmodern city within a capitalist, democratic state—also impinge on Irene's consciousness in an increasingly liberating way. In her autobiographical essays Müller contrasts the power of state control in the village where she grew up (a village she described as '[d]ie erste Diktatur, die ich kannte'[35]) with the relative freedom she experienced when she moved into the city to study and work.[36] This is consonant with the sociologist Georg Simmel's positive view of urban anonymity as promoting important forms of individualism, both diversity of lifestyle and tolerance of eccentricity. Western cities give particular new freedoms, especially to women, as Elizabeth Wilson notes in her study of women's place in some of the world's great cities, and Irene's encounter with the city is certainly conditioned by her gender.[37]

Despite her initial sense of distance from what she sees, Irene's positioning in relation to the city is, for example, rather different from that of Walter Benjamin's *flâneur*, who, in the nineteenth century, strolled the streets and arcades of the ultimate modern city, Paris, gathering fleeting impressions but standing apart from the alienation of the crowds. The *flâneur* enjoyed a privileged, controlling gaze which held the crisis of the modern world at bay, and, as Maria Kublitz-Kramer has observed, was always by definition male, for his gaze and his pen objectified woman.[38] In her study of contemporary novels by women about city life she observes that women are not seeking to take up the public place of

[34] 'that the air has eyes when everything is under surveillance' (*R* 149).

[35] 'the first dictatorship I knew' (Haines and Littler, 'Gespräch mit Herta Müller', 17).

[36] 'Das Ticken der Norm', in Müller, *Hunger und Seide*, 88–100 (92).

[37] Wilson, *The Sphinx in the City: Urban Life, the Control of Disorder, and Women* (London: Virago, 1991), 7.

[38] Kublitz-Kramer, 'Die Freiheiten der Straße: Stadtläuferinnen in neueren Texten von Frauen', in Friedmar Apel, Maria Kublitz-Kramer, and Thomas Steinfeld (eds.), *Kultur in der Stadt* (Paderborn: University of Paderborn Press, 1993), 15–36 (19).

men traditionally denied them through their confinement in the home, but are rather—as is appropriate in the postmodern age—redefining space and breaking down the old binary oppositions of inner and outer, centre and margin.[39] This is consonant with Donatella Mazzoleni's reconceptualization of the city as 'habitat', an extension of the bodily experience of space. In metropolitan life there is, for Mazzoleni, 'a "knot" of spatial experience, a point at which the most elementary distinction of space—the distinction between "inside" and "outside", which is the very distinction between "I" and "the world"—grows weaker'.[40] In this context Irene can be read as a postmodern female embodied subject: her gaze does not seek to dominate or unify what she sees; rather, chaotic urban diversity becomes intrinsic to her subjectivity, and spatial boundaries, including at times bodily boundaries, are experienced as fluid. Embodiment is crucial, for as a woman in the city she is threatened by male sexuality in a way that a *flâneur* never could be: at one point, for example, she is taken for the prostitute who is available for the *flâneur*'s pleasure (*R* 153),[41] and she is, as we have seen, aware of the ever-present threat of violence.

The name Irene—the adjective irenic means 'aimed at peace'—is deliberately chosen. It is central to Müller's most significant intertext, Italo Calvino's postmodern novel *Invisible Cities* (1972), in which the Venetian envoy Marco Polo reports to the Tartar emperor Kublai Khan about the cities in his empire. The descriptions are given to reassure the emperor of the extent and glory of his dominion, but it turns out that they resist any such appropriation. Calvino's novel suggests the impossibility of ever knowing and conquering the 'other', represented here in the form of cities, all of which have female names. Like Berlin in Müller's novel, the cities all resist male conquest; the locality of place asserts its difference from the abstract space of fatherland/empire. The extract from Calvino's novel quoted in the text is also indicative of the distance inherent in Irene's identity:

> **Irene is a name for a city in the distance, and if you approach, it changes. | For those who pass it without entering, the city is one thing; it is another for those who are trapped by it and never leave. There is the city where you arrive for the first time; and there is another city which you leave never to return. Each deserves a different name; perhaps I have already spoken of Irene under other names; perhaps I have spoken only of Irene.**[42]

[39] Kublitz-Kramer, 'Die Freiheiten der Straße', 36.

[40] Mazzoleni, 'The City and the Imaginary', trans. John Koumantarakis, *New Formations*, 11 (1990), 91–104 (101).

[41] Harnisch, '"Ausländerin im Ausland"', 517.

[42] Calvino, *Invisible Cities*, trans. William Weaver (San Diego, Calif.: Harcourt Brace, 1974), 125; *R* 94.

It is Franz, Irene's German lover, who cites this, and he does so to express his frustration at not being able to possess Irene in the same way that he appropriates the spaces he inhabits, so that when Irene visits Marburg she finds him everywhere, limiting her freedom, imposing thoughts of him on her (*R* 143). Kublai Khan's imperialist aim is described as a dematerialization as well as decoding of the cities of his empire. He wants to discover the model for all possible cities, the 'norm' from which all other cities may be deduced. Marco Polo opposes to this the view that cities are like dreams, resistant to all manifest interpretation. His ideal city is 'a city made only of exceptions, exclusions, incongruities, contradictions'.[43] This accords with Irene's occupation of a precarious position as a permanent traveller in the pluralist city, unable ever to take the city for granted. By contrast, those who truly inhabit the city enjoy a physical intimacy with it based on routine (*R* 138–9).

The fluidity of Irene's identity is further thematized in her liking for collage, which she indulges by cutting up images on postcards and pasting them together in new formations: 'Die Verbindungen, die sich einstellten, waren Gegensätze. Sie machten aus allen Photos ein einziges fremdes Gebilde. So fremd war das Gebilde, daß es auf alles zutraf. Sich ständig bewegte.'[44] The new unity created by the collage is startling and unstable; it makes possible 'das Fortwirken von Gegensätzen' through the senses.[45]

A useful model for exploring Irene's fluid, vulnerable, embodied subjectivity further is Rosi Braidotti's 'nomadic subject', though the correspondence is not entire. The nomadic subject is Braidotti's autobiographically inspired term for a subject in transit which resists assimilation into dominant ways of representing the self and is propelled forward by desire. Identity for the nomadic subject is a retrospective notion, not built upon separation and domination, but made up of the map of where one has already been, 'an inventory of traces'.[46] Braidotti defines her materialist concept of identity as follows: 'The nomad does not stand for homelessness, or compulsive displacement; it is rather a figuration for the kind of subject who has relinquished all idea, desire, or nostalgia for fixity. This figuration expresses the desire for an identity made of transitions, successive shifts, and coordinated changes, without

[43] Calvino, *Invisible Cities*, 69.

[44] 'The connections which appeared were opposites. Out of all the photos they made a single strange construct. So strange was the construct that it applied to everything. Kept on moving' (*R* 47).

[45] 'the continued functioning of opposites' (Friedmar Apel, 'Turbatverse: Ästhetik, Mystik und Politik bei Herta Müller', *Akzente* (1997/2), 113–25 (117)).

[46] Braidotti, *Nomadic Subjects: Embodiment and Sexual Difference in Contemporary Feminist Theory* (New York: Columbia University Press, 1994), 14.

and against an essential unity.'[47] Braidotti anticipates new-materialist thinkers such as Christine Battersby in that she is interested in systems of thought that can accommodate change and go beyond dualism.[48] She adopts nomadism as 'a gesture of nonconfidence'[49] in the political symbolic order, a gesture comparable to Müller's rejection of organized politics. But her nomadic subject also seeks to reinvent politics, empower women, and enable new forms of interrelatedness, a move which Müller does not make.

Crucial to Müller and to Braidotti's political fiction of the nomadic subject is desire, which Braidotti defines as the unconscious energy sustaining conscious thought. By definition this desire is always deferred, resulting in a rejection of fixity.[50] Irene's desire is at first aimed at unsuitable and unattainable targets. She behaves in a voyeuristic and compulsive way, returning each of her remaining nights in 'das andere Land' to the place where she can observe a flasher, and rushing into a one-night stand with a West German tourist, Franz. She pursues Franz after her arrival in Berlin, though it is clear that he is not really interested in her, and she indulges in promiscuous behaviour in a search for tenderness. She imagines sleeping with the men on her plane (*R* 22–3), and spies on the sexual activities of her neighbours (*R* 113). But Irene's movements through the city are also propelled by desire: 'Irene spürte die Haut in ihren Kniekehlen. Und Takte. Es war Erregung, die Irene durch die Straßen trieb. Die Schritte waren ungleichmäßig, aber leicht.'[51] As the novel's title[52] and the Calvino reference imply, the possibility of identity without solidity or stasis is being explored. The asymmetry of walking on one leg is thematized also in the repeated references to shoes and to tread. For example, when Irene observes refugees rummaging in cheap-shoe baskets to find matching pairs, the distance between the shoes becomes representative of the gaps in identity: 'Und diese Entfernung blieb, von einem Schuh zum andern. Sie wuchs hinter den Rücken. Schloß auch die Schultern ein. | Auch in den Augen stand diese Entfernung.'[53] The intimate and public spaces of the city are experienced by Irene as an extension of her own

[47] Braidotti, *Nomadic Subjects*, 22.

[48] Battersby is, however, critical of Braidotti's overly hasty dismissal of metaphysics (see Battersby, *The Phenomenal Woman: Feminist Metaphysics and the Patterns of Identity* (Cambridge: Polity, 1998), 13, 189–91).

[49] Braidotti, *Nomadic Subjects*, 32.

[50] Ibid. 14.

[51] 'Irene felt the skin in the hollows of her knees. And beating. It was desire that drove Irene through the streets. Her steps were uneven, but light' (*R* 75).

[52] 'Traveller(s) on one leg'.

[53] 'And this distance from one shoe to the other remained. It grew behind their backs. Included their shoulders. In their eyes too stood this distance' (*R* 30).

body and psyche, not as that against which she defines her own subjectivity. Thus when she goes to view a flat in Berlin the rooms pass through her consciousness, rather than being the passive objects of her gaze (*R* 38), and when falling asleep in the new flat she experiences architectural space as the concretization and extension of her body (*R* 42). Sometimes the spatial dislocation is liberating, even funny, for example when she falls out of bed because her bed was located differently in relation to the room in her bedroom at home (*R* 120). In any case, movement rather than control is the issue: 'Wenn der Schädel stillstand, wuchs der Asphalt. Wenn der Asphalt stillstand, wuchs die Leere im Schädel. | Mal fiel die Stadt über Irenes Gedanken her. Mal Irenes Gedanken über die Stadt.'[54]

Braidotti's nomadic subject is polyglot, a further factor militating against fixity, for 'the polyglot has no vernacular'.[55] Irene moves between three linguistic codes: the German she brought with her, the German spoken in West Berlin, and the language of her homeland, for which she has an especial fondness. The gap between Irene's German, learned in the linguistically isolated village community in 'das andere Land', and that spoken by West Germans is alienating, for example when she first meets Franz: 'Es war eine Nähe gewesen in zwei Sprachen, die sich nicht verstanden.'[56] She has particular difficulty understanding slang (*R* 115–16), the language of officialdom (*R* 122), and the language of advertising (*R* 107). But her awareness that another language uses imagery in quite a different way enables her to undermine the fixity of the German language; for example, when she evades the categories on the *Bundesnachrichtendienst* official's form she imports an image from her other language to express in German the hopelessness of the official's attempt to tie her down in words (*R* 28). On another occasion she prefers German because the double meaning of the word 'Blatt' ('leaf' and 'page') does not impose a choice on the speaker (*R* 102). This recourse to another linguistic world is a source of mystery and annoyance to her friend Thomas, who can only imagine expressing himself in his mother tongue (*R* 97, 103), but Irene comes to revel in the richness of her multilingualism which gives her a private space and enables her to resist assimilation to the mainstream. Müller elsewhere quotes

[54] 'When the skull stood still, the asphalt grew. When the asphalt stood still, the emptiness in the skull grew. Sometimes the town set upon Irene's thoughts. Sometimes Irene's thoughts set upon the town' (*R* 63).

[55] Braidotti, *Nomadic Subjects*, 13.

[56] 'There had been a closeness in two languages which did not understand each other' (*R* 10).

with approval Jorge Semprun's statement, 'Nicht Sprache ist Heimat, sondern das, was gesprochen wird',[57] and appropriates this phrase for the title of her latest publication, *Heimat ist das, was gesprochen wird* (2001).

The location of *Heimat* in language is not a denial of the past or of the material bases of identity. Irene accepts her roots without nostalgia, declaring, 'Ich bin nicht heimatlos. Nur im Ausland',[58] and is impatient with those who do not, for example her friend Stefan, whose rootlessness is achieved only by a studied neglect of his mother (*R* 80–1). By the same token an Italian with whom she chats before he makes a pass at her has little cause to complain of being 'heimatlos', for, despite being a second-generation immigrant, he has a German family with whom he refuses to identify, preferring to look to the past for an unattainable idyll of belonging (*R* 60–2). Irene feels no more sympathy for the rootless and aggressive street boy, one of many, who accosts her, and spots, presumably from her accent, that she is a foreigner (*R* 72). She categorically rejects notions of *Heimat* based on affiliation to a state, however: her ultimate rejection of Franz, the man with whom she had hoped to form a lasting attachment when she met and slept with him in Romania, is at least in part because he identifies with Germany and the fatherland. She protests, 'Wo trägst du es, dein Vaterland, wenn es plötzlich gegen deinen Willen da ist.'[59]

Irene feels most in sympathy with Thomas, a gay man who is also an outsider. Like Irene, Thomas is emotionally vulnerable, a prey to depression and feelings of abjection (*R* 68–70), but also fluid in his sense of identity. They share a distaste for the people around them who 'den Horizont bewohnen' ('inhabit the horizon', *R* 129). Both love fashion; though Thomas is enslaved to a compulsive cycle of consumption and disappointment, Irene, whilst aware of the fetish character of women's clothes, also sees fashion as potentially liberating, a fund of alternative identities, all provisional and holding the excitement of the new (*R* 75). It is Thomas who makes the most upbeat statement about the role of desire: 'Manchmal könnte man meinen, wir haben keinen Verstand. Und brauchen auch keinen. Nur sinnliche Kraft, um zu leben. Weißt du, wo man das merkt, auf windigen Straßen, auf Bahnsteigen im Freien und

[57] 'It is not language that is home, but what is spoken' (Semprun, *Frederico Sanchez verabschiedet sich*, quoted in Herta Müller, 'Wenn sich der Wind legt, bleibt er stehen oder Wie fremd wird die eigene Sprache beim Lernen der Fremdsprache' <http://www.dhm.de/ausstellungen/goethe/katalog/mueller.htm> 1–3 (2), accessed May 2004).

[58] 'I haven't lost my homeland. I'm just abroad' (*R* 61).

[59] 'Where do you carry it, your fatherland, when it is suddenly there against your will' (*R* 124).

auf Brücken. Dort bewegen die Menschen sich so schamlos und leicht, daß sie den Himmel fast berühren.'[60]

Conclusion

Trauma theory and nomadic subjectivity have certain preoccupations in common, not least their theorizing of the viability of an identity based on aporia and of the desirability of giving expression to unique experience. There is an affinity too between the Holocaust victim who refuses to understand and narrate what has happened, thereby giving active resistance to 'the platitudes of knowledge',[61] and Braidotti's nomadic aesthetics, which disengage 'the sedentary nature of words, destabilizing commonsensical meanings, deconstructing established forms of consciousness'.[62] Together trauma theory and nomadism provide useful, overlapping models for exploring this novel by an author who once described the ideal relationship to one's surroundings as 'eine Fremdheit, an die man sich gewöhnt'.[63] Irene's 'Fremdheit' is internal and a sign of damage, and she is never 'cured' of the trauma which produced it, but neither does she have any nostalgia for an illusory wholeness. With the help of the fluidity of identity allowed by the western city, she translates her 'Fremdheit' into something which allows her to live. 'Der fremde Blick' is not a marker of separation between Irene and what she sees, it signifies a continuing estrangement of the self and of the very relationship between self and other, arising from trauma but sustained by postmodern city life.

The lack of ownership of her own life can at times still seem overwhelmingly stressful, as when she feels '[d]aß sie in irgendeinem Augenblick, der entscheidend gewesen sein mußte, alles versäumt hatte',[64] and she greets the news that she has been granted German citizenship with indifference (*R* 157); however, she becomes more content to inhabit her surroundings without understanding their design: 'Seit ich hier lebe, ist das Detail größer als das Ganze. Das macht mir nichts

[60] 'Sometimes you could think we don't have a mind. And don't need one either. Just sensual power, to live. Do you know where you notice this, on windy streets, on railway platforms in the open air and on bridges. There people move so shamelessly and lightly that they almost touch the sky' (*R* 132–3).

[61] Caruth, intr. to pt. 2 of Caruth (ed.), *Trauma*, 155.

[62] Braidotti, *Nomadic Subjects*, 15.

[63] 'a strangeness/alienation one gets used to' (Haines and Littler, 'Gespräch mit Herta Müller'), 20.

[64] 'that at some moment or other, which must have been decisive, she had missed everything' (*R* 112).

aus. Nur den Dingen, die zeigen das nicht gern.'[65] The nomadic lifestyle seems now less threatening, more alive with possibilities, as the closing words of the novel show: 'Menschen, die nicht mehr wußten, ob sie nun in diesen Städten Reisende in dünnen Schuhen waren. Oder Bewohner mit Handgepäck. | Irene lag im Dunkeln und dachte an die Stadt. | Irene weigerte sich, an Abschied zu denken.'[66] Irene's desire is now experienced as the kind of pleasure in the moment that Thomas describes, for example when she starts to feel happy on the street (*R* 124, 133). But the *jouissance* she experiences from the risk-taking involved in crossing the road on a red light—'Irene . . . [l]ief knapp vor den Autos her. Atmete rasch, hatte sowohl das Gefühl, sich in Lebensgefahr zu begeben, als auch, sich das Leben zu retten. | Weder tot noch lebendig, dachte Irene. Es war fast Freude'[67]—is, like so much of her behaviour, ambiguous, for it can be interpreted both as the compulsive repetition characteristic of trauma and as a hint that she can cope: she is getting used to the idea that she will survive each day, and can inhabit her world with more confidence, to the extent of taking risks.

Müller once commented that reading is as much about what is not written as what is written: 'Das Gesagte muß behutsam sein, mit dem, was nicht gesagt wird . . . Das, was mich einkreist, seine Wege geht, beim Lesen, ist das, was zwischen den Sätzen fällt und aufschlägt, oder kein Geräusch macht. Es ist das Ausgelassene.'[68] Much that is of import in *Reisende auf einem Bein* is between the lines: the Romanian trauma, for example, while not named, is present throughout, as are the moments of trauma in Germany's past with which Irene connects. With its risky exploration of the dissolution of boundaries in politics, history, language, and in the self, *Reisende auf einem Bein* indicates the presence of 'the unforgettable forgotten'[69] in the make-up of its protagonist and in the snapshot it presents of West Berlin and of Europe in the late 1980s.

[65] 'Since I have been living here the detail is bigger than the whole. That doesn't bother me. It only bothers the things, they don't like to show it' (*R* 162).

[66] 'People who no longer knew if they were now travellers in thin shoes in these towns. Or inhabitants with hand luggage. | Irene lay in the dark and thought of the town. | Irene refused to think of leaving' (*R* 166).

[67] 'Irene . . . [r]an narrowly in front of the cars. Breathed quickly, had both the feeling she was risking her life and also saving it. | Neither dead nor alive, thought Irene. It was almost delight' (*R* 161).

[68] 'What is said must be careful with what is not said . . . What encircles me and goes on its way when reading is what falls between the lines and leaps up, or makes no noise. It is what is left out' (Müller, *Der Teufel sitzt im Spiegel: Wie Wahrnehmung sich erfindet* (Berlin: Rotbuch, 1991), 19).

[69] Lyotard, *Heidegger and 'the jews'*, 26.

6 Emine Sevgi Özdamar, 'Mutter Zunge' and 'Großvater Zunge' (1990)

Introduction

The protagonist of the first two, interlinked stories in Emine Sevgi Özdamar's *Mutterzunge* is a Turkish woman, living in East Berlin, who attends Arabic classes with a Koran scholar in order to reconnect with her Turkish heritage. This presents a dilemma for those readers for whom the abolition of the Arabic script in 1928 and the secularization of twentieth-century Turkey might seem the very conditions on which female emancipation has been founded. Indeed, as an emancipated Turkish woman intellectual, the unnamed protagonist bears some comparison with her author. Born in Malatya, Turkey, in 1946, Emine Sevgi Özdamar is the most prominent of the growing number of non-Germans writing in German. 'Minority' or 'migrant' writing is a phenomenon which has increased rapidly since the 1980s in the aftermath of the recruitment of *Gastarbeiter* (guest-workers) by the Federal Republic between 1955 and 1973.[1] However, designation of this work is itself problematic, as terms such as *MigrantInnenliteratur* ('migrant literature') tend to fix the writing of non-Germans in a marginal relationship to the mainstream, instead of extending the definition of German literature itself. Even positive reception has often been couched in an orientalizing discourse which sees the exoticism of an oral or naive, story-telling tradition as a mere embellishment of German culture. Much of the early so-called *Gastarbeiterliteratur* was indeed confessional and limited in scope, but since the 1980s the writing of non-Germans has become more complex and diverse, demanding the attention of the literary-critical community.

As a first-generation Turkish-German writer who has spent much of her adult life in either East or West Germany, yet having achieved critical acclaim, Özdamar presents perhaps the strongest challenge to conventional definitions of German Literature. She first came to Germany in 1965 as a factory worker in West Berlin, where she experienced the

[1] The contract with the Turkish government was not signed until October 1961. For more detail on the recruitment of foreign labour see David Horrocks and Eva Kolinsky (eds.), *Turkish Culture in German Society Today* (Oxford: Berghahn, 1996).

beginnings of the student movement before returning to Istanbul in 1967 to train as an actress. After the closure of many theatres in the aftermath of the 1971 military coup, she again left Turkey for Germany in 1976, where she began working with Brecht's pupil Benno Besson at the Volksbühne in East Berlin as an actress and assistant director. While working at the Bochum Schauspielhaus (1979–84) she wrote her first play, *Karagöz in Alamania* (premièred in 1986), a prose version of which is printed in *Mutterzunge*. This first prose volume appeared in 1990, closely followed in 1991 by her second play, *Keloğlan in Alamania*. In the same year she was awarded the prestigious Ingeborg Bachmann prize for her first novel, *Das Leben ist eine Karawanserei—hat zwei Türen—aus einer kam ich rein—aus der anderen ging ich raus* (1992). This depiction of a childhood in Turkey in the 1950s and early 1960s charts the declining fortunes of a family against the turbulent backdrop of the country's first experiment with multi-party democracy. The story ends as the young woman protagonist leaves for Germany to work as a *Gastarbeiterin* in Berlin. This is the starting point for the second novel, *Die Brücke vom Goldenen Horn* (1998), which is set against the backdrop of the student movement in Europe and political upheaval in Turkey. Özdamar's third novel, *Seltsame Sterne starren zur Erde* (2003), charts the theatrical career of a young Turkish woman in 1970s Berlin. While not strictly autobiographical, all three novels unmistakably mirror the author's experience, first of migration within Turkey, then of migration across national boundaries to western Europe, and finally of her acting and directing career. This chapter will explore the impact of geographical and linguistic migrations on the female protagonist of the first two stories in *Mutterzunge*. It will locate the stories in the cultural and historical contexts of Özdamar's writing, and assess the usefulness of psychoanalytical, post-colonial, and new-materialist feminist thinking to illuminate the texts. Özdamar's depiction of the consequences of *actual* migration can be understood also as a form of intellectual and cultural nomadism. Her construction of female subjectivity is also emphatically corporeal, in a way which suggests unexpected parallels between Turkish literary traditions and the concerns of recent feminist theory.

The first two stories in *Mutterzunge*, entitled 'Mutter Zunge' and 'Großvater Zunge', revolve around the dilemma of linguistic dislocation: 'Wenn ich nur wüßte, wann ich meine Mutterzunge verloren habe.'[2] The protagonist is living in East Berlin, and has become so at home in the German language that even her most intimate memories of her mother's words come back to her now, 'wie eine von mir gut gelernte

[2] 'If only I knew when I lost my mother tongue' (*M* 7).

Fremdsprache'.[3] Her position between Turkish and German culture is mirrored in the divided city of Berlin, where two radically contrasting realities existed side-by-side. However, it is impossible to grasp the full impact of her sense of cultural loss without reference to the history of the Turkish Republic, as established by Atatürk in 1923. Mustapha Kemal 'Atatürk' ('father of the Turks') led Turkey in the War of Liberation (1919–22) after the collapse of the Ottoman Empire in the First World War. The republic he founded was characterized by radical reform, and driven by westernization, secularism, and nationalism. This included the abolition of Islamic symbols (such as the veil), the secularization of education, and the wholesale importation of western legal codes. Most important for Özdamar's text were the orthographic reforms introduced in 1928, which replaced the Arabic script (used throughout the Ottoman Empire) with the Latin script. In addition to increasing literacy, the introduction of the Latin alphabet was seen as a significant step in the country's alignment with western Europe. Language purists also initiated a continuing process of eliminating foreign influences from the Turkish vocabulary, introducing new Turkish words where only loanwords existed.

From a western perspective, many of Atatürk's reforms, although imposed from above, had a liberating effect on women, whose lives were no longer to be subjected to Islamic law (Turkish women were fully enfranchised in 1934, over ten years earlier than women in France, Italy, or Belgium). Indeed, the female protagonist of 'Mutter Zunge' and 'Großvater Zunge' is a product of Atatürk's westernizing reforms, but at the same time she participates in a critique of Kemalism which was widespread in 1980s Turkey. Although Turkish intellectuals still favour 'öz Türkçe', an 'authentic' Turkish, cleansed of Arabic and Persian influence, since the 1980s this has come to be seen as problematic: 'the ideology of reclaiming an "essential" Turkish language stripped of its history and organic development has come under attack, for it entails a practice of denying, forgetting, and erasing vital cultural heritages'.[4]

[3] 'like a foreign language which I have learned very well' (*M* 7).

[4] Azade Seyhan, 'Geographies of Memory: Protocols of Writing in the Borderlands', in Klaus J. Milich and Jeffrey M. Peck (eds.), *Multiculturalism in Transit: A German-American Exchange* (New York/Oxford: Berghahn, 1998), 193–212 (209). Deniz Göktürk is more sceptical about recent criticisms of Atatürk's orthographic reforms, suspecting they arise from politically reactionary motives (Göktürk, 'Multikültürelle Zungenbrecher: Literatürken aus Deutschlands Nischen', *Sirene*, 12/13 (1994), 77–92 (85)). Elsewhere Seyhan has also noted that Özdamar's text might have been construed as a fundamentalist religious gesture if published in Turkey (see Seyhan, 'Scheherazade's Daughters: The Thousand and One Tales of Turkish-German Women Writers', in Gisela Brinker-Gabler and Sidonie Smith (eds.), *Writing New Identities: Gender, Nation and Immigration in Contemporary Europe* (Minneapolis, Minn./London: University of Minnesota Press, 1997), 230–48 (246).

Thus the lack of access to collective memories and a shared cultural heritage is not only an experience of Turkish diasporic communities, but also that of younger generations of Turks resident in Turkey. This is the context in which the critique of Atatürk in 'Großvater Zunge' can be understood: 'aber er hätte die arabische Schrift nicht verbieten müssen. Dieses Verbot ist so, wie wenn die Hälfte von meinem Kopf abgeschnitten ist.'[5]

The problem for female readers of Özdamar's text is that her protagonist is apparently rejecting an aspect of Atatürk's reforms which contributed at least in part to the extension of literacy and education to women. How are we to explain the prioritization of cultural continuity over female emancipation in a woman who appears so modern in her political outlook ('Brecht war der erste Mensch, warum ich hierher gekommen bin')?[6] Indeed, does this apparent impasse signal the limits of western feminist theory, when confronted with a non-European Islamic culture? The desire to embrace the patriarchal 'Großvater Zunge', and willingly to take up a female subject position within Islam, is difficult to reconcile with Lacanian feminist theory, for which Islam represents a patriarchal symbolic order, one in which the position of women is arguably even more circumscribed than in Christianity. But Elizabeth Boa has argued that to apply psychoanalytical feminist theory to Özdamar's representation of Islam would amount to epistemological violence; that is, the imposition of an inappropriate framework of knowledge on the object of study. To read the story only in terms of the oppressive, patriarchal power invested in the Arabic script would be to disregard the importance of cultural and linguistic continuity in the text.[7] A further reason for caution when applying psychoanalysis in this context is that it presupposes a radical disjuncture between mind and body, the psyche and the real, a split which Özdamar's text explicitly challenges. The following textual analysis will explore these tensions, and propose a conceptual framework which draws on recent Australian feminist theory. This theory is both materialist in orientation and marked by its specific context of inclusion and exclusion, the nomadic indigenous peoples of Australia having been dispossessed by colonists and settlers. Attending as much to issues of racial difference as to gender, this is a feminist critique which attempts to respect culturalist claims.

[5] 'but he shouldn't have banned the Arabic script. This ban is as if half of my head has been cut off' (*M* 27).

[6] 'Brecht was the first person I came here for' (*M* 11).

[7] Boa, 'Sprachenverkehr: Hybrides Schreiben in Werken von Özdamar, Özakin und Demirkan', in Mary Howard (ed.), *Interkulturelle Konfigurationen: Zur deutschsprachigen Prosaliteratur von Autoren nichtdeutscher Herkunft* (Munich: iudicium, 1997), 115–37.

The other key context within which writers of the Turkish-German diaspora may be viewed is the field of post-colonial studies. Whereas the discussion of Indo-Anglian, francophone, Latin American, and lusophone writing has become an integral part of English, French, Spanish, and Portuguese Studies respectively, it remains a moot point whether Turkish-German writing can be considered to exist in a 'post-colonial' relation to German culture. While Turkey has never been a German colony, it has arguably been subject to German imperialism, where this is understood not as colonial rule but as economic subordination to sustain the growth of West German capitalism. Moreover, the history of German interests in Turkey's strategic position and mineral resources stretches back well before the twentieth century; for example one might recall Bismarck's plan to build a railway through the country to exploit Iraqi oilfields or Germany's alliance with the Ottoman Empire in the First World War. It is probably with this history in mind that Özdamar made an explicit connection between colonialism and migrant labour in a 1996 interview: 'It is true that the older colonial powers have managed the business of immigration much more successfully. The Germans came by their colonies relatively late in the day, and they have ended up creating new colonies on their home territory.'[8] Özdamar's texts do reflect this perception of German-Turkish relations, though with very little pathos. Her play with orientalizing images serves to expose the power relations they uphold, but her protagonist does not merely represent an oppressed minority. She is rather a nomadic intellectual who ultimately accepts her own hybridity, in place of the restoration of an intact identity.

Gender, language, and identity

Much has been written about Özdamar's poetic style, in particular her literal translation of Turkish idioms into German, her use of Turkish and Arabic vocabulary, and her deliberate flouting of German grammar. These alienating effects express a political as well as an aesthetic agenda; they are calculated to pose obstacles to comprehension and make the German-speaking reader share the linguistic estrangement experienced by foreigners in Germany. Even the title *Mutterzunge* is a slightly odd neologism in German, as a language which does not use the word

[8] This interview is published in English in Horrocks and Kolinsky (eds.), *Turkish Culture in German Society Today*, 45–54 (52–3).

'tongue' as a synonym for 'language'. Many passages in Özdamar's work leave the non-Turkish-speaking reader with a sense of 'loss', not having access to all the potential meanings of the words. In some cases knowledge of the Turkish idiom opens up an entirely new meaning to expressions, such as that in the opening scene: 'Ich saß mit meiner gedrehten Zunge in dieser Stadt Berlin.'[9] While this might seem to hold negative, or at least ambiguous, connotations of deformity in German, 'Zunge drehen' may refer here to the Turkish idiom 'dili dönmek' (usually used in the negative 'dilim dönmüyor', which means 'I cannot pronounce').[10] So the narrator positively affirms her ease with the sounds of the German language as well as commenting on its difficulty. Indeed, 'Mutter Zunge' opens with a lament for the loss of her mother tongue, coupled with an acknowledgement that she has adopted a western perspective, as seen in her perception of Istanbul as 'dark', to which her mother remarks: 'Istanbul hatte immer diese Lichter, deine Augen sind an Alamanien-Lichter gewöhnt.'[11]

From the outset the protagonist's desire for cultural continuity is tempered with a critical view of Turkey, expressing a deeply ambivalent attitude rather than simple nostalgia for an idealized lost homeland. An upsurge of political extremism in the 1960s, followed by a military coup and the imposition of martial law in 1971, had led to what Erik Jan Zürcher has called 'a veritable witch-hunt against anyone with leftist or even progressive liberal sympathies' in Turkey.[12] Özdamar's most recent novel depicts a protagonist who leaves Turkey in the 1970s in response to this situation, and she reflects on the impact of political violence on the language itself: 'Man sagt, in fremden Ländern verliert man die Muttersprache. Kann man nicht auch in seinem eigenen Land die Muttersprache verlieren?'[13] This illuminates further the protagonist's dilemma in 'Mutter Zunge', as she tries to ascertain when she lost her mother tongue. The three Turkish words she initially retrieves signify

[9] 'I sat with my twisted tongue in this city, Berlin' (*M* 7).

[10] This is Seyhan's interpretation in 'Geographies of Memory', 204–5. Kader Konuk suggests that the reference is to the verb 'çevirmek', meaning to turn, rotate, or to translate. Thus 'gedrehte Zunge' could simply mean 'translated language' (Konuk, '*Das Leben ist eine Karawanserei*: Heimat [*sic*] bei Emine Sevgi Özdamar', in Gisela Ecker (ed.), *Kein Land in Sicht: Heimat—weiblich?* (Munich: Fink Verlag, 1997), 144–57 (146)).

[11] 'Istanbul has always had these lights, your eyes are accustomed to German lights' (*M* 7). It should be noted that 'Alamanien-' and 'Alamania' are Germanized forms of the adjective 'alman' and the noun 'Almanya', and that Özdamar is using a hybridized language, not simply importing Turkish words into German.

[12] Zürcher, *Turkey: A Modern History* (London: Tauris, 2001; 1st pub. 1993), 272.

[13] 'They say that one can lose one's mother tongue in a foreign country. Can't one also lose one's mother tongue in one's own country?' (Özdamar, *Seltsame Sterne starren zur Erde* (Cologne: Kiepenheuer & Witsch, 2003), 23).

solidarity with opponents of the Turkish government, as well as fear of discrimination in the West. 'Görmek' ('to see') is associated with sensory deprivation, being uttered by prisoners cut off from the world outside; 'kaza geçirmek' ('to experience life's accidents') recalls the wisdom of a communist friend in Istanbul, who alerts her to the link between suffering and creativity; 'ISCI' ('WORKER') is stamped in her passport when she first travels to Germany, and when the train is searched by German officials she feels branded by this Turkish word as well as by its designation of her occupation: 'ich überlege mir, ob ich sagen soll: "ich bin Italienerin" '.[14] References to a mother whose son was executed for political opposition in the 1980 military coup (*M* 8) underline still further the protagonist's oppositional status, while her commitment to Brecht's theatre in East Berlin also locates her in opposition to the capitalist West. Specifically, she feels no nostalgia for being a woman in Turkey, where, as an independent, politically active woman, she is suspected of being a prostitute (*M* 11).

Despite considering herself a modern, emancipated woman, however, she resolves to learn the Arabic script, the abolition of which separates her culturally from her grandparents' generation. She finds an Arabic teacher, Ibni Abdullah, who makes his living from teaching 'orientalists' and environmentally conscious Germans seeking alternatives to western consumerism. The cultural transition from West back to East is reversed, as she has to cross from East to West Berlin to receive her tuition. Ibni Abdullah is both a teacher and embodiment of Islam; his name means 'son of Abdullah' (Muhammad's father), his room is described as 'eine kleine Moschee' ('a small mosque') in which even the cushions are 'artig' ('well-behaved') (*M* 13), and only the view from the window betrays the existence of secular reality. At the same time the room is intensely sensual with its smell of roses, silk hangings, and cushions, a seductive setting for the love story which follows. But the language into which she seeks to be initiated is unequivocally that of the law of Islam, a symbolic order for which female desire is dangerous and destabilizing excess, and must therefore be controlled. Her tuition begins with a parodic imitation of Muhammad's revelation; when first commanded by the Angel Gabriel to read the words of Allah in a dream Muhammad protested that he was illiterate, just as the protagonist claims she cannot read the script (*M* 16). Miraculously, however, on the third attempt he was able to read the ninety-sixth Sura of the Koran. Like Gabriel, Ibni Abdullah commands: 'Lese, Gott hat es uns geschickt.'[15]

[14] 'I consider whether I should say: "I'm an Italian" ' (*M* 10).

[15] 'Read, God has sent it to us' (*M* 16). For an account of this passage in the Koran see Tahire Kockturk, *A Matter of Honour: Experiences of Turkish Women Immigrants* (London and New Jersey: Zed Books, 1992), 35.

The letters that come out of her mouth are signifiers detached from their signifieds, and they are visual as well as aural images, foregrounding the pictorial aspect of Arabic script. As the Muslim religion does not tolerate representations of the divine, Islamic calligraphy takes the place of religious art. It is this aspect of the scripts, rather than their symbolic content, which fascinates and beguiles both protagonist and reader:

> **Manche sahen aus wie ein Vogel, manche wie ein Herz, auf dem ein Pfeil steckt, manche wie eine Karawane, manche wie schlafende Kamele, manche wie ein Fluß, manche wie im Wind auseinanderfliegende Bäume, manche wie laufende Schlangen, manche wie unter Regen und Wind frierende Granatapfelbäume, manche wie böse geschreckte Augenbrauen, manche wie auf dem Fluß fahrendes Holz, manche wie in einem türkischen Bad auf einem heißen Stein sitzender dicker Frauenarsch, manche wie nicht schlafen könnende Augen.[16]**

This description is one of several passages in 'Großvater Zunge' which recur (almost verbatim) in relation to the grandmother in *Das Leben ist eine Karawanserei.*[17] The above images recall the grandmother's folk religion, with its emphasis on love and a spiritualized nature, as well as her earthy humour. As Soheila Ghaussy has argued, the suppression of the symbolic meaning of the scripts and emphasis instead on their sensuous materiality both resists the patriarchal discourse of the Koran and asserts the corporeal aspect of language.[18] The Arabic letters take on a life of their own, sometimes effecting a comic reversal of the similes in the above quotation, as when Ibni Abdullah's perplexed face resembles a letter. This occurs when his feelings for the protagonist become incompatible with and inexpressible within the religious context of their studies (*M* 17, 21).

[16] 'Some looked like a bird, some like a heart with an arrow stuck on it, some like a caravan, some like sleeping camels, some like a river, some like trees buffeted by the wind, some like snakes in motion, some like pomegranate trees shivering in the rain and wind, some like angry startled eyebrows, some like wood travelling on the river, some like the fat bottoms of women sitting on a hot stone in a Turkish bath, some like eyes which can't sleep' (*M* 16).

[17] See Özdamar, *Das Leben ist eine Karawanserei—hat zwei Türen—aus einer kam ich rein—aus der anderen ging ich raus* (Cologne: Kiepenheuer & Witsch, 1992), 18. The grandmother is transmitter of the Arabic language and Islamic religion to the child, but she also represents an idiosyncratic, mystical form of Islam which bears little relation to the faith of Ibni Abdullah. The fairy tale of the 'Geduldstein' (*M* 31–3) also occurs in the novel, and the husband's brutal punishment of his wife echoes that of the grandfather in *Das Leben ist eine Karawanserei.* Yet the grandmother becomes quite liberated in the course of the novel, and encourages her granddaughter to study hard at school, so that she will never have to wash some man's feet (*Das Leben ist eine Karawanserei*, 213).

[18] Ghaussy, '"Das Vaterland verlassen": Nomadic Language and "Feminine Writing" in Emine Sevgi Özdamar's *Das Leben ist eine Karawanserei*', *German Quarterly*, 72/1 (1999), 1–16 (11).

The growing love between pupil and teacher leads to the end of their professional and personal relationship, but it is also the occasion for many of the text's most poetic effects. It is important to acknowledge both levels on which the story works: the logic of the incompatibility between their desire and Ibni Abdullah's intellectual discipline on the one hand, and the articulation of desire in the poetic imagery of the text on the other. Indeed, this is where the parallels with theories of patriarchal language and repressed feminine desire are most compelling, although these must be balanced against the specificity of the context to be elaborated below. The protagonist falls in love with her teacher, but language fails her in the expression of that love: 'ich habe kein Wörterbuch gefunden für die Sprache meiner Liebe'.[19] Once, when almost overwhelmed by desire, her helplessness is again related to the limitations of language: 'ich konnte ihn nicht fassen, meine Hände lagen wie Buchstaben ohne Zunge auf meine Knien'.[20] On this occasion she resorts to recounting a dream, allowing the encoded contents of her unconscious to speak to him of her passion, and leading to the consummation of their love. When he later withdraws from her, she again laments the shortcomings of language: 'Mit welcher Sprache soll mein Mund sprechen, daß mein Geliebter es sieht.'[21] She resorts to inscribing her repressed desire on a tear-stained, blank sheet of notepaper (*M* 34).

Her dilemma is compounded by the fact that the language she is learning is that of orthodox Islam, and most of the Koranic quotations in the text concern the sin of mankind and the wrath of Allah. Readers from a Judaeo-Christian background will notice echoes from biblical tradition, such as the story of Jusuf (Joseph) and Zeliha (Potiphar's wife), as well as telling differences (such as the legitimacy accorded here to Zeliha's desire). Significantly for this emancipated woman, however, the Arabic scripts represent discipline, denial, and retribution. When Ibni Abdullah leaves her alone in his room they stand guard over her, admonishing her for her inattentiveness, yet at the same time distracting her with their picture-language of hearts and arrows, and women's eyes (*M* 42). Even as the Koranic texts speak of fire and brimstone and the punishment of unbelievers, patterns of combination and repetition of elemental imagery develop to disrupt this unequivocal message. For example, fire is as frequently associated with passion as with punishment. The Koran warns: 'Was die Elenden anlangt, so sollen sie ins

[19] 'I haven't found a dictionary for the language of my love' (*M* 30).

[20] 'I couldn't take hold of him/understand him, my hands lay on my knees like letters without tongues' (*M* 22).

[21] 'What language should my mouth speak for my beloved to see it?' (*M* 38).

Feuer kommen',[22] but in a song it also speaks of the heart as a phoenix, repeatedly consumed by fire (*M* 22). When tormented by her love, the protagonist says: 'Liebe ist ein Hemd aus Feuer',[23] the only relief for which is his reciprocal desire: 'das Feuer, das aus meinem "Ach" rauskam, kann nur Ibni Abdullahs Feuer löschen'.[24] Allah's avenging fire and the fire of human passion become intertwined in the poetic vocabulary of the text.[25]

Stone and water also acquire layers of significance related to the love which the law of Islam attempts to circumscribe; the former by association with the grandmother's story of the 'Geduldstein' ('patience stone') (*M* 32), signifying the positive Islamic quality of patience, then with the protagonist's prayer: 'entweder mach mein Herz zu Stein, oder gib mir ein Geduldstein',[26] and her inner plea to Ibni Abdullah: 'Drücke mir einen Stein auf das Herz.'[27] Patience, so revered by Islamic tradition (as echoed by her grandfather, *M* 43), is also associated with indifference and insensitivity. Stone becomes a barren landscape waiting for the return of the sea in a poetic passage which abounds with images of fertility and fluidity, as the voices of the Arabic texts awaken the excess of her desire:

> **die Schriften sprachen miteinander ohne Pause mit verschiedenen Stimmen, weckten die eingeschlafenen Tiere in meinem Körper, ich schließe Augen, die Stimme der Liebe wird mich blind machen, sie sprechen weiter, mein Körper geht auf wie ein in der Mitte aufgeschnittener Granatapfel, in Blut und Schmutz kam ein Tier raus. Ich schaue auf meinen offenen Körper, das Tier faßt meinen offenen Körper, leckt meine Wunden mit seiner Spucke, ich hatte Steine unter meinen Füßen, ein Meer soll sich mal zurückgezogen haben, eine unendliche Landschaft blieb nur mit Steinen, ihr Glanz hatte sie verlassen, die Steine schrien: 'Wasser, Wasser'. Ich sah, wie das Meer aus dem Mund dieses Tieres rauskam. Das Meer floß über die gestorbenen Steine, die Steine bewegten sich, das Wasser hebt mich hoch, ich lag da, über dem Körper vom Wasser schlief ich ein.[28]**

22 'As for the wretched, they shall go into the fire' (*M* 29, 31).

23 'Love is a shirt of fire' (*M* 38). This is a translation of the Turkish 'aşk ateşten gömlek'.

24 'The fire which came out of my "Oh" can be quenched only by Ibni Abdullah's fire' (*M* 25).

25 This ambiguous fire image may relate to different Turkish idioms, such as *içim yanıyor* (it is burning in me) and *içimdeki ateş/içimde bir ateş var* (the fire in me/there is a fire in me), which suggest a state of regret or longing, and a powerful desire or will to action respectively.

26 'either turn my heart to stone or give me a patience stone' (*M* 32). Being turned to stone is a punishment from God which occurs in many Turkish expressions.

27 'Press a stone on my heart' (*M* 38).

28 'the scripts were speaking to each other continuously in various voices, they wakened the slumbering beasts in my body, I close my eyes, the voice of love will make me blind, they go on speaking, my body splits open like a pomegranate cut down the middle, in blood and filth an animal emerged. I look at my open body, the animal takes hold of my open body, licks my wounds with its spit, I had stones under my feet, a sea is said to have retreated once, leaving an endless

This elemental imagery points to the legacy of Ottoman literature in Özdamar's work, but it also resonates with Luce Irigaray's imaginative evocation of Presocratic philosophical discourse. In *Elemental Passions* (1982), Irigaray's hymn to erotic love, she uses elemental images to counter static, oppositional, and hierarchical representations of the relations between the sexes. She draws in part on the thought of Empedocles (*c*.493–*c*.433 BC), who taught that reality was composed of four elements, fire, air, earth, and water, which continually mingle and separate under the influence of love and strife. By adopting the language of ancient alchemy and a logic of perpetual becoming, Irigaray shows what is at stake in more modern ontologies based on fixed essences and binary thinking.[29] So, for example, her poetic female voice opposes the fluidity of air, fire, and water to rock-solid earth: 'Is fire not joy? Is burning with you not grace?'[30] In her analysis of the Ottoman mystic romance Victoria Holbrook has also noted the influence of pre-modern science on elemental imagery in allegorical depictions of inner journeys.[31] Her study lends support to the view that pre-modern practices (such as Ottoman poetry) may indeed share textual qualities with post-modern critiques of modernity.[32]

Özdamar could be said to make tactical use of the elemental to question Ibni Abdullah's interpretation of Islam, in particular his separation of body and mind, of carnal and spiritual love. It should be noted that the Islamic notion of the subject does not share the body/mind dualism of Christian philosophy, and asceticism plays virtually no role in Islamic tradition, except in some forms of mystical Sufism.[33] Perhaps Ibni Abdullah's resistance to the protagonist's active sexuality has more to do with his masculinity than with his religion. When he responds to orgasm with horror, as if to the sight of death (*M* 37), one is reminded of Irigaray's challenge to the bodily containment associated with male subjectivity: 'What terrifies you? That lack of closure. From which

landscape with only stones, its lustre had deserted it, the stones cried out: "Water, water". I saw the sea coming out of the animal's mouth. The sea flowed over the dead stones, the stones moved, the water lifts me up, I lay there, on top of the body of the water I fell asleep' (*M* 24–5).

29 See Irigaray, *Elemental Passions*, trans. Joanne Collie and Judith Still (London: Athlone, 1992; 1st pub. in French 1982). For a discussion of Irigaray's use of the elemental see Elizabeth Grosz, *Sexual Subversions: Three French Feminists* (St Leonards, NSW: Allen & Unwin, 1989), 168–72.

30 Irigaray, *Elemental Passions*, 80. The 'you' addressed in this text is the male beloved whose world-view is being challenged.

31 Victoria Rowe Holbrook, *The Unreadable Shores of Love: Turkish Modernity and Mystic Romance* (Austin, Tex.: University of Texas Press, 1994), 134.

32 Holbrook, *The Unreadable Shores of Love*, 4.

33 See Marshall G. S. Hodgson, *The Venture of Islam: Conscience and History in a World Civilization*, i (Chicago, Ill.: University of Chicago Press, 1974), 393–400.

springs your struggle against in-finity [*sic*]. Origin and end, form, figure, meaning, name, the proper and the self: these are your weapons against that unbearable infinity.'[34] To a mechanistic view of time and the body Irigaray opposes a view of the subject as porous and open to the fluid density of unfolding space-time. These different conceptions of embodiment seem to play a part in the growing tension between the protagonist and Ibni Abdullah, which is also a clash between the competing social projects of Islamism and western modernity.

Embodiment and sexual difference

The sensuousness of Özdamar's prose and her insistence on corporeally grounded metaphors invite comparison with other developments in recent feminist theory which also challenge the body/mind distinction. Feminist philosophy has traced the radical body/mind distinction in western thought back to Plato, but sees it continued also in the thinking of Descartes, Kant, and Lacan. Christine Battersby has pointed to the parallels between Kant's thinking on the self and personhood and Lacan's model of subjectivity.[35] Kant saw personhood as a mental construct based on autonomy and closure, and believed that the self needed to exist in an oppositional relationship to permanent and inert matter. Similarly, in Lacan's account of subjectivity the self is only constructed by means of a radical break with the other, initially the infant's mother, but also with the real, to which the subject has no access after entering the symbolic. In both schemes of thought the body is inert matter, only rendered meaningful retrospectively by the signifying processes of language/mind. As the Italian philosopher Adriana Cavarero notes, one consequence of this radical body/mind separation is to render sexual difference invisible and reinforce the false universalism of a masculine norm:

> **At this point [in Plato's Socrates] Western philosophy has already celebrated its glorious triumph over matter. By trivializing the necessary bodily dimension of living, it now inhibits the symbolic translation of sexual difference. In other words, a separated and dematerialized embodiedness can more easily conceal its sexual connotation, always marked by difference. Hence the male gender can easily claim to be neutral and universal.[36]**

[34] Irigaray, *Elemental Passions*, 71.

[35] Battersby, *The Phenomenal Woman: Feminist Metaphysics and the Patterns of Identity* (New York: Routledge, 1998), 61–3, 86–9.

[36] Cavarero, *In Spite of Plato: A Feminist Rewriting of Ancient Philosophy*, trans. Serena Anderlini-D'Onofrio and Áine O'Healy (Cambridge: Polity, 1990), 26.

Moreover, the logical conclusion of such a devaluation of the body is a glorification of death, as the ultimate liberation of the soul from its bodily fetters. What this philosophical tradition is unable to account for is the events of gestation and birth, in which matter shows itself capable of radical novelty independent of mind. The corporeal ontology of Australian philosophers Elizabeth Grosz, Moira Gatens, and Genevieve Lloyd is founded on a Spinozist turning away from the 'critical linguisticism' of Anglo-American philosophy.[37] In place of the Lacanian (Kantian) view of the body as resistant to signification, only knowable via language, they question the boundary between the real and representation, suggesting that meaning emerges at the level of the corporeal. Spinoza saw the mind as an idea of the body, and the body as the content of the mind; thus both are sexually differentiated and particular. The body is neither brute and determining prelinguistic being nor the mere effect of ideological representation, it has its own dynamic and effects its own self-representation.

Rather than looking in Özdamar's prose for evidence of *écriture féminine* in the form of silences and rhythms which betray the presence of a repressed 'feminine', therefore, one might detect in her poetic images an agency accorded to matter, and the assertion of a sexually embodied desire. In these stories specifically, the protagonist experiences her body and mind as inseparable. Significant moments of emotional turmoil are recalled as physical trauma rather than purely mental pain. When she watches old cine-film footage from 1936 with German friends, for example, she is made physically ill by their unproblematic nostalgia for such a dark period of German history (*M* 18). This moment of physical suffering is also the moment when she realizes that Ibni Abdullah has 'entered' her body and she has begun to identify with his difference, rather than with her German environment. When she is overwhelmed by the sensuous beauty of the script Ibni Abdullah reprimands her for poor concentration (*M* 17), but this merely underlines their radically different attitudes to embodiment. For him the body is a hindrance to knowledge and spirituality, for her the medium of her mental life, both conscious and unconscious.

It is important also in this context to understand the symbolic role of women in Islam, as circumscribed by the key terms 'modesty' and *mahrem*, or gender segregation. While Islam does not share the radical

[37] See Claire Colebrook, 'From Radical Representations to Corporeal Becoming: The Feminist Philosophy of Lloyd, Grosz and Gatens', *Hypatia*, 15/2 (2000), 76–93. By 'critical linguisticism' she refers to the priority accorded to language in most post-structuralist and postmodern accounts of subjectivity.

body/mind distinction of Christianity, it nevertheless upholds essential differences between the sexes and their social roles, crediting women with more sexual power, but men with social dominance. The Arabic word *fitna*, denoting both 'beautiful woman' and 'chaos', is at the heart of the Islamic imperative to control female sexuality; if uncontrolled it will result in social disorder. The related concept of *mahrem* replaces the public/private division in the West, determining social organization in such a way as to banish women from a stranger's gaze. Atatürk's westernizing reforms in the 1920s posed a challenge to *mahrem*, in that women were prominent and 'visible' in the founding of the new republic. The secularization of the education system also had implications for veiling, which has become contentious again since the revival of Islamism in the 1980s.[38]

When Özdamar's protagonist presents herself to Ibni Abdullah it is with a gesture of traditional submission to the teacher's will, as invoked by three Turkish expressions: 'eti senin, kemiği benim' ('his/her flesh is yours, the bones are mine'), 'dayak cennetten çıkmadır' ('spanking hails from heaven'), and 'hocanın vurduğu yerde gül biter' ('roses bloom where the teacher touches'). Thus respect for the disciplining power of the *hodca* (teacher/priest) mingles with Ibni Abdullah's sensual appeal: 'Seine Hand roch nach Rosen. Ich lief hinter diesem Duft.'[39] Whilst he offers her friendship as well as tuition, he is clearly disturbed by her physical presence. As she copies the Arabic letters he stares at her exposed wrists: 'Ibni Abdullahs Gesicht sah wie ein zorniger Buchstabe aus, der seine eine Augenbraue hochgezogen hatte.'[40] His face embodies the discrepancy between the outrage of the script and his desire for her body. It is only after falling in love with him that the protagonist becomes acutely aware of her difference in Berlin, and longs for integration into the Muslim Arabic community: 'Ich ging den arabischen Frauen mit Kopftüchern hinterher, ihre schwangeren Töchter neben ihnen, ich will unter ihre Röcke gehen, ganz klein sein, ich will ihre Tochter sein in Neukölln.'[41]

When Ibni Abdullah returns from a visit home to see his mother the protagonist is conscious of her female modesty, sitting personified in the room with them in a hermetically sealed Islamic world: 'Er, ich

[38] For detail on the complexities of veiling see Ruth Mandel, 'Turkish Headscarves and the "Foreigner Problem": Constructing Difference through Emblems of Identity', *New German Critique*, 46 (1989), 27–46.

[39] 'His hand smelled of roses. I followed this scent' (*M* 13).

[40] 'Ibni Abdullah's face looked like an angry letter which had raised its one eyebrow' (*M* 17).

[41] 'I walked behind the Arabic women with headscarves, their pregnant daughters beside them, I want to walk under their skirts, be very small, I want to be their daughter in Neukölln' (*M* 19–20).

und die Scham sitzen in dem Schriftzimmer. Die Vorhänge zum grauen Hof sind zu.'[42] Once they have consummated their love he encloses her behind a curtain, the symbolic equivalent of veiling her from other men's eyes (*M* 23), and persists in urging her to cultivate the Islamic virtue of patience. He regards her almost as a votive object, to be contemplated to inspire him to prayer: 'Du, mein Rosenbaum im Garten des Gebetes.'[43] Even as she is tormented by her desire the mosque-like room makes her ashamed of her exposed hair and flesh: 'Ich schämte mich vor meinen offenen Haaren, vor meiner nackten Haut, ich dachte, alle Farben vom Schriftzimmer schreien auch aus Scham.'[44]

At the same time the text repeatedly challenges the gender dichotomy which Islam seeks to uphold. Ibni Abdullah lies next to the protagonist 'wie eine Mutter, die ihr Kind gut zugedeckt hat',[45] and appears to be both male and female as he sleeps (*M* 34). This could be taken to imply a platonic, asexual love, but inevitably it also disrupts gender identities. Similarly, the stories of their respective sexual initiation reverse the conventional gender definitions: she was active in seeking to lose her virginity, he the passive victim of a voracious older woman (a story echoing that of Yusuf and Zeliha). This could also be seen as a play on the stereotype of the sexually predatory oriental woman. But such cultural stereotypes would seem to be invoked only to undermine them. In a humorous exchange of reproaches each accuses the other of being 'sehr deutsch' ('very German'), by which she means cold and formal (*M* 38) and he means sexually promiscuous (*M* 40). More importantly, there is a fundamental difference between Ibni Abdullah's notion of 'die heilige Liebe, reine Liebe' and her embodied sexual desire.[46] As a *hodca,* Ibni Abdullah is dedicated to a life of the mind and soul; indeed, his livelihood depends on his ability to attract students of the Koran. His sexual involvement with the protagonist becomes incompatible with his intellectual discipline: 'Mein Körper ist verrückt geworden, wenn du weiter in mich kommst, spätestens in einem Monat verliere ich meine Arbeit, ich bin ein armer Mann.'[47] It is clearly not only his religious belief—which would impose no such restrictions on his sexual

[42] 'He, I, and shame are sitting in the script room. The curtains are drawn on the grey courtyard' (*M* 21).

[43] 'You, my rosebush in the garden of prayer' (*M* 28).

[44] 'I was ashamed of my loose hair, of my naked skin, I thought all the colours of the script room are also crying out in shame' (*M* 40).

[45] 'like a mother who has tucked up her child well' (*M* 31).

[46] 'holy love, pure love' (*M* 40).

[47] 'My body has gone mad, if you come further into me, in a month at the most I will lose my work, I am a poor man' (*M* 40).

activity—but his material livelihood which is at stake. He leaves her alone more and more as her presence excites his body to the detriment of his work.

Even as the protagonist longs to be with him in his homeland, her fantasies cut to the very heart of Muslim *mahrem*, as she imagines herself veiled, but half dressed as a man, making love with him on the prayer mats of a mosque, and knowing that she will bear the guilt (*M* 20). He is explicitly associated with Muhammad, with sunlight shining from his face, but the passage is also overtly erotic, as she prays to him to descend from his spiritual home: 'Sehr hoch Fliegender, setz dich nieder vor meiner Tür auf meine Erde, wo du ruhen kannst, sind meine Augenpupillen, meine Tränen sollen dein Trinkwasser sein.'[48] Thirst is a frequent metaphor for desire, particularly when Ibni Abdullah can no longer resist his pupil's charms (*M* 22), and in the fantasies of the protagonist she is a sea bringing refreshment to a parched seabed (*M* 24). But when she begins to initiate sex he is disturbed by his own lack of control, and he has to leave her: 'Deine Anwesenheit regt mich so auf, ich kann nicht im Zimmer bleiben.'[49] When he pleads with her for a 'spiritual' love she counters with: 'Wenn die Körper sich vergessen, vergessen die Seelen sich nicht? . . . Wie soll ich mit einem schweigenden Körper laufen?'[50] After the protagonist leaves his room for the last time, unable to bear sexual rejection, she seeks out the greatest possible discomfort in order to kill off the bodily presence of her lover within her. While the conflation of sacred and profane love and the profusion of natural and elemental imagery in the text can be attributed to an oral Turkish folk tradition preserving traces of Ottoman culture, there are striking similarities between Özdamar's representation of embodied female subjectivity and a dynamic, material world and the materialist concerns of recent feminist thought. If meaning emerges at the level of the body then there can be no false universalism accorded to reason and thought, which is always already marked by sexual difference. And if human being is viewed as a mode of nature, not radically opposed to the material world, different forms of sociability may become possible, not based on the binary conceptions of self and other which dominate western cultures.

[48] 'You who fly very high, sit down on my earth before my door, where you can rest are the pupils of my eyes, my tears shall be your drinking water' (*M* 20).

[49] 'Your presence excites me so much, I cannot stay in the room' (*M* 38).

[50] 'If bodies forget each other, do not the souls forget each other also? . . . How am I to walk with a silent body?' (*M* 41).

'Islam with a Turkish accent'

The question remains as to whether the outcome of 'Großvater Zunge' is a successful piecing together of the protagonist's ethnic and linguistic roots (as suggested by several critics) or whether it resists such a conciliatory reading. With its depiction of a tense and fraught cultural encounter between traditional Islamic values and modern, secular identity, does it not construct a Turkish subject who has become irrevocably hybridized in the German diaspora? Like the protagonist, Ibni Abdullah is a displaced person; both have lost loved ones at the hands of military regimes and appreciate the relative political stability of western Europe. But whereas he harbours hopes for a harmonious pan-Islamic world order, she is sceptical, both of the religious way of life and of the 'freedoms' afforded by western capitalist democracy. Her experience of student politics in West Berlin and of radical theatre in the East has irreversibly estranged her from her Turkish roots. But these roots are themselves internally fractured; as a metropolitan intellectual brought up in a traditional Muslim society she embodies the contradictions of Turkish modernity.

Furthermore, the Arabic Islamic culture to which she seeks to return is itself problematic, because not identical with the reality of Islam in the Ottoman Empire. Stuart Hall writes of the dialogue with 'Africa' which has become a myth of lost origin for the British-Caribbean diaspora, as a dialogue which is 'always already fused, syncretized, with other cultural elements'.[51] This could be said also of Ottoman Islam, which retained elements of the shamanism of the nomadic Turkic tribes of Anatolia. It is true also of the Ottoman language, which was itself a hybrid of Turkish with Arabic and Persian loanwords and constructions. In a certain sense, then, we may speak of a colonial relationship on two fronts: that of western economic imperialism in the twentieth century on the one hand and that of the religious dominance of Sunni Islam throughout the Ottoman Empire on the other.

Post-colonial theory is interested in highlighting the dialogue of dominance and resistance, the imperfect transmission of cultural values from one culture to another. This is what complicates the protagonist's attempt to restore a link between the language of her grandparents' generation and that of her own by learning Arabic from an Arab. She compiles lists of words shared by Turkish and Arabic, for which

[51] Hall, 'Cultural Identity and Diaspora', in Patrick Williams and Laura Chrisman (eds.), *Colonial Discourse and Postcolonial Theory* (New York/London: Harvester Wheatsheaf, 1994), 392–403 (400).

there is often a modern Turkish equivalent, as for 'mazi' ('the past'), which coexists with Turkish 'geçmiş', and 'sine' ('breast'), which has the Turkish synonym 'göğüs'. When the Latin alphabet was introduced, instead of simply transcribing Ottoman Turkish words in the new alphabet, they were adapted to the sounds of spoken Turkish. Thus when the protagonist pronounces Arabic words Ibni Abdullah remarks: 'Es hört sich ein klein bißchen anders an', to which she replies: 'Bis diese Wörter aus deinem Land aufgestanden und zu meinem Land gelaufen sind, haben sie sich unterwegs etwas geändert.'[52] The Turkish language has eight vowels, whereas Arabic has only three, which explains why the word pronounced 'sabr' ('patience') in Arabic is 'sabír' in Turkish. This is the 'feminine virtue' on which both the protagonist's grandfather and Ibni Abdullah insist, in accordance with their ideal of the submissive Muslim woman. The linguistic slippage which occurs between the languages implies also a different interpretation of Islamic values in the two cultures.

Orthodox Sunni Islam was not imported wholesale into Anatolia, but customized and popularized into a folk religion by the Turkic tribes who migrated westwards from Mongolia in the ninth and tenth centuries and were gradually converted to Islam by the Arabs they encountered. The Turkoman people who settled in Anatolia remained heterodox in belief, as Azade Seyhan has noted in relation to *Das Leben ist eine Karawanserei*:

> **One of the most insightful instances of Özdamar's narrative is her portrayal of Islam with a Turkish accent and of Islamic customs in Turkish costumes. A nomadic people of the Central Asian steppes, the pre-Islamic Turks practiced various shamanistic religions. Furthermore, their social structure was not patriarchal by any measure. Orthodox Islamic practice could never be properly hooked up with this nomadic history . . .**[53]

This is seen in the 'parallel texts' which juxtapose Koranic verses with Turkish folk song in the course of the protagonist's tuition. Passages from the Koran are interspersed with poetic texts which are like the voice of a collective unconscious disrupting the symbolic order of Islam. When the Koran speaks of Allah's judgemental wrath, her inner voice speaks of his creative goodness (*M* 23–4); when the Koran speaks of the endless damnation of sinners, the folk song in her head speaks of the endlessness of desire (*M* 31). The juxtaposition suggests a dialogue

[52] 'It sounds a tiny bit different'; 'Since these words stood up in your country and walked to mine, they have changed somewhat on the way' (*M* 27).

[53] Seyhan, 'Lost in Translation: Re-Membering the Mother Tongue in Emine Sevgi Özdamar's *Das Leben ist eine Karawanserei*', *German Quarterly*, 69 (1996), 414–26 (422).

between the dominating power of Sunni Islam and the resistance to its hegemonic claims in the Ottoman Empire, where heterodox sects coexisted. For Homi K. Bhabha such moments of disparity between colonizer and colonized are moments of disruption which may give rise to resistant post-colonial identities. A different, but related, phenomenon which can be observed in the text is the sense of temporal disjunction which Bhabha designates 'the signifying time-lag of cultural difference' or the sense of 'belatedness' that often accompanies minority or diasporic consciousness.[54] Özdamar herself has expressed the experience of cultural difference in terms of temporality, overtly opposing to the acceleration of western modernity the leisurely pace of her narratives. The very location of 'Großvater Zunge', set in the divided Berlin, symbolizes the incommensurability of cultures. When the protagonist passes from one Berlin reality to the other, she notes with surprise: 'Ah, hier hat es auch geregnet.'[55] This unexpected sameness within difference underlines the complexity of the East–West divide in Özdamar's writing.

Conclusion

The quest to rediscover the childhood of Turkish in the vocabulary it still shares with Arabic does, undoubtedly, restore a sense of cultural continuity to the protagonist of Özdamar's tale. But the text also invites us to question the possibility of return to an originary self, the love story revealing tensions between westernized femininity and Islam on the one hand and between different interpretations of Islam on the other. Ibni Abdullah's desire for a spiritual love conflicts with the protagonist's poetic folk religion which resists the separation of body and mind. The importance to the protagonist of embodied subjectivity is also in some part the product of Özdamar's professional identity as an actress. She has spoken in an interview of the performative aspect of language as a key factor in her decision to write in German: 'You must remember that my first encounter with German was via the theatre. I experienced the language as it were bodily, either by speaking lines myself or hearing them from the bodies of fellow actors. You could almost say that words

[54] Bhabha, '"Race", Time and the Revision of Modernity', in Bhabha, *The Location of Culture* (London: Routledge, 1994), 236–56 (237).

[55] 'Oh, it has rained here too' (*M* 16). In *Seltsame Sterne starren zur Erde* there are beautiful evocations of the time lag between East and West Berlin, which would explain the protagonist's surprise at this simultaneity.

themselves have bodies, and when they are spoken on stage they are especially beautiful.'[56] In addition to the somatic relationship with language implied here, there is also the suggestion that taking on a new language is akin to playing a new role, assuming a new identity. Thus, although constrained to communicate in German, in their reiterated exchange of proverbs regarding the proximity of death Ibni Abdullah and the protagonist perform a common 'oriental' identity as the basis of their relationship (*M* 14). In the view of post-structuralist feminist theorist Judith Butler this would beg the question as to whether *all* identity is performance and all categories of identity are the results thereof: 'There is no gender identity behind the expressions of gender; that identity is performatively constituted by the very "expressions" that are said to be its results.'[57] It is perhaps such an awareness of the instability of identity which inspires the protagonist to seek a sense of permanence and belonging in the Arabic script in the first place. But her encounter with Ibni Abdullah makes her suddenly self-conscious of 'aping' German culture, and prompts her to ask passers-by: 'Meine Herren, spielt in meinem Gesicht ein Affe?'[58] This evokes Homi K. Bhabha's positive re-evaluation of colonial mimicry, not as unconscious adaptation but as a potentially disruptive form of imitation which is at the same time a mockery of and a threat to the dominant culture.

More insistent than the imagery of aping in the stories, however, is that of the bird, that figure of boundary crossings and migration. In the poetic mantra which recurs twice in the story the bird embodies love: 'Die Liebe ist ein leichter Vogel, er setzt sich leicht irgendwo hin, aber steht schwer auf.'[59] Birds also signify freedom from love, as the protagonist prays for the wings of a bird to escape the agony of unrequited passion (*M* 34). Then again they signify vulnerability, in Ibni Abdullah's epithet, 'Meine Schöne mit der Ferse der Taube'[60] and in the way he interpellates her as his fledgling pupil: 'Ich war wie ein neugeborener nasser Vogel, der sehr große Geduld haben muß.'[61] However, she is also a bird of passage who is at home in transit, on the highways, and in the

[56] Horrocks and Kolinsky (eds.), *Turkish Culture in German Society Today*, 47.

[57] Butler, *Gender Trouble: Feminism and the Subversion of Identity* (London: Routledge, 1990), 25.

[58] 'Gentlemen, is there an ape playing in my face?' (*M* 19). For further discussion of this image see Claudia Breger, '"Meine Herren, spielt in meinem Gesicht ein Affe"?: Strategien der Mimikry in Texten von Emine Sevgi Özdamar und Yoko Tawada', in Cathy S. Gelbin, Kader Konuk, and Peggy Piesche (eds.), *AufBrüche: Kulturelle Produktionen von Migrantinnen, Schwarzen und jüdischen Frauen in Deutschland* (Königstein/Taunus: Ulrike Helmer Verlag, 1999), 30–59.

[59] 'Love is a light bird, it sits down easily no matter where, but gets up again with difficulty' (*M* 34, 38).

[60] 'My beauty with a dove's heel' (*M* 31).

[61] 'I was like a newborn wet bird which has to be very patient' (*M* 25).

anonymous city-limits (*M* 25). It is significant that her final gesture of defiance is to throw the Arabic scripts on to the motorway, that symbol of modernity and mobility. At the end of the story the protagonist might be considered, in Rosi Braidotti's terms, a 'nomadic polyglot', her aesthetic style 'based on compassion for the incongruities, the repetitions, the arbitrariness of the languages s/he deals with'.[62] She designates herself a 'Wörtersammlerin' ('a collector of words', *M* 46), and her trilingual lexicon affords her only momentary cultural proximity, not perfect translation. In the protagonist's encounter with a young woman mourning her lost love at the end of 'Großvater Zunge', the relation of German 'Ruh' ('peace') to Turkish/Arabic 'ruh' ('soul') is not an exact correlation, merely a semantic familiarity. This signals that the cultural identity she had sought in the Arabic language is multilayered and fractured. Beyond the cultural rift brought about by Atatürk's secular republic there is a history of the incomplete imposition of a monolithic religion on to the shamanistic beliefs of the Turkic tribes, and of a language which accommodated and adapted to foreign influences. Hence, the story is not one of return to an intact cultural tradition, but of recognition that Turkish identity is an accretion of layers of cultural history, each betraying traces of the last. What might at first have appeared a reactionary step, a return to patriarchally defined femininity, represents a challenge to that tradition, and an assertion of identity as culturally hybrid and unstable, but at the same time historically located, embodied, and gendered.

[62] Braidotti, *Nomadic Subjects: Embodiment and Sexual Difference in Contemporary Feminist Theory* (New York: Columbia University Press, 1994), 15.

Chronology

1918	The First World War ends with the defeat of Germany and the collapse of the Ottoman Empire. Women in Austria and Germany granted the right to vote.
1919	The Weimar Republic founded in Germany. Death of Rosa Luxemburg.
1923	The Turkish Republic founded by Mustapha Kemal 'Atatürk'.
1926	Ingeborg Bachmann born in Klagenfurt, Austria.
1929	Christa Wolf born in Landsberg/Warthe, Poland. Women in Romania granted the right to vote.
1933	Adolf Hitler's *Machtergreifung* (seizure of power) in Germany heralds the beginning of the National Socialist era, which leads to the Second World War and the Holocaust/Shoah.
1934	Women in Turkey granted the right to vote.
1938	*Anschluß* (annexation of Austria by Germany).
1939	Start of the Second World War.
1942	Anne Duden born in Oldenburg.
1945	End of the Second World War. Occupation of Germany and Austria by the allied powers. Atomic bomb dropped on the Japanese town of Hiroshima. Christa Wolf moves to Mecklenburg, Germany.
1945–8	The cold war begins.
1946	Emine Sevgi Özdamar born in Malatya, Turkey. Elfriede Jelinek born in Mürzzuschlag, Austria.
1948	Berlin airlift.
1949	Two German states founded, the Federal Republic of Germany in the West and the German Democratic Republic in the East.
1952	Bachmann, Paul Celan, and Ilse Aichinger read at the Niendorf meeting of the *Gruppe 47*.
1953	Herta Müller born in Nitzkydorf, Romania. Duden's family leave the GDR for the FRG and settle in Oldenburg. The FRG starts to recruit *Gastarbeiter* (guest-workers).
1955	Austrian independence.
1960	First military coup in Turkey.
1961	Building of the Berlin Wall. The FRG starts to recruit *Gastarbeiter* from Turkey.

1963	John F. Kennedy, President of the USA, visits Berlin.
1965	Özdamar first comes to Berlin as a factory worker.
1966	Start of the Ceauşescu regime in Romania.
1967	Özdamar returns to Istanbul to train as an actress.
1968	The student movement in the FRG heralds the start of the second women's movement.
1971	Second military coup in Turkey. Alice Schwarzer's abortion campaign in the FRG.
1972	*Simultan* (Ingeborg Bachmann).
1973	Death of Bachmann. The FRG stops the recruitment of *Gastarbeiter*.
1975	*Die Liebhaberinnen* (Elfriede Jelinek).
1976	Özdamar takes up permanent residence in Germany.
1978	Duden moves to London.
1980	Third military coup in Turkey.
1982	*Übergang* (Anne Duden).
1983	*Kassandra* and *Voraussetzungen einer Erzählung: Kassandra* (Christa Wolf).
1987	Müller leaves Romania for West Germany.
1989	*Reisende auf einem Bein* (Herta Müller). The *Wende* (turning point): fall of the Berlin Wall; collapse of the GDR state. Fall of the Ceauşescu regime in Romania; death of Nicolai and Elena Ceauşescu. Effective end of the cold war.
1990	*Mutterzunge* (Emine Sevgi Özdamar). Reunification of Germany (3 October). The *Literaturstreit* (literary dispute) sparked off by the publication of Wolf's *Was bleibt*.
1991	Jelinek leaves the *Kommunistische Partei Österreichs* (Austrian Communist Party).
1998	Jelinek bans her plays from being performed in Austria in protest at the election of a government including Jörg Haider's *Freiheitliche Partei Österreichs* (Austrian Freedom Party).
2003	Germany refuses to support US and British action in the Second Gulf War.

Glossary

Note
The principal thinker associated with a particular theory or the originator of a term in its current use is given in parentheses.

Abject (Julia Kristeva): that which must be expelled and kept at bay in order for the subject successfully to gain and maintain its integrity. For Kristeva this explains the disgust and fear with which such things as body fluids and excreta are viewed. The abject also preserves an archaic memory of birth, that first and violent separation.

Agency: the ability to act as a subject. Second-wave feminism diagnosed that under patriarchy women are denied agency and it remains part of the aim of Enlightenment feminism to overcome this.

Autofiction: a mode of fiction which reworks elements of the author's biography in such a way that these are still visible. The term is employed by Herta Müller to characterize her fiction.

Body/Embodiment/Corporeal subject: see **New materialists**.

Deconstruction (Jacques Derrida): a form of textual analysis which undoes the hierarchical binary oppositions on which texts depend for meaning; closely associated with post-structuralism. Of interest to post-structuralist feminism are Derrida's attacks on the 'metaphysics of presence' and 'logocentrism' of western philosophy, and his proposal that meaning is never present in the sign but is produced within language by a constant process of *différance*.

Desire (Jacques Lacan): a longing that persists after needs have been satisfied, which is integral to the subject and signifies the split at its heart. Unlike Sigmund Freud's 'libido', desire only emerges on entry into the symbolic order and subjection to its law. Lacan saw male desire as wholly determined by phallic function, male pleasure being limited to the residual *jouissance* allowed within language. Female desire, in contrast, is not entirely subject to the symbolic order, leaving open the possibility of an 'Other *jouissance*' beyond the boundaries set by language.

Différance (Jacques Derrida): the operation of language by means of difference and deferral; signs have meaning only in relation to others in the system, but also their meaning is never fixed, each signifier referring to a potentially infinite set of signifieds and other signifiers. It is spelled thus to emphasize the written, rather than the spoken, aspect of language.

Difference: a key term for post-structuralist feminism. While second-wave feminism sought equality for women, post-structuralist feminism is alive not just to sexual difference but also to multiple differences between women, for example of class, race, and ethnicity, and to post-structuralist theories of the production of meaning in language through *différance*.

Discourse (Michel Foucault): a group of statements that together form an institutionalized body of knowledge, such as medicine or natural history, through which relations of force and power are exercised. The existence of discursive practices in societies creates the subject positions occupied by individuals.

Ecriture féminine (Hélène Cixous): an experimental kind of writing which attempts to inscribe the femininity which has been repressed and marginalized in patriarchal culture. It has been identified in writing by male authors of the European avant-garde, but because of its association with the body, in particular the maternal body, it is open to the charge of essentialism.

Ego/Ego ideal/Ideal ego (Jacques Lacan): Freud defined the ego as the conscious part of the subject, and attributed agency to it. For Lacan it is an object, and a narcissistic attachment to false images, not to be reinforced in analysis. The child's ego is formed first from identification with an ideal ego (in the mirror stage), which is the promise of future unity and the source of all subsequent identifications. For Lacan the ego ideal is a symbolic introjection, allowing the subject to look at itself from the point of view of the perfection for which it strives (this can be compared with the Freudian superego).

Enlightenment: the movement of intellectual liberalization in Europe which occurred in the seventeenth and eighteenth centuries. Immanuel Kant defined the Enlightenment as man's (*sic*) emancipation from a self-incurred immaturity. It sought to free mankind from all forms of traditional authority, superstition, and injustice, and placed its faith in man's reason. Both feminism and Marxism are latter-day Enlightenment discourses and attempt to continue its unfinished business. However, the Enlightenment has been critiqued by Max Horkheimer and Theodor Adorno, who argued that it has led to man's domination of nature and to a widespread alienation, by postmodernists, such as Jean-François Lyotard, who see it as an outdated grand narrative, and by post-structuralist feminists, such as Luce Irigaray, who see it as a masculine universalist discourse.

Epistemology: the branch of philosophy which deals with the nature of knowledge (as opposed to ontology, which is concerned with the nature of things). Feminist epistemology, often influenced by Michel Foucault's thesis that any epistemology is also a form of power, challenges the supposed value-neutrality of knowledge. It argues that women's perspectives may produce a different knowledge, though this is in turn open to critique from a post-structuralist perspective for simply giving a new foundational base to knowledge. Christine Battersby detects in much feminist theory an 'epistemological bias' which militates against female agency, the product of the influence of 'the two Jacques', Derrida and Lacan, who both place the feminine outside the bounds of the knowable.

Essentialism: the belief that things and people have a true and permanent nature. Second-wave feminism either rejected essentialism, arguing that what were seen as 'natural' or 'innate' differences between men and women were the result of culture, not nature, or reinforced it, attempting to validate women's experience and sexual difference. The French feminist thought of Hélène Cixous, Luce Irigaray, and Julia Kristeva sometimes draws on essentialism in its attempt to assert a legitimate place for the feminine in culture. Gayatri Spivak also called at one point for a 'strategic essentialism' to be employed so that women could challenge hegemonic discourses. More recently, Christine Battersby has argued that a notion of female essence (though, crucially, a fluid and historically changing one) is necessary to theorize the conflict between the real (experience) and the discursive (which mediates experience).

Exchange of women: the theory developed by Gayle Rubin and Luce Irigaray, building on the work of anthropologist Claude Lévi-Strauss, that, socially and symbolically, the relations between men which constitute patriarchy are sustained by treating women as commodities, whose value derives from their place in an economy based on exchange.

Frankfurt School: a group of Marxist thinkers, including Theodor Adorno, Max Horkheimer, and Herbert Marcuse, who were associated with the Institute for Social Research in Frankfurt and then went into exile during the Second World War, before returning to the FRG in the 1950s. Their work, often collectively referred to as Critical Theory, has been influential on post-war, and particularly post-1968, intellectual life in Germany and Austria.

Heimat: homeland, or roots. The concept has long been central to Austrian and German definitions of identity.

Heteroglossia/Dialogism (Mikhail Bakhtin): the existence of conflicting, intersecting discourses in a text. A dialogic as opposed to a monologic text reflects a multiplicity of social voices without privileging any one of them.

Historical materialism: Marxist philosophy; a teleological form of thought which sees human history as moving forward dialectically in a series of stages to a point where capitalism will inevitably be overthrown and replaced with a socialist society. Eastern-bloc societies were founded on a version of historical materialism called Marxist-Leninism.

Holocaust/Shoah: the systematic persecution and murder of approximately six million Jews by the National Socialist regime in Germany and its collaborators between 1941 and 1945. Others targeted included Roma, Poles, the handicapped, homosexuals, and political and religious dissidents. The Hebrew word for extermination, *Shoah*, is often preferred to the Greek 'Holocaust', which means 'to be consumed by fire' and has religious connotations.

Hybridity (Mikhail Bakhtin): the coexistence of two linguistic registers, or voices, in the same utterance.

Hybridity (Homi Bhabha): term derived from nineteenth-century biology, and used in racial theory to condemn miscegenation. It has been re-evaluated positively by Bhabha to mean the margin where cultural differences come into contact and conflict. Post-colonial and migrant identities are, for Bhabha, based on hybridity, and offer a release from singular identities based on class, nationality, or gender into an in-between cultural space.

Hylomorphism: the view, deriving from Immanuel Kant and pervasive in western culture, that active form imposes itself on inert matter. Christine Battersby opposes to this top-down view a theory of mobile identities emerging from patterns of becoming; embodied selves which persist through material mutation, rather than minds giving meaning to brute matter.

Hysteria (Sigmund Freud): a form of neurosis, traditionally diagnosed only in women. For Freud hysteria was an indicator of the inadequacy of gender identity to support the differences between the sexes. For Jacques Lacan it is the hysteric who has insight into the fundamental lack in desire and knowledge, revealing the incapacity of any human subject to satisfy the ideals of symbolic identifications.

Ideology: a set of beliefs belonging to a class or interest group; often used pejoratively to designate false consciousness. In Marxist discourse the term denotes the world-view of the capitalist class, which obscures the real relations of production, which are based on exploitation. For Louis Althusser ideology 'represents the imaginary relationships of individuals to their real conditions of existence'.

Imaginary (Jacques Lacan): the pre-Oedipal realm where the infant is at one with its mother before entry into the symbolic; a blissful state associated with completion and plenitude. It corresponds roughly to Julia Kristeva's notion of the semiotic, which refers to the rhythmic, tonal, and physical aspects of language, and is associated with the prelinguistic child's connection to the maternal body. The imaginary is also part of Lacan's structural model of subjectivity, along with the symbolic and the real.

Instrumental reason (Max Horkheimer and Theodor Adorno): reason which has been pursued to excess and becomes in itself totalitarian, governed by the logic of means and ends and seeking domination. A key component of Horkheimer and Adorno's critique of the Enlightenment.

Interpellation (Louis Althusser): the act of being 'hailed' by an 'ideological state apparatus', such as the media or the family, in responding to which a subject comes into being. Thus, according to Althusser, subjects are the product of ideology and cannot exist outside it. For Judith Butler this explains the attachment of subjects to power structures which enslave them, though she argues that resistance is possible.

Intertextuality (Julia Kristeva): the multiple and complex relationships between a text and other texts, which it may, for example, refer to, quote from, imitate, or parody.

Jouissance (Jacques Lacan): a primordial, overwhelming sense of pleasure and pain experienced as the subject comes into being as a result of the traumatic encounter with the Other's desire. *Jouissance* must be replaced by desire for sustainable subject-formation. Something of the *jouissance* lost on entry to the symbolic is refound in language, and in some readings of Lacan and in Luce Irigaray the female subject has access to another form of *jouissance* which is unsymbolizable.

Law of the father (Jacques Lacan): the breaking of the mother/child dyad which signals entry into the symbolic order. Represented by the phallus, it regulates sexual relations, prohibiting incest, thereby replacing the state of nature with that of human culture. It gives rise to desire even as it imposes limits on it.

Logocentrism (Jacques Derrida): a characteristic of systems of thought which are based on the assumptions that language can deliver extralinguistic truth and that meaning is independent of the language which produces it.

Marxist-feminism: a revisionist trend which seeks to address the blind spots in Marxist theory concerning gender and sexuality and reconcile the class-based analysis of Marxism with the gender-based approach of feminism.

Masquerade: see **Mimicry**.

Mimicry (Luce Irigaray): a strategy for women. By mimicking the feminine style assigned her by the symbolic order a woman can counter its hegemonic claims. Judith Butler advocates a politics of the masquerade, through which a woman stages gender as a performance, revealing the constructedness of identity. See also **Performativity**. Homi Bhabha also uses mimicry in the context of colonial identities whose subversive potential lies in their imperfect reproduction of the colonizer's culture.

Mirror stage (Jacques Lacan): denotes two things. (1) The stage in the development of the subject when the child first recognizes its specular image and identifies with the illusion of coherence and control which it presents. It is the beginning of the process of misrecognition which founds subjectivity. (2) As a permanent structure of the psyche it inaugurates the imaginary, which sustains the subject's libidinal relationship with its body image.

Modernism: a wide-ranging artistic and literary movement in the early part of the twentieth century. Influenced by psychoanalysis and the crisis of the First World War, writers and artists employed avant-garde techniques to challenge the conventions of nineteenth-century realism and explore the alienation of modern life.

Mythologies (Roland Barthes): a volume of essays (1959) in which Barthes playfully examines the ideological meanings encoded in everyday cultural artefacts and reveals how they have come to appear natural; a parallel project to Bertolt Brecht's use of alienation techniques in the theatre, though less straightforwardly political in intent.

Myths: traditional belief systems of many societies, widely thought to have been superseded in their truth claims by science and philosophy but resurrected periodically at times of social crisis because of their ability to address fundamental issues. Giani Vattimo discerns three contemporary attitudes to myth: archaism, which seeks a return to myth; cultural relativism, which does not privilege either mythic or scientific knowledge; and limited rationality, which reads myth as a specific, narrative form of discourse. Myths work with paradigms, which make them partly translatable across cultures, tend as narratives towards perfection, or closure, and speak of possible worlds. Many feminist thinkers and writers, such as Adriana Cavarero, Hélène Cixous, and Christa Wolf, have attempted to rewrite myths from a female perspective.

Negative dialectics (Theodor Adorno): a dialectical style of argument which acknowledges unavoidable tensions between polar opposites (for example, between the universal and the particular) while refusing to affirm any underlying unity or synthesis of the opposites, although Adorno always held open the possibility of their reconciliation.

New materialists: those theorists, such as Christine Battersby, Rosi Braidotti, Adriana Cavarero, Moira Gatens, Elizabeth Grosz, and Genevieve Lloyd, who attempt to recoup the body, traditionally seen as inferior to the mind, as a source of signification in its own right, and to undo the mind/matter hierarchy. They propose a corporeal subject existing on a plane of immanence, rather than a transcendent subject for whom the body is unimportant/accidental.

Nomadic subject (Rosi Braidotti): a subject in transit which resists assimilation into dominant ways of representing the self and is propelled forward by desire. The nomadic subject is embodied and polyglot and seeks new forms of interrelatedness.

Patriarchy: any social, political, or symbolic system in which women's interests are subordinated to those of men. The term is associated more with second-wave feminists than with post-structuralist feminists, who are wary of its universalizing pretensions and the dangers it brings of ahistorical thinking.

Performativity (Judith Butler): the theory that aspects of subjectivity (such as gender) are continually performed, and that any inner depth or essence to identity is the product of an illusion.

Phallus (Jacques Lacan): see **Law of the father**.

Post-colonial theory: a body of theory associated with, among others, Edward Said, Gayatri Spivak, and Homi Bhabha which examines the lasting influence of imperialism and colonialism on the identities, societies, and literature of the colonized and the colonizers.

Postmodernism: a new phase of modernism in the second half of the twentieth century, reflecting the age of the mass media, or that which breaks with it, opposing modernism's attachment to high culture, aesthetic innovation, and search for deep meaning. Postmodernism rejects all master narratives in favour of playful pastiche, surface images, and fragmentation.

Post-structuralism: a broad trend in critical thinking, drawing on deconstruction, psychoanalysis, Marxism, and the discourse theory of Michel Foucault, which refuses the validity of any universal foundations to knowledge and emphasizes the instability and contingency of meanings and of the subject.

Psychoanalysis: a discourse deriving from the work of Sigmund Freud and Jacques Lacan which seeks to explain the workings of the mind and the acquisition of subjectivity; also a clinical practice. Some feminists have criticized the role of psychoanalysis in regulating women's sexuality and critiqued the biologism inherent in Freud's work and the negative place assigned to the feminine by Lacan; others have stressed the revolutionary potential of a theory which accords importance to unconscious processes and shows subjectivity as constructed rather than given.

Real (Jacques Lacan): Lacan's third order, apart from the imaginary and the symbolic. The real consists of that which resists symbolization and conceptualization. Like Immanuel Kant's noumenal being, it is the unknowable being-in-itself of things.

Second women's movement: the women's movement that arose in Europe and the USA as a result of a general politicization at the time of the students' movement in 1968 (as opposed to the first women's movement around the turn of the twentieth century, which campaigned for women's suffrage). The second women's movement called for equality for women and campaigned on such issues as the right to abortion and equal pay.

Sex/gender distinction: the distinction, of great importance to the second women's movement, between biological sex and culturally constructed gender, often summed up in Simone de Beauvoir's pithy statement: 'One is not born a woman, one becomes one.' Judith Butler, however, collapses the distinction between sex and gender, insisting that there is only gender, even sex being discursively constructed. New-materialist feminism also questions the sex/gender distinction, but on the basis that it upholds the distinction between brute matter and representation.

Socialist realism: a prescriptive type of literature promoted by eastern-bloc states such as Romania and the GDR. Authors were required to depict the struggle for socialism in a positive light using techniques from nineteenth-century realism.

Subject: a way of conceptualizing a socialized human individual other than a small infant. Theorists of the subject, such as Louis Althusser and Jacques Lacan, tend to show the individual to be a product of impersonal processes or language, rather than a unified self in possession of a unique identity. The usefulness of the term lies in its ambiguity, as grammatically both passive and active: the subject is *subjected to* the forces which construct it, while also being *a subject which acts*. See also **New materialists, Nomadic subject, Unique existent**.

Symbolic order (Jacques Lacan): the order of culture and language which the individual, leaving behind the blissful imaginary realm of the mother–child bond, enters in order to become a subject, and which constitutes its subjectivity. The symbolic order is characterized by lack or loss and the distinction between self and other. Entry into the symbolic requires taking up a subject position in language which is governed by the law of the father, signified by the phallus. Woman, as associated with the imaginary figure of the mother, represents loss and lack, and cannot be represented in the symbolic. Feminist theorists have responded to this in different ways, by identifying the disruptive force of the feminine in language (Hélène Cixous) or by arguing for the construction of a female symbolic (Luce Irigaray).

Trauma: psychological shock resulting from an event experienced as so horrific that the mind cannot comprehend it. Symptoms include flashbacks and feelings of alienation, numbness, and detachment. Treatment may involve the writing of a trauma narrative; literature *of* trauma, by contrast, expresses the trauma through gaps and silences in the text without seeking to represent or master it.

Unique existent (Adriana Cavarero): individual subject, which is unique, embodied, exposed, and relational.

Further Reading

Introduction

For further surveys of women's writing in German apart from Weedon's see Jo Catling (ed.), *A History of Women's Writing in Germany, Austria and Switzerland* (Cambridge: Cambridge University Press, 2000); Hiltrud Gnüg and Renate Möhrmann, *Frauen Literatur Geschichte: Schreibende Frauen vom Mittelalter bis zur Gegenwart* (Frankfurt am Main: Suhrkamp, 2003); and Sigrid Weigel, *Die Stimme der Medusa: Schreibweisen in der Gegenwartsliteratur von Frauen* (Reinbek bei Hamburg: Rowohlt, 1989). Two useful reference sources are Friederike Eigler and Susanne Kord (eds.), *The Feminist Encyclopaedia of German Literature* (Westport, Conn.: Greenwood, 1997) and Elke P. Frederiksen and Elizabeth G. Ametsbichler (eds.), *Women Writers in German-Speaking Countries: A Bio-Bibliographical Critical Sourcebook* (Westport, Conn.: Greenwood, 1998). On the Frankfurt School see Andrew Arato and Eike Gebhardt (eds.), *Essential Frankfurt School Reader* (Oxford: Blackwell, 1978) and Paul Connerton, *The Tragedy of Enlightenment: An Essay on the Frankfurt School* (Cambridge: Cambridge University Press, 1980). Two recent texts by Jewish women writers are Esther Dischereit, *Joëmis Tisch: Eine jüdische Geschichte* (Frankfurt am Main: Suhrkamp, 1988) and Barbara Honigmann, *Roman von einem Kinde: Sechs Erzählungen* (Hamburg: Luchterhand, 1989). On women's writing in Switzerland see Christine Flitner, 'Women's Writing in German-Speaking Switzerland: Engaging with Tradition: Eveline Hasler and Gertrud Leutenegger', in Weedon (ed.), *Post-War Women's Writing in German: Feminist Critical Approaches* (Oxford: Berghahn, 1997), 305–25. Useful reference sources for critical theory are Sonya Andermahr, Terry Lovell, Carol Wolkowitz, *A Glossary of Feminist Theory* (London: Arnold, 2000); Chris Baldick, *The Concise Oxford Dictionary of Literary Terms* (Oxford: Oxford University Press, 2001); Dylan Evans, *An Introductory Dictionary of Lacanian Psychoanalysis* (London: Routledge, 1996); Sarah Gamble (ed.), *The Routledge Companion to Feminism and Postfeminism* (London: Routledge, 2001); Maggie Humm, *The Dictionary of Feminist Theory* (New York: Harvester Wheatsheaf, 1995); J. Laplanche, J. B. Pontalis, and D. Lagache, *The Language of Psychoanalysis* (London: Karnak, 1988); David Macey, *The Penguin Dictionary of Critical Theory* (London: Penguin, 2000); and Elizabeth Wright (ed.), *Feminism and Psychoanalysis: A Critical Dictionary* (Oxford: Blackwell, 1992).

Chapter 1

For general works see Monika Albrecht and Dirk Göttsche (eds.), *Bachmann-Handbuch: Leben—Werk—Wirkung* (Stuttgart/Weimar: Metzler, 2002); Ingvild

Folvord, *Sich ein Haus schreiben: Drei Texte aus Ingeborg Bachmanns Prosa* (Hannover/Laatzen: Wehrhahn, 2003). On *Simultan* see Bärbel Thau's *Gesellschaftsbild und Utopie im Spätwerk Ingeborg Bachmanns: Untersuchungen zum 'Todesarten-Zyklus' und zu 'Simultan'* (Frankfurt am Main: Lang, 1986) which draws on Hélène Cixous to analyse Bachmann's prose style. On Judith Butler, Sara Salih, *Judith Butler* (London/New York: Routlege, 2002) is a useful introduction to her thought. On Mikhail Bakhtin see Ken Hirschkop and David Shepherd (eds.), *Bakhtin and Cultural Theory* (Manchester: Manchester University Press, 1989). On Bakhtin and feminism see Dale Bauer, *Feminist Dialogics: A Theory of Failed Community* (Albany, NY: State University of New York Press, 1988); Dale Bauer and S. Jaret McKinstry (eds.), *Feminism, Bakhtin and the Dialogic* (New York: State University of New York Press, 1991); Wayne Booth, 'Freedom of Interpretation: Bakhtin and the Challenge of Feminist Criticism', in G. S. Morson (ed.), *Bakhtin: Essays and Dialogues on his Work* (Chicago, Ill: University of Chicago Press, 1986), 145–76; Karen Hohne and Helen Wussow (eds.), *A Dialogue of Voices: Feminist Literary Theory and Bakhtin* (Minneapolis, Minn.: University of Minnesota Press, 1994).

Chapter 2

On Austrian women's writing see Jacqueline Vansant, *Against the Horizon: Feminism and Postwar Austrian Women Writers* (New York: Greenwood, 1988). An excellent general article on *Die Liebhaberinnen* not already mentioned is Ilse Nagelschmidt, 'Vom Schreiben gegen das Ausgesetztsein: *Die Liebhaberinnen* von Elfriede Jelinek', *Diskussion Deutsch* (1993), 385–91. Jelinek's Marxist-feminism is also examined in Linda C. DeMeritt, 'A "Healthier Marriage": Elfriede Jelinek's Marxist Feminism in *Die Klavierspielerin* and *Lust*', in Jorun B. Johns and Katherine Arens (eds.), *Elfriede Jelinek: Framed by Language* (Riverside, Calif.: Ariadne, 1994) 107–28. Jelinek's reception abroad is treated in Daniela Bartens and Paul Pechmann (eds.), *Elfriede Jelinek: Die internationale Rezeption* (Graz: Droschl, 1997). A useful recent study of her prose work is Ute Schestag, *Sprachstil als Lebensform: Strukturuntersuchungen zur erzählenden Prosa Elfriede Jelineks* (Bielefeld: Aisthesis, 1999). On Jelinek and Austria see Pia Janke (ed.), *Die Nestbeschmutzerin: Jelinek und Österreich* (Salzburg: Jung und Jung, 2002). On the concept of *Heimat* see Elizabeth Boa and Rachel Palfreyman, *Heimat, A German Dream: Regional Loyalties and National Identity in German* (Oxford: Oxford University Press, 2000). For other humorous texts by women writers from the same period see e.g. Gisela Elsner, *Die Riesenzwerge* (Reinbek: Rowohlt, 1964); Irmtraud Morgner, *Leben und Abenteuer der Trobadora Beatriz nach Zeugnissen ihrer Spielfrau Laura* (Berlin: Aufbau, 1974); and Christa Reinig, *Entmannung: Die Geschichte Ottos und seiner vier Frauen* (Darmstadt: Luchterhand, 1977). Jelinek is still one of the only writers in German to publish regularly on her own website (see http://ourworld.compuserve.com/homepages/elfriede/ accessed May 2004).

Chapter 3

For a discussion of Duden and national identity see Stephanie Bird, *Women Writers and National Identity: Bachmann, Duden, Özdamar* (Cambridge: Cambridge University Press, 2003). On aesthetics see Rita Felski, 'Why Feminism Doesn't Need an Aesthetic (and Why it Can't Ignore Aesthetics)', in P. Z. Brand and C. Korsmeyer (eds.), *Feminism and Tradition in Aesthetics* (University Park, Penn.: Pennsylvania State University Press, 1995), 431–45, and Cornelia Klinger, 'Aesthetics', in Alison M. Jaggar and Iris Marion Young (eds.), *A Companion to Feminist Philosophy* (Oxford: Blackwell, 1998), 343–52. On Lacan see Jean-Michel Rabaté (ed.), *The Cambridge Companion to Lacan* (Cambridge: Cambridge University Press, 2003). For a more detailed discussion of the role of abjection in Duden's work see Margaret Littler, 'Trauma and Terrorism: The Problem of Violence in the Work of Anne Duden', in Heike Bartel and Elizabeth Boa (eds.), *Anne Duden: A Revolution of Words: Approaches to her Fiction, Poetry, and Essays* (Amsterdam: Rodopi, 2003), 43–61. This is the first collection of essays to appear on Duden's work, and includes three essays on the poem cycle *Steinschlag*. On the role of music in Duden's work see Suzanne Greuner, *Schmerzton Musik in der Schreibweise von Ingeborg Bachmann und Anne Duden* (Hamburg: Argument, 1990). Susanne Baackmann, *'Erklär mir Liebe': Weibliche Schreibweisen von Liebe in der deutschsprachigen Gegenwartsliteratur* (Hamburg: Argument, 1995) examines the treatment of love in texts by Bachmann, Duden, Unica Zürn, and Ulla Hahn. On Duden and Verena Stefan see Elsbeth Dangel, 'Übergang und Ankunft: Positionen neuer Frauenliteratur. Zu Anne Dudens *Übergang* und Verena Stefans *Wortgetreu ich träume*', *Jahrbuch für Internationale Germanistik*, 22/2 (1990), 80–94. Klaus Briegleb, 'Der Weg in die absolute Prosa: Peter Weiss und Anne Duden', in Klaus Briegleb and Sigrid Weigel (eds.), *Gegenwartsliteratur seit 1968* (Munich: Hanser, 1992), 140–50, and Timm Menke, 'Anne Dudens Erzählband *Übergang*: Zum Verhältnis von Angst und Postmoderne in der Literatur der achtziger Jahre', *Orbis Litterarum*, 41 (1986), 279–88, are both concerned with Duden's aesthetics. Andrea Allerkamp, *Die innere Kolonisierung: Bilder und Darstellungen des/der Anderen in deutschsprachigen, französischen, und afrikanischen Literatur des 20. Jahrhunderts* (Cologne: Böhlau, 1991) contains a section on *Übergang* (pp. 35–44).

Chapter 4

Kassandra can be a daunting text because of its density and range of reference. A number of study guides are available; for example, Ulrike E. Beiter, *Christa Wolf: 'Kassandra'* (Munich: Mentor, 1996); Rosemarie Nicolai, *Christa Wolf: 'Kassandra'*, 3rd edn. (Munich: Oldenbourg, 1995). General introductions to Wolf's work are: Gail Finney, *Christa Wolf* (New York: Twayne, 1999); Sonja Hilzinger, *Christa Wolf* (Stuttgart: Metzler, 1986); Therese Hörnigk, *Christa Wolf* (Göttingen: Steidl, 1989); Margit Resch, *Understanding Christa Wolf: Returning Home to a Foreign Land* (Columbia, SC: University of South Carolina Press, 1997). Wolf's most recent novel is *Leibhaftig* (Munich: Luchterhand, 2002). A comprehensive recent biography is Jörg Magenau, *Christa Wolf: Eine Biographie* (Berlin: Kindler, 2002). A standard work on GDR literature is Wolfgang Emmerich, *Kleine Literaturgeschichte der DDR* (Berlin: Aufbau, 2000). A significant contemporaneous GDR novel which deals with women and myth is Irmtraud Morgner, *Amanda: Ein Hexenroman* (Hamburg: Luchterhand, 1984). Virginia Woolf's essay *Three Guineas*, written just before the outbreak of the Second World War, raises similar questions about men and militarism, and what women can do to avert war (*A Room of One's Own, Three Guineas* (London: Penguin, 1993)). Marina Warner's *Managing Monsters: Six Myths of our Time* (London: Vintage, 1994) is a fascinating study of myth in the modern world.

Chapter 5

For background information on Romania see Martyn Rady, *Romania in Turmoil: A Contemporary History* (London: Tauris, 1992) and Dennis Deletant, *Ceauşescu and the 'Securitate': Coercion and Dissent in Romania, 1965–1989* (London: Hurst, 1995). Two useful recent general overviews of Müller's work are Norbert Otto Eke, '"Sein Leben machen | ist nicht, | sein Glück machen | mein Herr": Zum Verhältnis von Ästhetik und Politik in Herta Müllers Nachrichten aus Romänien', *Jahrbuch der Schillergesellschaft*, 41 (1997), 481–509, and Petra Günther, 'Kein Trost, nirgends: Zum Werk Herta Müllers', in Andreas Erb (ed.), *Baustelle Gegenwartsliteratur: Die neunziger Jahre* (Opladen: Westdeutscher Verlag, 1998), 154–66. The novels of Müller's former husband Richard Wagner, who left Romania with her, make an interesting comparison; see e.g. *Ausreiseantrag. Begrüßungsgeld: Erzählungen* (Berlin: Aufbau, 2002). Müller's 1994 novel *Herztier* is available in a prize-winning English translation by Michael Hofmann, *The Land of Green Plums* (London: Granta, 1998), and is usefully interpreted in Valentina Glajar, 'Banat-Swabian, Romanian, and German: Conflicting Identities in Herta Müller's *Herztier*', *Monatshefte*, 89/4 (1997), 521–40. Müller's collages can be viewed in *Der Teufel sitzt im Spiegel* (Berlin: Rotbuch, 1991), which also contains her main statements on aesthetics, and in *Der Wächter nimmt seinen Kamm* (Reinbek bei Hamburg: Rowohlt, 1993). Bibliographies on Müller can be found in Norbert Otto Eke (ed.), *Die erfundene Wahrnehmung: Annäherung an Herta Müller* (Paderborn: Igel, 1991); Brigid Haines (ed.), *Herta Müller* (Cardiff: Cardiff University Press, 1998); and in a special issue of *Text + Kritik*: *Herta Müller, Text + Kritik*, 155 (2002). A wide-ranging and illuminating interview is Beverley Driver Eddy, '"Die Schule der Angst". Gespräch mit Herta Müller, den 14 April 1998', *German Quarterly*, 72 (1999), 329–39. Rosi Braidotti's work on nomadism is continued in *Metamorphosis: Towards a Materialist Theory of Becoming* (Cambridge: Polity, 2002).

Chapter 6

For further discussion of *Mutterzunge* see Margaret Littler, 'Diasporic Identity in Emine Sevgi Özdamar's *Mutterzunge*', in Stuart Taberner and Frank Finlay (eds.), *Recasting German Identity: Culture, Politics and Literature in the Berlin Republic*

(Rochester, NY: Camden House, 2002), 219–34. Stephanie Bird's *Women Writers and National Identity: Bachmann, Duden, Özdamar* (Cambridge: Cambridge University Press, 2003) contains two chapters on Özdamar. See also Kader Konuk, *Identitäten im Prozeß: Literatur von Autorinnen aus und in der Türkei in deutscher, englischer und türkischer Sprache* (Essen: Die Blaue Eule, 2001). For more detail on Atatürk's reforms see Günsel Renda and Max C. Kortepeter (eds.), *The Transformation of Turkish Culture: The Atatürk Legacy* (Princeton, NJ: Kingston University Press, 1986); Andrew Finkel and Sirman Nükhet (eds.), *Turkish State, Turkish Society* (London: Routledge, 1990). Nicole Pope and Hugh Pope, *Turkey Unveiled: Atatürk and After* (London: John Murray, 1997) is a journalistic but approachable introduction to recent Turkish history. For more detail on the symbolic role of women in Islam see Nilüfer Göle, 'Islamism, Feminism and Post-Modernism: Women's Movements in Islamic Countries', *New Perspectives on Turkey*, 19 (1990), 53–70. Informative though this is, Göle's argument enlists postmodernism in a questionable way to represent religion in general and Islam in particular as the repressed 'other' of western Enlightenment. For detail on the impact of Atatürk's reforms on women see Çiğdem Balım-Harding, 'Representations of Turkish Women: Objects of Social Engineering or Individuals?', in Grace Jantzen (ed.), *Bulletin of the John Rylands University Library of Manchester: Representation, Gender and Experience*, 80/3 (1998), 107–27, and Tahire Kockturk, *A Matter of Honour: Experiences of Turkish Women Immigrants* (London/New Jersey: Zed Books, 1992). For an account of the early phase of *Gastarbeiterliteratur* see Helmut Kreuzer, 'Gastarbeiter-Literatur, Ausländer-Literatur, Migranten-Literatur? Zur Einführung', *LiLi: Zeitschrift für Literaturwissenschaft und Linguistik*, 14/56 (1984), 7–11, and Heidrun Suhr, 'Ausländerliteratur: Minority Literature in the Federal Republic of Germany', *New German Critique*, 46 (1989), 71–103. On post-colonial theory, and especially the question of language, see Gayatri Chakravorty Spivak, 'How to Read a Culturally Different Book', in Frances Barker, Peter Hulme and Margaret Iversen (eds.), *Colonial Discourse/Postcolonial Theory* (Manchester: Manchester University Press, 1994), 126–50. Two recent works on minority writing in German are Petra Fachinger, *Rewriting Germany from the Margins: 'Other' German Literature of the 1980s and 1990s* (Montreal/Kingston: McGill/Queens University Press, 2001) and Azade Seyhan, *Writing outside the Nation* (Princeton, NJ: Princeton University Press, 2001), which contains revised and expanded versions of some of the material by her quoted in this chapter.

Select Bibliography

Primary texts discussed

Bachmann, Ingeborg, *'Todesarten'-Projekt*, iv, ed. Monika Albrecht and Dirk Göttsche, under the direction of Robert Pichl (Munich: Piper, 1995), 57–471.

Duden, Anne, *Übergang* (Berlin: Rotbuch, 1982).

Jelinek, Elfriede, *Die Liebhaberinnen* (Reinbek bei Hamburg: Rowohlt, 1989).

Müller, Herta, *Reisende auf einem Bein* (Berlin: Rotbuch, 1992).

Özdamar, Emine Sevgi, *Mutterzunge: Erzählungen* (Berlin: Rotbuch, 1990).

Wolf, Christa, *Kassandra. Voraussetzungen einer Erzählung*, ed. Sonja Hilzinger, *Werke*, vii (Munich: Literaturverlag, 2000).

English translations

Duden, Anne, *Opening of the Mouth*, trans. Della Couling (London: Pluto, 1985).

Jelinek, Elfriede, *Women as Lovers*, trans. Martin Chalmers (London: Serpent's Tail, 1994).

Müller, Herta, *Traveling on One Leg*, trans. Valentina Glajar and André Lefevere (Evanston, Ill.: Northwestern University Press, 1998).

Özdamar, Emine Sevgi, *Mother Tongue*, trans. Craig Thomas (Toronto: Coach House, 1994).

Wolf, Christa, *Cassandra: A Novel and Four Essays*, trans. Jan van Heurck (London: Virago, 1984).

Critical theory and feminist theory

Belsey, Catherine, and Moore, Jane (eds.), *The Feminist Reader: Essays in the Politics of Literary Criticism*, 2nd edn. (Basingstoke: Macmillan, 1997).

Bennett, Andrew, and Royle, Nicholas, *Introduction to Literature, Criticism and Theory*, 2nd edn. (Harlow: Prentice Hall, 1990).

Brooks, Anne, *Postfeminisms: Feminism, Cultural Theory, and Cultural Forms* (London: Routledge, 1997).

Culler, Jonathan, *Literary Theory: A Very Short Introduction* (Oxford: Oxford University Press, 1997).

Deutscher, Penelope, *Yielding Gender: Feminism, Deconstruction, and the History of Philosophy* (London: Routledge, 1997).

Eagleton, Mary, *Feminist Literary Theory: A Reader*, 2nd edn. (Oxford: Blackwell, 1996).

Flax, Jane, *Thinking Fragments: Psychoanalysis, Feminism, and Postmodernism in the Contemporary West* (Berkeley and Los Angeles, Calif.: University of California Press, 1990).

Fuss, Diana, *Essentially Speaking: Feminism, Nature, and Difference* (London: Routledge, 1989).

Gatens, Moira, *Imaginary Bodies: Ethics, Power, and Corporeality* (London: Routledge, 1996).

Humm, Maggie, *A Reader's Guide to Contemporary Feminist Literary Criticism* (New York: Harvester Wheatsheaf, 1994).

—— *Practising Feminist Criticism; An Introduction* (London: Prentice Hall/ Harvester Wheatsheaf, 1995).

Jaggar, Alison M., and Young, Iris Marion (eds.), *A Companion to Feminist Philosophy* (Oxford: Blackwell, 1998).

Moi, Toril, *What is a Woman?* (Oxford: Oxford University Press, 1999).

Price, Janet, and Shildrick, Margrit, *Feminist Theory and the Body: A Reader* (Edinburgh: Edinburgh University Press, 1999).

Weedon, Chris, *Feminist Practice and Poststructuralist Theory* (Oxford: Blackwell, 1987).

—— *Feminism, Theory, and the Politics of Difference* (Oxford: Blackwell, 1999).

Index